Trawling for

A Clyde Odyssey

Stephen Younger

Foreword

A month or so ago, in typically wet, windy Scottish weather, I travelled with my wife and family for the Christmas half term holiday to the Clyde. Whilst there I made my irregular pilgrimage to Tighnabruaich, which had been my home for many years in the 1980s. I did the usual photo shoot with 'my team' at the end of the old pier under the large battered sign announcing to the world that this was 'Tighnabruaich, Kyles of Bute'. I tried to interest my children, telling them something of my life long ago, before they were born, of the adventures and excitement, in a time without mobile phones, tablets and social media. A time of rudimentary computers and navigational aids. A time when there was still a fishing fleet.

I stood on the end of the pier, with my hand atop the solid wood bollard standing ready to accept mooring ropes from passing ships. My fingers instinctively moved to where the metal handle that had been there thirty years ago should be. I remember putting my absolute faith in this handle as daily I would use it to swing my body over the end of the pier to find the steel ladder suspended below, so that I could descend to the Glendale.

The handle was still there, cold as ever, and my mind registered and recognised the familiar imperfections in its surface that I had long ago forgotten. A great sense of déjà vu sent a little shiver down my spine. I looked down and I could see in my mind's eye the old trawler with her blue and red hull, rocking back and forth against her mooring lines on the grey waters. Her white painted wheelhouse, standing starkly out against the grey of the water and the leaden sky. I could also see the tall figure of a young man, clad in yellow oilskins, wearing a Newcastle United woolly hat, his pale smiling face staring up at me. "Alreet Boss," he called acknowledging my arrival. "We're all ready to go." I came back to reality, there was no fishing vessel at the end of the pier, just my family braving the grey and windy day and my very active imagination.

My re-kindled memories of the *Glendale* years were due in no little way to reading Steve's manuscript that he had very kindly sent me. I was really thrilled that he had bothered to put pen to paper, even if I was just a little jealous that he had done it and not I (I am actually far too lazy to embark on such a task). However, as soon as I had digested his first chapter and having had quite a few chuckles in the process, I knew immediately that my inactivity had paid off. Steve's wonderful writing style was a joy and his perception of events were so much more interesting and accurate than mine could ever have been. If I hadn't known it before, Steve's book confirmed that he really had enjoyed his two-year sabbatical afloat.

The book takes you through Steve's first visit aboard the 'Glendale' for his two-day interview, through his first year; initially as an apprentice boathand, then latterly as a qualified skipper to whom the boat and passengers were entrusted earlier than either he or I anticipated. To say he achieved this at record speed, whilst learning to cook and leading natural history and birding expeditions, gives some idea of the abilities of the then twenty-two-year-old. I was lucky indeed to call him a shipmate and even to this day to be able to call him one of my very best friends. How fate could so easily have had a different outcome after his interview!

It has been tempting in this foreword to divulge some details that he has obviously sought fit to omit (mostly about himself). However, as he has on the whole been kind to me (apart from a few personal observations about me and my humour), my temptation has subsided. Steve's story is of a delightful period in our lives, even though much is now remembered through rose-tinted spectacles. Please enjoy the tales, they are all true. I've enjoyed reliving them so much that I've accidently gone and bought another boat just so I can be 'The Skipper' again.

The Skipper
Yacht 'Deja Vue'
December 2016

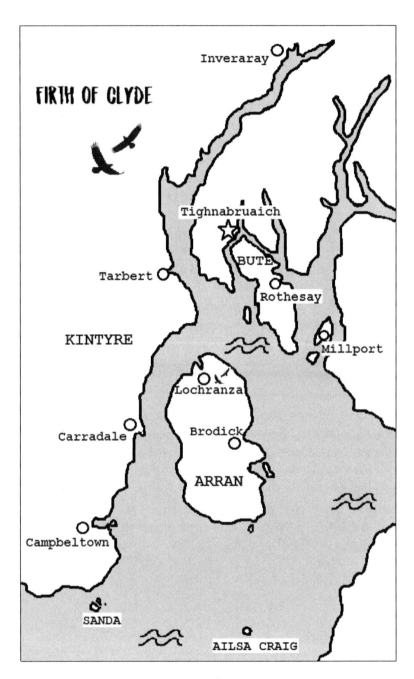

FIRTH OF CLYDE

Inveraray

Tighnabruaich

BUTE

Tarbert

Rothesay

KINTYRE

Millport

Lochranza

Carradale

Brodick

ARRAN

Campbeltown

SANDA

AILSA CRAIG

1. Job Application

'The successful applicant will be bone idle, have no work experience whatsoever, and have a Polytechnic degree in Environmental Studies. Birdwatching and Subbuteo skills an advantage.' Despite months of half-hearted searching, I could not find anything in the newspaper appointments sections which remotely resembled this particular job description.

I left Sunderland Poly in June 1986, and after spending a 'Gap Month' travelling around Europe with some friends, it was time to face up to the reality of looking for work in post-miners'-strike Tyneside. It wasn't helpful that I had not the slightest idea what I wanted to do for a living, although I was pretty good at recognising things that I didn't want to do. Nothing too menial, and definitely nothing too mundane. Compared to the great unemployed, I had things relatively easy, living at home and with sympathetic parents, but I was beginning to realise that even their patience wasn't limitless.

My job-search routine involved walking to the library in North Shields once or twice a week, to check the ads in magazines and newspapers, a round trip of about three miles. I had applied for a handful of posts, and in about half of those cases, I had received the courtesy of a rejection letter. Prospects were not good.

I was by no means alone in my plight; indeed, most of my friends found themselves in a very similar position to mine. One of those friends was Chris, whom I had known since before he had invited me to his fifth birthday party, and with whom I had recently undertaken an InterRail adventure in Europe. He was slightly more energetic than I was in his job-search, and he woke me at around 11am one September morning with a ring on the doorbell.

Chris had already been to the library, and had brought me a copy of an ad in the 'New Scientist' magazine. A company called Beagle Cruises was advertising a vacancy for a 'Ship's Naturalist / Ornithologist aboard a converted fishing boat in South-West Scotland'. I read on. The successful applicant would have a strong knowledge of wildlife, especially birds. That was a requirement which I could meet. Experience in handling a boat would be an advantage, as would cooking ability. And it was stressed that this would be no soft option – physical (and dirty) work would be expected, and the career would not be financially lucrative.

Having seen countless job ads which asked for a minimum of two years' experience working in one area or another, this one came as something of a breath of fresh air, so I thanked Chris and set to on preparing an application. As I did so, though, doubts started to creep in as to whether I really was such a good match for the list of skills which were required.

Birdwatching was by far and away my biggest strength. It was a hobby which I had pursued enthusiastically since I was eight or nine, and in spite of my tendencies not to blow my own trumpet, it was something which I knew that I was good at. Then it struck me that it could be very difficult to describe expertise in birdwatching in a job application, and I imagined that my potential competitors could easily bluff their way with unfounded claims of their knowledge. I decided to highlight my familiarity with the seabirds that might be seen from the boat, and tried to prove my credibility by mentioning the fact that I contributed records of sightings which were regularly accepted by the Tyneside Bird Club.

Despite having spent my entire life within a couple of miles of the sea, I didn't exactly have the brine coursing through my veins. My relationship with the sea was defined by the fact that it added to the variety of birds which I could meet with close to home, while my view of trawlers was that they were boats which were followed by gulls, occasionally tempting a Glaucous or Iceland Gull into the harbour at North Shields Fish Quay.

As for actually handling boats, aside from skippering a pedalo on Tynemouth Boating Lake, I could not claim to have any experience at all. My seafaring had largely been limited to frequent trips on the Shields Ferry, but I thought it best to gloss over the fact that I had found it necessary to pop a couple of 'Sea Legs' on a recent two-mile voyage to the Farne Islands. Neither did I mention my own nagging doubts about the wisdom of living on a boat in the knowledge that I could not swim more than a length without hyperventilating.

My cooking expertise was similarly limited. I could just about survive on student ready-meals or the odd fry-up, and had experimented with ingredients for toasties, but I had never prepared food for anyone other than myself. I thought it best not to make any reference to cooking so as not to draw attention to such an obvious weakness.

A slightly odd feature of the application process was a request to supply a photograph. The only photo which I had to hand was a rather sour-faced passport mug shot, and I felt obliged to add a P.S. to the application to explain that I didn't always look as miserable as this.

I need not have doubted myself, though, as my efforts in assembling my application portfolio were rewarded within a couple of days of posting it. I received a phone call from a well-spoken lady called Peggy from Beagle Cruises. She gave me the good news that for the first time, I had been selected for an interview, and went on to explain the arrangements. Although I was an interview novice, even I could sense that this was going to be somewhat out of the ordinary.

I was to spend two nights aboard the boat, which would give me the chance to display all the requisite skills for the job. My availability was hardly going to provide any obstacles in scheduling the interview, so we agreed a date in October on which I would travel up to the south-west of Scotland.

The interview day arrived, and started much like any other day of unemployment, with a lie-in. What was left of the morning was spent packing my bag and having an early lunch with my Mam, before it was time to start a journey which would end on the floating premises of my interviewers. I needed to catch four trains and a ferry, and in the days before mobile phone communication, I had to stick to a precise schedule and keep fingers crossed that there would be no delays or missed connections.

I left home with an odd mixture of emotions, ranging from curiosity to trepidation, but for now, I had to concentrate on getting to Gourock in time for the 4:55 ferry to Dunoon, where I had agreed to meet my interviewer. I considered myself quite an experienced independent traveller at the time, but I knew from my European tour a few weeks earlier that travel plans had a habit of going awry. A most spectacular example had been when I was navigating while attempting to drop off a hire car in Istanbul, and had somehow managed to take a wrong turn which resulted in us travelling into the wrong continent.

The first leg of the journey was simple and familiar enough, as I slung my bag over my shoulder and set out on a walk of a mile or so to West Monkseaton station. From there, I caught a square, yellow Metro to Newcastle Central Station, and arrived with plenty of time to spare to catch a quiet, lunchtime train from Newcastle to Edinburgh. This was the longest and most enjoyable part of the trip, with views out over the dunes to Holy Island and the imposing cliffs of St Abb's Head. The Gannet-guano stained Bass Rock stood sentinel at the mouth of the Forth, and soon we were approaching Scotland's capital.

At Edinburgh Waverley, I had only a short wait for a connection to Glasgow Queen Street. The train pulled away through Edinburgh's west end, past the rugby stadium at Murrayfield, and then out across the low hills and moors which separate Scotland's two great conurbations. On arrival at Queen Street, I successfully navigated on foot through the unfamiliar streets of Glasgow as I made the short walk to Central Station. It was with some relief that I boarded the orange train which would take me along the southern shore of the Clyde to the ferry terminal.

Some forty-five minutes later, my train made its way around the edge of Gourock harbour before coming to a halt alongside the quay. I had a little time to kill, so I had a coffee, and watched as the cars were arranged into queues ready to board the ferry. Soon, the black-and-white-hulled, red-funnelled Caledonian MacBrayne ferry *Jupiter* swung into the harbour, and edged backwards towards the quay to get into position for cars to roll on and roll off.

I boarded as a foot passenger, and as soon as the last car was safely on board, the engines rumbled and we were underway. The Clyde had appeared quite narrow from the train, and not a great deal wider at Gourock, but once we cleared the pier, the river suddenly turned south and broadened dramatically. Gannets and Fulmars skimmed over the waves, taking advantage of the assistance offered by the breeze. The sight of these 'proper' seabirds so far up the Clyde proved that we were already very much in a marine environment.

2. The Interview

After a twenty-five-minute voyage, we docked at Dunoon, where my interviewer was waiting to meet me. He was at an advantage, having already seen a photo of me, and he soon recognised the slightly ill-at-ease, wide-eyed stranger among the crowd. I was not sure what to expect of a converted trawler Skipper, but whatever it was, the Skipper was not it. The man who introduced himself was stocky, almost jowly, in his mid-twenties and with small, bright blue eyes amid the freckles under a mop of mouse-coloured hair.

"You must be Steve, or is it Stephen?" he asked in an accent which was well-spoken almost to the point of being plummy. I wasn't expecting to have to make a decision quite so early in the process, but I chose Steve.

The Skipper shook my hand warmly, and led me to a Murray-mint coloured Volvo, which was liberally dotted with rust patches as a result of long periods parked on the sea front. As we set off through Dunoon, the Skipper quickly put me at ease, and we were soon chatting a friendly chat. He pointed out some of the local sights in what seemed to be an intriguing town which was dominated by the presence of large numbers of American military personnel. We passed the Holy Loch, where a large US warship was permanently moored and had a sleek, black, nuclear submarine tied up alongside.

A sharp left turn took us away from the waterside and through some Forestry Commission land, and we then emerged into what was an increasingly wild Scottish landscape. A sheep suddenly jumped out from the verge into the narrow road, and the Skipper slammed on the brakes. "The way is baa'ed. There's no pulling the wool over his eyes," he quipped. The Skipper evidently had a penchant for rubbish jokes, which was something I could relate to.

The Volvo rounded the heads of Lochs Striven and Riddon, and then climbed to a viewpoint, where we pulled into a lay-by to take in an utterly breath-taking view of highlands and islands. Less than half an hour earlier we had been in Dunoon, a town which looked across to the Clydeside conurbation, but now we were overlooking an apparent wilderness where three bodies of sea water met one another.

Loch Riddon stretched away to our left, while across the water in front of us was the Isle of Bute, separated from the mainland by two narrow straits. These were the East and West Kyles of Bute. We had a clear line of sight down both Kyles, and in the far distance, Arran's jagged mountains loomed on the horizon. At the centre of these mountains was the striking profile of the 'Sleeping Warrior', complete with helmet, rugged facial features and a rather rounded belly.

Bute itself looked to be a wild place of low hills, with bracken- and heather-clad slopes rising abruptly from the shore. Three small islands complemented the view in the near-distance, where the mouth of the loch met the head of the Kyles. These were the Burnt Islands, a group of low, rounded rocks from which a handful of small pine trees sprouted.

Far below us was a pier, and, just visible at its end, was what appeared to be an ordinary fishing boat. This was my first glimpse of my potential place of employment, the *Glendale*.

*

The boat was based in Tighnabruaich on the shores of the West Kyle of Bute. Attempting to pronounce Tighnabruaich was one of the first challenges of my interview, but it was a question to which there did not seem to be a single answer. Depending on to whom you spoke, the correct pronunciation was either 'Tye-na-brewech' (with a hard 'ch'), 'Tinna-brewech', or even 'T'na-brewech'. The name itself was a concatenation of three Gaelic words: 'Tigh' for house, 'na' meaning 'on the' and 'bruaich' meaning brae or hill.

My first impression of Tighnabruaich was of a quiet, rather idyllic place, which was laid out in a narrow ribbon along the foreshore. It was surprisingly long, stretching almost three miles from the boatyard in the north to Kames in the south, but it was seemingly never more than three buildings deep. There were few shops, and a lot of rather grand-looking Victorian houses set behind immaculate lawns along the sea front.

We descended through the 'suburbs' of Tighnabruaich to shore level, and approached the pier along the road by the sea front. The Skipper parked the Volvo in a tiny car park above the rocky beach by the pier head, and I stepped out to take my first lungful of Tighnabruaich air. There was an instantaneous other-worldliness about the place, enhanced by the lack of traffic, and an impression of being cut off from the outside world by hills behind the village and the waters of the Kyles to the front.

We walked through what appeared to be an open garage under a house, before emerging onto the wooden slats of a long, T-shaped pier, flanked by low, white-washed railings. Despite our approach, the *Glendale* did not seem to grow significantly. Even looking down on the deck from the end of the pier, she was surprisingly small at 52 feet long. She looked a little tired after a long season, with patches of rust staining the blue and red paint of the hull. To all intents and purposes, she looked like any other trawler, complete with a stack of prawn creels in one corner of the deck. The most obvious difference was in the centre of the deck. Instead of a gaping, hollow fish-hold, there was a neat, raised wooden roof painted in the same glossy blue as the hull, complete with a matrix of small, square windows which reflected the evening sky above.

The boat was tied up to the pier with two large ropes, but she was lying a few feet away from the pier end, being blown out by a slight breeze. The Skipper took up one of the ropes and leaned on it until the boat started to swing back towards us, and the gap began to disappear. We descended a metal ladder which clung to the end of the pier, and straddled a guard rail before stepping onto the deck. The boat felt quite solid underfoot, but bobbed very slightly under the weight of its new arrivals, before swinging gently from the pier as the ropes tightened in the light breeze.

The Mate, whose imminent departure had led to the vacancy for which I was being interviewed, then emerged from a varnished hatch and welcomed me on board. He struck me as being a man of the outdoors, dressed in khaki trousers and a dark green woolly jumper, with slightly unkempt, curly, sand-coloured hair and a bristly moustache. He was slightly older than the Skipper, and while being perfectly civil and friendly, lacked some of the affability and confidence of his colleague. He had worked on the *Glendale* for just one season, but had decided to leave so that he could marry and start a new life with one of the guests who had visited earlier in the season.

We descended below decks through the hatch via a small staircase, and I was immediately impressed by the highly-polished and varnished interior, which provided a startling contrast to the rusty scene outside. The saloon, where the fish-hold once was, was the most impressive part of the boat. A large, mahogany table was folded away, creating the biggest area below decks in which I could stand to my full height of 6'5". The walls behind the table were finished with varnished pine panelling, and light penetrated from above through the square windows built into the ceiling, as well as two smaller, round 'portholes' in the deck above some of the darker recesses.

In the corner of the saloon was the galley, featuring a four-ring gas hob which was home to a 'bagpiping' kettle, and this soon came to the boil with a vaguely musical wheeze. The Mate retrieved some mugs which were suspended from hooks in order to prevent breakages on the high seas, and we settled down around the table for a cup of tea. On a wall behind the table was a slightly dog-eared chart of the cruising area, from which I was given an overview of the regular ports of call during a Beagle Cruise.

15

I sipped my tea while the Skipper set the scene and the schedule for my interview. We would set off shortly on a two-hour voyage, sailing down the Kyles and then up Loch Fyne to the fishing port of Tarbert. Here we would be entertaining some friends of the boat for an evening meal. The next day would give me a chance to show my wildlife knowledge, both from the deck of the boat and on a short walk on a nearby island called Inchmarnock. So far so good, but it was my final assignment which made me feel uneasy. I was to be tested on my cooking skills by providing a meal for the Skipper and the Mate.

Briefing over, I was taken on a tour of the *Glendale*. The cabins were described in the brochure as being 'palatial', although a coffin was brought to mind before any thought of a palace. Each of the three cabins had two narrow bunks built into them, hemmed in on all sides by more varnished pine-panelling. In fairness, the 'Honeymoon Suite' in the bows was marginally less claustrophobic than the port and starboard cabins, with a lower bunk which could, at a push, pass as a double bed. The all-in-one toilet / shower was compact, but had character, and I was given my first demonstration of the pump-action flushing mechanism.

We returned to the saloon, and then made our way through a small door and into the dark, diesel-saturated engine-room. Having already been conscious of my limited cooking and non-existent nautical experiences, I now had to add a complete lack of engineering know-how to my list of nice-to-have skills on which I might be found wanting during the interview. I watched as the engine was fired up, and after a brief splutter and strain, a distinctive rhythm was established. A few key features of the engine were pointed out to me, but I felt unable to pass any meaningful comment, as I did not really know a cylinder from an alternator. I opted to nod and look quietly impressed.

Despite its small size, the different sections of the boat were varied in style and character, and emergence into the crew's quarters at the 'blunt end' provided a further contrast to what had gone before. The woodwork lacked the varnish and polish seen in the guests' quarters, and here things were much more as they had been during the *Glendale*'s fishing days. Each crew member slept in a wooden recess, making the 'palatial' claims of the guests' cabins suddenly seem a little less far-fetched. In pride of place at one end of the cabin stood the ship's fridge. The Skipper explained that good, fresh food was a big part of the holiday experience on board.

In the corner, almost directly under a hatch up to the wheelhouse, was a tiny room which contained the crew's toilet, and in common with the rest of the crew's quarters, the best that could be said for it was that it was functional. We climbed a vertical, black, metal ladder into wheelhouse, from where I continued in my silent observer mode as the Skipper and the Mate went about untying us from the pier, arranging the ropes into neat, coiled piles on deck as they went. The *Glendale* was on the move, first gently nudging her bow into the pier, and then moving away backwards (or 'astern' to use the nautical term) and out into the Kyle. It was still early evening as we swung around and down the Kyles, bound for Tarbert, Loch Fyne.

I was allowed to steer the boat, and was told to aim for a distant, red navigation buoy at Ardlamont Point. There were few instructions – only to keep an eye on the depth reading and to shout if the alarm sounded to indicate that the water had become too shallow. Although I did not know it at the time, there was little danger of this, as Loch Fyne is a deep, deep channel, and we would be moving over a trough which plunged to around 200 metres during our short trip.

We entered Loch Fyne, and I was shown how to use the compass, which was suspended from the ceiling. I was to proceed on a heading of 330, which seemed a simple enough instruction, but it proved to be trickier than I expected. I found myself constantly drifting slightly off course, and then over-correcting the wheel before finally settling back onto the correct bearing.

For a while, I was left alone with my instruments, which were few, and those that actually worked were even fewer. By far the most impressive was the radar, which gave a clear, glowing image of adjacent shorelines and 'targets' representing yachts and navigation buoys. The radar screen was shaded by a cylindrical cover, over which I placed my face to view the picture at its clearest. I enjoyed my first experience of helmsmanship, although I guessed that conditions might not always be this favourable.

As I relaxed and became accustomed to handling the boat, I began to see some birds. We passed a couple of Black Guillemots, paradoxically white in their winter plumage, and propelled by bright red feet. I liked Black Guillemots, even though I'd only had brief or distant views of a couple before. These had been in their jet-black summer plumage, with their contrasting, clear white oval wing-patches. I liked the fact that this was a bird with three great names. As well as the English name, they were frequently referred to by the popular Gaelic 'Tystie', while *Cepphus grylle* was one of a few scientific bird names which I could remember.

I successfully navigated up Loch Fyne, and as we approached Tarbert in the gathering dusk, I was relieved of my duties at the wheel, as the Skipper took the helm to guide us through the narrow harbour entrance. Slick rope-handling was again in evidence as we took our place among the local fishing fleet, tying up to a trawler similar in size to ours. The *Glendale* suddenly seemed to be in her true element, and blended in with her old fishing boat friends and relatives on the fish quay.

We disembarked, climbing up one of several vertical ladders and onto a broad, quiet fish quay, before making our way across the road to the Islay Frigate, a large pub which overlooked the quay. Three pints of heavy were ordered, but before they were poured, I was facing an unexpected and unscheduled interview test. The Skipper had been distracted by a Scottish girl, who smiled back at him through the fringe of her permed, black hair. It seemed that he had encountered an old flame.

I guessed that the appropriate behaviour in response to this test would involve giving him some space and making myself scarce. I was able to acquit myself quite well, occupying the next half-hour playing pool with The Mate. I was soon introduced to our guests who would be coming aboard for the evening, a couple who ran a cafe next door to the pub, who were well-established friends of the boat. The Cafe Owner had a distinct Teesside accent, and he and his wife both struck me as being friendly, if a little eccentric.

After an enjoyable few pints, it was time to return to the boat, with the Old Flame being added to the guest list, and the wine and the conversation continued to flow freely as meal preparations were made. The Cafe Owner, it turned out, was a keen bird man, who was the local RSPB representative and performed a lot of seabird survey work around the Tarbert area. Black Guillemots were a favourite of his, too, and he had actually considered renaming his Cafe to 'the Cepphus Grylle'. They're very, very Tystie.

The Cafe Owner had brought with him one of the courses for the evening meal. He had chosen to bring a pot of frogs' legs in garlic butter, my first experience of this particular delicacy, and we all concluded that they did indeed taste a bit like... chicken. The Skipper followed up with an impeccable, wholesome and flavoursome hotpot. The gastronomic standard had been set.

After several nightcaps, the Cafe Owner and his wife said their goodbyes, and walked back to their house across the road from the quay. The Skipper continued with his hospitality towards the Old Flame in the 'Honeymoon Suite', while I retired to my palatial coffin in the port cabin, too tired to reflect on the day's events, and with little indication as to how the interview was progressing. Rather than allowing the pressure to get to me regarding the outcome of the interview, I made up my mind to enjoy the trip in its own right. At the same time, despite the fact that this was my first job interview, I did realise that this experience was not giving me a great deal of practise at my interview technique should I need to go for a more conventional job in future.

The following morning, I awoke to find that daylight had penetrated the decks and into my cabin. A small, glass prism was set in the wooden planking of the ceiling, which scattered the light into the little room surprisingly effectively. I managed not to bump my head on the upper bunk, and rolled off my bed onto the small floor space in which I managed to dress without fully unfurling my limbs.

My first experience of breakfast on board was a fairly relaxed affair, particularly as the Skipper was not an early riser. Instead, the Mate took charge of porridge preparation, using what I was assured was the only authentic Scottish porridge-stirring technique, in an exclusively clockwise direction using a local wooden implement know as a spurtle. This banter was obviously well-practised, and I imagined that spurtles and bagpiping kettles were all part of the holiday experience.

After breakfast, I was shown some photo albums, which included a record of the conversion of the *Glendale* from an empty shell of a decommissioned trawler to a well-appointed holiday boat. I could sense the pride in the Skipper's voice as he talked me through the transformation, and the pictures hinted at the scale of the project which he had masterminded. Parts of the boat's structure still just about recognisable from where I sat, but the interior seemed to have undergone a complete metamorphosis.

There was also an intriguing picture of The Skipper and his father on the quay at Tarbert, taken during a family holiday some years earlier. The unremarkable, anonymous-looking, purple fishing boat tied up to an otherwise empty fish quay in the background had a profile which was already familiar to me. It was the *Glendale*, quietly waiting for a buyer to take her on new adventures now that her fishing days were behind her.

The Skipper was a keen sailor, and had visited the Clyde for yachting holidays on several occasions, both with his father and with friends. It was on one such trip, after an exhilarating day's sailing (and a fair amount of alcohol), that the Skipper and a University friend called Carl sat in a harbour-side bar in Rothesay, and decided that this was the life for them. His friend was a keen birdwatcher, and seemingly simplistic plans were hatched to combine their two passions into a holiday offering which would appeal to many.

The Skipper's father shared his enthusiasm for sailing and for the Clyde, so it was not a difficult task to sell the vision to him, and he agreed to give the financial backing needed to get the idea afloat. The original plan was to purchase a sailing boat, but the timing of the *Glendale*'s availability, and recognition of its potential for conversion, meant that the plans had to be modified slightly.

During the 18 months after the purchase of the *Glendale*, The Skipper and Carl oversaw her conversion at the tiny boatyard in Tighnabruaich. The choice of location proved to be a masterstroke, as it gave them a means of getting to know a wide range of locals, particularly the craftsmen who fitted out the boat. The first season of cruising holidays had been in 1984, so my visit was at the end of the third season, and I was applying to become the third permanent crew member after Carl and my present interviewer.

Breakfast dishes were finally washed and stowed, and it was time to go back ashore and into the shops of Tarbert to prepare for my evening assignment. I was to provide dinner for the Mate, the Skipper and the Old Flame that evening aboard the boat, and after the sophistication of the previous evening's menu, I felt more than a little intimidated. I struggled to find inspiration from the regular diet provided for me at home, which was healthy, if unimaginative, largely comprising pork chops and various dishes involving mince, vegetables and not a lot else.

I was taken to butchers and greengrocers, and given a completely free rein and a limitless budget to conjure up a culinary treat. So I bought some pork chops and some vegetables.

The shopping was taken back on board where it was put into the fridge, and after a pub lunch at the Islay Frigate, it was time to leave Tarbert. This time we retraced our previous evening's wake down Loch Fyne, but instead of heading back up the Kyles to Tighnabruaich, we made for an anchorage between Bute and a small island off its west coast. This was Inchmarnock, about two miles long and less than half a mile across. It had recently become uninhabited, although its two farm houses remained largely intact.

Getting ashore on Inchmarnock involved a maiden voyage for me on the second boat in the Beagle fleet. 'Gordon' was an eighteen-foot orange inflatable, not unlike an inshore lifeboat in size and appearance. The Skipper explained that there had been some debate over a name for this boat, but they finally decided to keep things simple and use the name of her manufacturer which featured on a badge at her bow. It did sound rather odd referring to a *Gordon* as a 'She', but I quite liked the name.

Gordon's 55 horsepower engine meant that she was quite quick, and I was given my first taste of this speed as we dashed up and down the calm waters of narrow strait between Inchmarnock and Bute. The wind rushed through my hair at eighteen knots, and a large plume of spray was kicked up in our wake. The Mate then ran the inflatable up the gently-sloping sandy beach under Mid-Park Farm, and carried her anchor up beyond the high water mark.

We made our way up an overgrown path and past the recently-abandoned farmhouse. The sun blazed low in the late afternoon sky, its golden glow enhancing the yellowing tones of the dense stands of coppiced hazel. Deep red was added to the autumnal palette thanks to hedgerows full of flowering fuchsias. There was a stillness to this deserted island, which combined with the onset of autumn to create a feeling of stepping back into the past.

It was time for me to do some work, and I had about an hour ashore to find some birds to identify. There were not many about, and what was on show was quite mundane. A Kestrel, a couple of Buzzards and a few 'small brown jobs' in the fields. A distant raptor was perched on a fence, silhouetted against the sinking sun.

"What's that, then?" asked The Mate. I thought it was probably a Buzzard, but then why would he be asking me that when we had already seen a few Buzzards? And he had mentioned that Hen Harriers were quite regular here in an earlier conversation.

"Hen Harrier," I said. It was a Buzzard. Which was a bit annoying. That incident aside, I felt I had coped quite well on the bird front on the interview as a whole, standing on deck and picking out distant mergansers and auks. I hadn't magicked up a rarity, but I hoped that it would be fairly clear that I knew my avian onions. Apart from that one Buzzard.

I helped push *Gordon* off the beach, and the Mate lowered the outboard into the water for our short trip back to the *Glendale*. It was time for me to get busy in the galley, and I was to spend most of the journey back up to Tighnabruaich below decks. I had never had to peel so many potatoes before, so I sat down with a large pan of water between my feet, and started peeling. I began to notice that the water in the pan was sloshing around, and I was beginning to feel dizzy. A brisk breeze was stirring the surface of the sea, and little by little, nausea was beginning to take hold.

Rather than risk the ignominy of being seasick on my first full day on board, I took the pan up on deck, and continued with peeling potatoes in the fresh air. I tried to make light of the situation, and the Skipper and his Old Flame seemed to be amused by my reaction, although it must have been obvious to them that my sea legs might not be sturdy enough to withstand conditions which could undoubtedly get far worse than this.

The boat became steadier again as we entered the calm waters higher up the Kyles, so down I went again to complete preparations below decks. Pork chops under the grill. Vegetables chopped and thrown into the pan. Potatoes peeled and boiled. Pretty basic stuff, but I managed to avoid any mishaps. We tied up to the pier, and dinner was served. The Skipper muttered something about hating mixed vegetables. The mash was a bit lumpy. The Crew, the Skipper and the Old Flame tucked in and managed to eat what was presented to them, although to be fair, it would have been difficult for them to have mustered any real enthusiasm. Still, I had shown that I could do the basics without any real disasters, so perhaps some potential could be seen.

Further pub etiquette tests were laid on in the evening, and these primarily involved a check on my behaviour after a few pints and another opportunity to practise my pool skills. Then it was back along the front and down the pier for a second night aboard the *Glendale*. As I settled into my bunk in the port cabin, I noticed that there was a slight breeze, and water was slapping against the outside of the hull. I was concerned that the boat was now rocking, not a great deal, but just enough to make me feel rather odd again. At one point I was convinced I was going to lose the dinner I had so carefully prepared, but I felt sure that this would mean an instant rejection of my application. I knew that sea-sickness was something to do with balance and ears, so I shook my head hard, managed to convince myself that I felt better, and allowed the waters to rock me to sleep.

As the Skipper drove me back to Dunoon the following morning, I still had little indication as to how things had gone. On the positive side, I may have scored a B for birdwatching and perhaps a B- for ability to get on with the Skipper, but my cooking would have been C- at best, and it must have been obvious that I was a complete novice on the water.

I had thoroughly enjoyed my two days, but what would I do if I was offered the job? Well, almost by default I would have accepted it, but I knew that the environment I had encountered was completely alien. I was confident in my bird knowledge, but would I be able to impart this knowledge and become a guide? Then there were the nautical and culinary shortfalls; perhaps I could pick up these skills over time, but I had a long way to go. And perhaps most alien of all to a fresh, unemployed graduate was the prospect of discipline, hard work and tidiness.

The decision was now beyond my control and entirely in the hands of the Skipper and the Mate. They would know better than I whether I really was a genuine candidate to live this quite unique lifestyle on board.

3. The Offer

Not long after returning from Tighnabruaich, I had a call from the Skipper. He informed me that I was on the short-list, and while he gave no indication as to how short this list was, I was thrilled that at last, I had a lead. It was something positive I could tell people when they asked how the search was going. That I was in with a chance of actually securing a job on the basis of my hobby was a stroke of luck which I didn't really appreciate until I became a London commuter many years later.

Life over the two months that followed continued with a strong element of routine. I played Subbuteo on a Tuesday evening, five-a-side football on a Thursday, and watched Newcastle United on most Saturdays. Plus a trip to the dole office every other Thursday morning. A few non-eventful birdwatching outings and fruitless job applications were irregularly incorporated into this schedule.

I heard nothing more from Beagle Cruises for several weeks. My one and only lead was beginning to go cold, and no further job prospects were added to my pipeline. When Noddy Holder invited me to look to the future at Christmas, that future looked more uncertain than ever.

Eventually, the call came one evening between Christmas and New Year.

"We would like to offer you the job. Are you still available and would you be interested?" asked the Skipper. I was thrilled, but felt that I had to contain myself and give a down-to-earth response.

"Well I suppose I've got nothing better to do." I could almost hear the Skipper wince, as he wondered what he had just let himself in for. Showing an appropriate level of enthusiasm was added to the lengthy list of skills I was going to have to develop if I was to be a success in my new career.

The call was short and, aside from my spectacularly underwhelming response, unremarkable. I was a single man with few commitments, so I was glad of an opportunity to try something completely different. What I didn't realise at the time was just how much of a life-changing decision it had been, and what a voyage of discovery lay ahead.

The Skipper lived not too far from my home patch, in Sedgefield, County Durham, and I visited his family home on a cold, clear January day. The house was strategically situated in the centre of the village, and was very grand, with three storeys, ten bedrooms and a cosy beer cellar. The Skipper's father greeted me warmly before having to hurry off to his work as the village doctor.

I was introduced to Peggy the Purser, who had telephoned me a few months earlier to arrange my interview. She was a friendly lady, who kept busy during my visit assembling and posting brochures, as well as taking calls from potential guests. I could see that as well as being a family home, this building doubled up as the nerve centre for the Beagle Cruises operation, and despite first appearances of normality, it was, in fact, an understated hive of activity.

I met the Skipper's mother and sister, and was scratched by his sister's cat, before we got down to the business of discussing the season ahead. One of the main objectives of the day was to agree my working terms and conditions, and I drove a hard bargain. I would be earning £38 per week, to which I could expect to add up to £10 in tips. The basic pay alone represented a massive 45% increase on my dole income.

We went out for a pub lunch in the village to talk about plans for the early part of my new career. As we walked out of the house, I noticed another familiar character in the garage. *Gordon*, the fast orange inflatable, lay quietly under wraps on a trailer, patiently waiting for another season to come around.

I was told that bookings were actually down on the previous year, and there would be a slow start to the season, but we had at least agreed a start date. What lay ahead was as daunting as ever, but now it felt as if we were making some progress at last. With dates having been set, at least the whole venture was beginning to feel a little more real, but as I sat on the bus from Sedgefield back to Newcastle I did not really feel a great deal the wiser. In return, I was not sure that the Skipper was entirely confident that this rather non-committal youth whom he had hired would be man enough for the challenges which lay ahead.

*

My first day as a Beagle employee finally arrived on a grey Monday morning in February. The Skipper pulled his Murray-mint-coloured Volvo into the car park opposite my parents' house, with *Gordon* in tow on a trailer behind. We were already an hour or so behind schedule, which gave me a foretaste of the Skipper's attitude towards punctuality. I loaded a big grey hold-all into the car containing most of my worldly possessions, and said my goodbyes to my Mam. We headed along the Coast Road and through Newcastle, and then off out west along the A69, stopping at Longtown for a chippy pub lunch and a few games of pool.

The morning mists were well behind us as we pressed on up the A74, passing Lockerbie under clear blue skies. I was spending most of my first full day in paid employment in the passenger seat of a car, watching the scenery go by. The landscape became more industrial as we approached the Glasgow conurbation, passing close to the massive steelworks at Ravenscraig. As we approached central Glasgow, we pulled off the M8 and began a tour of the backstreets of the city.

Glasgow was a place I'd never visited before, but the Skipper knew it well, and we spent the next hour or so stopping at shops which specialised in goods for boats. We visited chandlery shops and a place for electronic gadgets near Celtic Park, before heading into the shadow of Ibrox to pick up paint supplies. I didn't know such places existed, but they seemed like little treasure troves full of all manner of boating stuff.

We re-joined the motorway for a short stretch, but exited again at Hillington in order to visit the Makro cash & carry. We filled the large trolley with bulk buys of soft drinks, cans of McEwan's Export and Tennent's Lager. It was the first time I'd ever been to a wholesaler's, and spent much of my time gawping in wonder at the unfeasibly massive jars of Hellman's Mayonnaise and Branston Pickle.

We lugged the supplies back to the car, quickly filling up the boot, and then piled the remaining crates and boxes onto the back seat. The old Volvo was now heavily laden, and sank on its axles, but the exhaust remained just clear of the tarmac as we continued down to the ferry at Gourock.

There had been a little more urgency in the drive after lunch, and little did I know that we were actually now working to a precise schedule. We had to catch a ferry from Gourock in order to make it to Tighnabruaich for 5pm, and Happy Hour at the Royal Hotel.

Almost as soon as we boarded the CalMac ferry, a crash-course in naming parts of a boat was provided by the Skipper. The words he spoke were quite foreign to me, as he pointed out oddly-shaped objects which, as a confirmed landlubber, I had completely overlooked in the past. Ropes were passed through fair leads and either tied around cleats or wound around capstans. There were gaps under the bulwarks so that water could run off from the gunwales. I listened intently, and committed some of the words to memory, but I still struggled to understand how any of this knowledge would be used in practice.

Lesson over, it was back to the car for a break-neck drive along the narrow road from Dunoon to Tighnabruaich. We walked into the bar at 5:03, and the Skipper was greeted as a returning hero. I knocked back a couple of pints of 80/-, but felt a little awkward in unfamiliar company. Still, if this was what life on a salary was about, I was not about to complain.

An hour later, we were on our way along the road towards the pier. This time, though, there was no *Glendale* moored at its end. She was out of the water for the winter, in a boatyard on the far side of the Isle of Bute. Instead, our destination was a big Victorian house, three doors beyond the pier, where we would be staying for the night. It was home to the most remarkable couple I had ever had the pleasure of meeting.

4. Starting Work

The Skipper had not told me much about this couple. All that I knew was that they were friends of his and supporters of the Beagle venture. Peter wore a blue boiler suit, and sported a crescent of fluffy white hair and fluffy white eyebrows under a slightly florid bald head. Jill had short, dark, slightly greying hair and a hint of a twitch. Both were exceedingly well-spoken and brimming with character, Peter's booming, slightly stammering voice being especially distinctive.

The Skipper and his old friends chatted away, making up for lost time, but Peter went to some lengths to make sure that I was not excluded from the conversation.

"So you're the new bird man, are you, Steve?" he asked. When I confirmed that this was indeed the case, he went on. "We had a Pheasant in the back garden the other day."

"Oh yes?" I responded.

"Oh yes. Strutting around. The arrogant bastard was annoying me, so I shot it."

I nodded and smiled. I was a little lost for words, being unaccustomed to Peter's eccentricities, but despite the unexpected words, his demeanour remained friendly and hospitable.

Back in 1982, when the Skipper and Carl had first arrived at their new base, Peter's friendly face appeared at the end of the pier. He explained that he was in a spot of bother with his own boat, which had run aground further down the Kyle. The crew of the *Glendale* duly helped out, and were offered use of the bath and a night's accommodation in return. That one night turned into 18 months, as they were integrated into the family. A bond had been formed which was to last for many years.

It later transpired that there had been nothing wrong with Peter's boat, and the rescue episode had been a ruse to get to know the enterprising young nautical new kids in town. Peter had a naval and sailing background which was second to none. He had served as a Frigate Commander in the Navy during and after the war, and had a number of incredible stories to tell from this time. The fact that he survived all of his assignments and lived to tell these tales seemed to be almost miraculous.

During the 1950s, Peter denied himself a comfortable pension by quitting the Royal Navy, a decision he took while based in Singapore. His first assignment back in Civvy Street was to deliver small yacht to a new owner in the UK, which entailed a 10,000 mile journey, with stops on the islands of Reunion and St Helena. It was during this voyage that he became convinced that he should attempt a round-the-world sailing trip, and set about the task of finding a boat and a crew to help him realise his dream.

After two potential crewmen had let him down, he decided to sail single-handed east to west across the Atlantic, from Rhu on the Clyde to Canada, an endeavour which was almost unheard-of at the time. After dodging the icebergs, Peter found a marina in Montreal in which to leave his boat, and flew home for the winter.

During that winter, he met Jill, and pragmatically killed two birds with one stone. Jill would double up to be his bride and his round-the-world crew. Their honeymoon saw them sail from Montreal and down the Eastern Seaboard of the USA, before navigating the Panama Canal and into the Pacific. The Panama yachting community advised them that treacherous tides and hidden reefs meant that it would be unwise to attempt to sail to the Galapagos. Then Peter established that very few of these people had actually made the trip themselves, so he decided to ignore that ill-informed advice, and successfully navigated the currents before spending several weeks among the 'Enchanted Isles'.

Without any electrical equipment, and with the help of only traditional navigational aids such as charts, a compass and a sextant, Peter successfully located the almost impossibly remote and tiny island of Pitcairn. Here they met the Christian descendants of the mutinous Bounty crew, before crossing another 2,000 miles of Pacific Ocean en route to Tahiti. By the end of their stay in Tahiti, Jill was six months pregnant, and they were forced to reconsider their options. The dream of circumnavigating the world was over, but the adventure certainly was not.

Their decision was to turn about and head east, and embark on a non-stop voyage of around 4,000 miles across the Pacific to Los Angeles. There they sold their story and film footage to a local TV company, and with the proceeds of this and the sale of their honeymoon boat, they made their way back to Scotland to continue their married lives together.

I listened to the story intently, and felt honoured to be given a viewing of the cine footage. I was also given a loan copy of Peter's book, 'The Restless Wind' which documented this amazing adventure. This was certainly not the type of company I was accustomed to, but the warmth of the hospitality offered by this couple put me completely at ease. This hospitality was extended further through a regular replenishment of beer, and extremely generous measures of whisky.

My second day at work began with a thumping hangover the next morning, but my spirits soon rose as I could see that the late February dawn had shed its light on the most wonderful view. The slope of the lawn gave the illusion that the garden ran down to the water's edge, beyond which was an uninterrupted view down the Kyles, with Arran's snow-capped mountains in the far distance.

It was only now that I began to appreciate something of the magic of this house. At its rear rose a steep, wooded bank, at the foot of which there stood a ramshackle wooden structure from which a smoky aroma emanated. Peter later opened its door to show us racks of salmon-sides, which were being gently and authentically smoked.

Inside the house, the staircase was dominated by an ancestral portrait. It was not until much later that I realised that the engagement ring worn on Jill's finger was the one worn by the distinguished lady who featured in this portrait. At the top of the stairs was a huge bathroom, whose centrepiece was a large bath with an odd cylindrical plug-cum-overflow. From that bath, or even from a perch on the toilet, the sumptuous views of the Kyles could be enjoyed through the window.

I was not really accustomed to such grandeur, but all too soon, it was time to leave it behind us and get back to the reality of work on the boat, and preparations for the season ahead. We caught the ferry across the Kyles from Colintraive to Rhubodach on the north end of Bute, before driving towards Rothesay. The car bumped across the tracks of the slipway of the rather smart boatyard at Ardmaleish, complete with a big, gleaming, modern trawler which looked to be almost ready for launch. Rounding the headland, the bay of Port Bannatyne stretched before us. On its far shore was another boatyard, much smaller and scruffier than the Ardmaleish yard. And in pride of place, on its slipway, stood the faded, rusty, barnacle-encrusted *Glendale*.

The *Glendale* had spent the winter out of the water at the yard, so that she could be left to dry out and undergo essential maintenance before the new season got underway. She was precariously balanced on a cradle, which itself was on a narrow, concrete slipway with rusty rails, bisecting a shallowly sloping, rocky shore. The keel was perched on a long, thin trolley, whose wheels were aligned with what was effectively a very narrow-gauge railway track. While it certainly did not look to be very safe, some stability was added by four large wooden poles tied to the side of the boat, and some shorter wooden wedges underneath the hull.

I was surprised by how big the boat looked now, and had not appreciated just how much of the hull there was below the waterline. Virtually every square inch of this area was covered by a layer of dead barnacles. And every one of these dead barnacles was going to have to be removed, before any painting could be started. The size of the task ahead now finally began to sink in.

We retrieved a ladder from the boatyard, and made our way up onto the deck and then down the main hatch and into boat. It was five months since my interview, and the interior looked much as I had remembered it, although now the *Glendale* was in a clammy, gloomy hibernation, awaiting our return before her revival for a new season. There was no electricity, so no warmth and little light. The fact that she was not fit for habitation meant that would have to find accommodation nearby for the time being.

With so much work to be done, and only three weeks in which to do it before launch date, I was struggling to see how we could get through it all. I literally didn't know where to start, but fortunately for me, the Skipper had seen it all before at the start of three previous seasons, not to mention the mammoth overhaul and original refit of the boat four years earlier. He had a long task list in his head, and was now keenly focused on getting through it all.

It was already late morning, but we decided to make a start with some tidying and readying of tools. I was issued with my regulation blue boiler suit, which, despite the fact that it had recently been laundered, retained oil stains and streaks of paint from earlier seasons. I quickly found that while one size did, in theory, fit all, it fitted some a lot better than me. A good two inches of the denim of my jeans poked out below the ends of the boiler suit legs, and other parts of the outfit were rather too snug for my liking.

Working life seemed full of surprises and unexpected challenges, and when nature called, I was to face another one. Without any running water on the boat, the on-board toilet was out of service, so we had to use the rather basic facilities which were on offer at the boatyard, or, rather, in a field next to the boatyard. A row of four Portaloos provided us with functional, but not very inspiring, toilets. They were reasonably well-maintained, but I was rather bemused to find the plastic fittings daubed with sectarian graffiti, something I had never seen before, and which indicated that I was in Protestant tribal territory. Once there, I faced a further challenge to extricate myself from my boiler suit, something which was a lot more easily said than done in the confines of a Portaloo. I tried to do whatever I could to keep future visits to the 'Catholic Throne' to a minimum.

Lunchtime soon arrived, and, still clad in our boiler suits, we decided that we should go and find some accommodation. We knocked on a few Bed & Breakfast doors in Rothesay. At one of these, we were told by the landlady that special rates were available for working men. My first proper day at work, and I had been correctly identified as a working man. I felt flattered enough to take a room there and then, but the Skipper was less impressed, and decided to carry on with our search.

Eventually we took a large, twin room in a hotel in Ardbeg, a suburb which linked the metropolis of Rothesay to the south and the smaller town Port Bannatyne to the north. It proved to be a good choice, being a very comfortable antidote to the day's hardships, with friendly staff and with decent breakfasts each morning.

As we returned to the boat, and The Skipper suddenly seemed to be a lot more focused, and he was ready to delegate my first tasks from the huge 'to do' list in his head. My first assignment was to take a scraper and some wire brushes, and set to on the barnacle infestation. I quickly realised that this actually presented me with two, quite different challenges to overcome. The smaller barnacles presented the first challenge, as they were almost impossible to prise from the hull, while the clumps of bigger barnacles near the keel came away much more easily, but were full of a decaying, foul-smelling gue. The challenge here was to avoid being splattered or drenched by this fermenting barnacle soup.

At dusk, we made our way back to the hotel at the end of the first day's work, having made some advances in the war on barnacles. The hotel had a welcoming bar, and it was here that I was to have my induction into the world of malt whiskies. I had never really touched whisky before, and could probably not have distinguished a blend from a malt, but I quickly learned about the basics. There were the 'common' malts, Glenfiddich and Glenmorangie (pronounced to rhyme with 'orangey') and 'rare' ones such as Linkwood and Rosebank. Perhaps it was because of the cold, fresh air that I quickly developed a preference for the warming, heavily peaty Islay malts from Lagavulin, Bowmore and Laphroaig.

I would have to pay particular attention to this subject, as we would regularly stock seven or eight bottles of various malts on board the *Glendale*. The tall tales printed on the labels of these bottles were particularly entertaining, each competing to explain exactly how their product was more authentically entrenched in Highland lore and tradition than the next. Each whisky seemed to be made of the purest or peatiest water and the freshest malted barley, while some boasted of taking on the taste of the sea by being stored in barrels at the tide's edge.

Back in 1987, the malt whisky industry was in decline. As we tasted several of the whiskies on offer in the hotel, I was told that some were getting rare, and that a number of distilleries were planned for closure. Since then, there has been a dramatic revival in the fortunes of the industry as a whole, and not only have once-mothballed brands been brought back on-line, but new distilleries are being built for the first time in over a century. It would be nice to think that our efforts on the *Glendale*, both personal and in introducing our guests to the delights of malt whisky, contributed in some way to this revival.

The weather was cold and bright, and working time was restricted to daylight hours. The Skipper was a reasonable man but quite a hard task-master, and while I was hardly a rebel, I was not used to being told what to do. I was also unprepared for the scrutiny and criticism which came my way. I was diligent, and taking pride in what I was doing, so I didn't take kindly to my paintwork being re-done or screws tightened. From the Skipper's point of view, of course, it made absolute sense to double-check what was being done by this untried and inexperienced novice. It was his business, after all, and its success depended on things being done in a certain way.

To lighten the mood, the Skipper took to referring to me as 'Number One', 'Old Bean' or 'Vieux haricot'. I just called him 'Boss'. I would not have called our relationship strained, but it would be fair to say that we spent several weeks sounding each other out and trying to make sense of one another's personalities.

We still had seven weeks to go before the first cruise, but just over two before the launch date, which had been agreed in advance with the boatyard. The vast majority of our available time was spent between the hotel and the boat. For lunch, we usually ventured into the urban sprawl of Rothesay, and a favourite option was Zavaroni's fish and chip shop. The fish was fried while we waited, and came as close to perfection as I imagined could be possible.

We also tried out a number of other establishments for lunch. On one occasion, we picked up some snacks from a seafood-selling ice cream van. The Skipper assured me that 'clammy-dos' were a local delicacy, although the huge horse-mussel did not look too appetising to me. I took one bite, and experienced the simultaneous textures of slime, rubber and grit, and not the slightest hint of any flavour. I could not stop myself from retching, and it was all I could do to find a quiet spot to spit the whole lot out. The Skipper found this all very amusing, and somehow managed to stomach his outsize mollusc with minimal fuss. I've never had another clammy-do since, but then again, I can't say I've seen anyone trying to sell one.

I liked Rothesay. It was clearly a seaside resort like many others, in that it was many years past its prime, an impression which was amplified by its deserted promenades and benches on grey days during February and March. There were some jewels to be found, though, such as the ornate and immaculate Victorian gents' toilets on the pier. I was unaware that such a sanitary masterpiece even existed, and the outside of the toilet block was quite anonymous, but once inside, the glass cisterns and fake marble surrounds to the huge individual urinals were quite spectacular. The contrast between these and the Portaloos by the boatyard could not have been starker.

The pier itself was in good working order, forming two sheltered, inner harbours, and connecting the island with the mainland via a regular CalMac ferry service. The ferries themselves were already familiar; *Jupiter*, *Juno* and *Saturn* divided their duties between the Gourock – Dunoon route and this one between Rothesay and Wemyss (pronounced 'Weems') Bay.

Over the next two weeks, the boat underwent a slow but total transformation. We had won the battle of the barnacles, and the underside was now coated in a layer of brick-red antifoul paint. We had opted for a new brand of slightly-less-toxic paint, as it would be in our best interests not to poison the marine life on which we were making our living. The sweet pear-drop smell of the paint was often quite overwhelming, but we persevered, and managed to keep to our schedule.

In recognition of my hard work, I was now receiving a weekly pay packet. The Skipper thanked me, and handed me a fistful of Scottish bank notes. I had seen these before, but there was still novelty to be had in the sight of different sets of notes from Bank of Scotland, Royal Bank of Scotland and Clydesdale Bank. I particularly liked the Clydesdale fiver, which seemed to depict a rat on the reverse side. £38 may have seemed a meagre return for such long hours, but I was being housed and fed, so I actually found myself with a few more pounds in my pocket at the end of each week.

The weather was kind to us, if a touch on the cold side. True to form, the west coast was generally frost-free, although on one occasion, a light covering of snow descended almost to sea-level. When it did rain, we would take the opportunity to make progress on the interior. We replaced the carpet-tiles, and applied a coat of paint to the surfaces, including dark brown paint on the huge oak beams, which would be responsible for countless bumps on heads and curses over the coming season.

When I arrived, my DIY and painting experience were non-existent, and I could not have told a Phillips screwdriver from flat-head, let alone work out which way to turn one to move the screw upwards or downwards. I was getting my hands well and truly dirty on a daily basis, but to counter this, I was introduced to the delights of a green, slimy substance called Swarfega. Despite its smell and texture, Swarfega seemed to possess magical properties, and could remove any amount of slime and grime from oily fingers and hands.

The days passed, but there always seemed to be so much more that needed to be done. Most of our time was spent on cosmetic tasks, to freshen up paintwork and polish wooden surfaces. The Skipper also had a long list of other tasks to complete, including the fitting of new electrical circuits to hook up appliances to our new generators. Some of these tasks came about as a direct result of feedback from guests over the years, such as requests for new lights to be installed in the saloon.

A regular visitor to the boatyard was Tony, a rather gnome-like engineer who lived in Tighnabruaich. The Skipper had commissioned him to assemble a contraption which, although I didn't appreciate it at the time, was about to revolutionise life on the *Glendale*. I remembered from my interview that the lights had begun to dim quite quickly on the boat as soon as the engine was killed, and the Mate had been asked to run it from time to time each evening. This was because all of the electricity on the boat was generated by the engine, and only so much of this energy could be retained after it was switched off. Tony was now installing a petrol generator which would make those problems a thing of the past. It wasn't clean, and it wasn't quiet, but it delivered new options and would improve the standard of living on the boat.

Within two weeks of starting, the Skipper trusted me enough to give me some jobs on my own, and I could feel that our progress was picking up momentum. I was now taking on some of the electrical wiring jobs on board, adding plug sockets, and even wiring a new light on a beam over the dining table in the saloon. We shared varnishing and painting jobs, and the interior, while still cold and clammy, was beginning to look very smart.

Back outside, we needed to make sure that the parts of the hull above the water line were ship-shape. After what felt like an age of sanding and priming, we applied a layer of grey undercoat, and suddenly, the *Glendale* was looking quite smart, if a little military. We could see the light at the end of the tunnel.

The time had come to make the *Glendale* look like the *Glendale* of the brochures, with the application of a coat of midnight blue paint to the hull, topped off with a broad stripe of monarch red on the bulwarks. We were making good progress, and the Skipper decided to make a trip into Glasgow for some supplies. I was left alone, in charge of the boat for the first time.

"Don't fall off the ladder" the Skipper quipped as he pulled away in his battered Volvo.

I was left to reflect on the fact that my working environment was undeniably a pleasant one. The boatyard was at the head of a quiet bay, with low hills to the north and west, gently rolling down to the shore. The entrances to the West Kyle, Loch Striven and the Clyde itself were hidden behind headlands, as was Rothesay, which was just out of sight to our south. The ferry from Wemyss Bay to Rothesay could be seen plying its route in the distance.   A large gathering of ducks, mainly Eider and Goldeneye, spent much of the time just offshore, and a smart drake Scaup joined them on several occasions.   On calm days, the calls of displaying drake Goldeneyes drifted across the water, intermingled with the comical, Frankie Howerd-like cooing of the Eiders.   Buzzards often drifted by, their mewing calls adding a final touch to the wildness and tranquillity of the atmosphere.

I was making good progress with the paintwork, and had positioned the ladder at the stern of the boat. The paint pot was suspended from a rung using a bent coat hanger, so that one hand was always free to hold the ladder and the other one could wield the paintbrush. I could usually cover a decent area from each ladder position by leaning out to the sides and extending my long arms.

As I reached out one more time, I suddenly felt the feet of the ladder swivel. Slowly at first, the ladder began to fall away. I made a rather graceful arc of paint on the hull with my brush hand, and frantically scrambled to gain a fingerhold with my other on the top edge of the hull.

I was now in a very tricky position. I was not going to be able to get down without a fall of 12 feet, and there was a real danger of landing on the rocks below. I also had visions of the paint pot following me and landing upside-down on my head. I needed help from somewhere, and it could have been hours before the Skipper would return. I decided that it would be best just to hang on, and found that the edge of the hull gave me two good fingerholds.

It felt like an age, but I could only have been hanging there for a few minutes at the most. As I frantically looked around for assistance, I noticed a movement in the boatyard. I let out a pitiful cry of "help!" with no response. My pleas became more urgent. "Help! HELP!" A man emerged from the boatyard and came across to assist. He took hold of the ladder, and as I let go of the boat, the ladder twisted quite violently on one of its feet. I clung on, and managed to descend quite safely, though if a little shakily. The Skipper was highly amused by this tale on his return from Glasgow soon afterwards. I didn't mind that I had given him the chance to have a laugh at my expense, as I was just glad to have emerged from the episode unscathed.

The day after we had completed the gloss work, we arrived at the boat to find that our latest efforts had been undone by an overnight frost. The gloss finish had been roughened up, so we had to set to on re-applying more monarch red and midnight blue, and kept a close eye on the weather forecast for more signs of frost or rain. My experiences from the previous day meant that I was a little more careful in positioning the ladder, and we completed the task of re-painting without any further drama.

We were luckier second time around, and the finishing touches were applied as we approached the launch date. A brilliant white water line separated from deep blue hull from the brick-red antifoul paint. The red bulwarks looked very smart to top things off, as did the wheelhouse with its new coat of white, and the wood-effect paint around the windows. The cover of the fish-hold, which was now the semi-glazed roof of the saloon, was painted dark blue between the sky-lights. The boat retained several winches and rusty capstans from its fishing days, and these were now resplendent in a coat of dove-grey paint. The deck was last to be painted as we waited for some tar caulking to set between planks before applying red deck-paint.

The very last task before launch undid some of the effect of our smart paintwork. We slung about ten old black tyres over the monarch-red bulwarks and midnight-blue hull to act as protective fenders on our port side. These were from an old school bus in Tighnabruaich, and added a touch of authenticity to our claims to being a 'genuine' trawler. We had completed our work for my first working deadline on schedule. I knew that the Skipper had been the brains behind this operation, but I secretly felt pleased with my contribution.

5. Launch & Shakedown

The day of the launch arrived. We checked out of our hotel and said our farewells to our hosts, who wished us luck for the season ahead. Back at the boatyard, which until now had been a quiet, almost sleepy place, we were greeted by a hive of activity. The Skipper met with the boatyard owner, and they went through the finer details of the launch plan, before we climbed the ladder for the last time. We were joined on board by engineer Tony, who had now completed the installation of a new generator and electrics on the boat.

The wooden poles which had supported the boat for the winter were removed, and a noisy winch was fired up. The Skipper explained to me that this would be quite a slow process, and that we were to be gradually allowed to inch down the slipway, controlled carefully by the winch, down the rails and into the water. Once at the bottom of the slip, we would wait for the rising tide to carry us away.

That was the plan, but almost immediately, I could see that things weren't going quite as expected. We should have been moving by now, but nothing was happening. The boatyard owner shouted up to us to explain that the wheels beneath us had flattened slightly over the winter, and were not turning. I couldn't see what was happening below the boat, but the adjustments (and brute force) applied by some of the boatyard crew had apparently been successful. We were now being lowered, a few inches at a time, towards the incoming tide. This was clearly going to be a lengthy process, so I went below decks to carry on with some tasks inside.

The inch-by-inch progress carried on for a while, but then, all of a sudden, we were on the move. Faster and faster, we went backwards down the slipway. I was in the crew's quarters, and managed to get up the ladder into the wheelhouse in time to see the world speeding by. We must have travelled around thirty metres, before splashing into the sea. Calm heads had been maintained throughout, but the whole episode had actually been very dangerous. Had we toppled over to one side at speed, there could have been some serious damage to the boat, not to mention the three of us who were on board.

So, after a more-dramatic-than-planned launch, we were at sea again. For a minute or so, the *Glendale* floated along quietly and serenely, back in her natural element. The air felt cooler and quiet descended on the decks, with the only noise being the gentle slapping of ripples of water against the newly-painted hull. It felt good to be back on the water after such a long time marooned ashore, and for the first time, I could feel myself warming to the ways of the salty dog. The water seemed surprisingly close after having been perched so high and dry on the slipway for the past few weeks, and our new element stretched in all directions around us, providing a sudden and real sense of freedom.

Then the engine coughed and spluttered a little before roaring into life, and we slowly edged out of Port Bannatyne Bay, past Ardmaleish and into the Kyles. We slowed down to pass through the narrow channel through the Burnt Islands, and soon, our home base of Tighnabruaich came into view. It was easy to see how the water could be the main mode of trade and transport in this area, as it had been during the 19th Century. Even now, there were no straight roads, and the sea provided a link between all of the main towns and ports in the Clyde.

A legacy of this history was the large number of piers that sprang up around its coastline. As the 20th Century progressed, a lot of these piers began to decay, and for the most part, those which did not serve commercial ferries or ports had been militarised, condemned or dismantled. We were grateful that our chosen base had been spared any of these fates.

There had originally been at least three piers in Tighnabruaich, with those at Kames and Auchenlochan being in addition to our home base.

Tighnabruaich Pier remained in good condition, and as well as serving as a base for the *Glendale* and a couple of local fishing boats, its main role was as a port of call for boats running pleasure trips from Glasgow. Most notable of these was the last surviving paddle-steamer, the *Waverley*, which ran a programme of summer cruises in the Clyde, and provided a throwback to the golden age of these waters.

Tighnabruaich proved to be an ideal base for the Beagle venture, as it was remote enough to carry a hint of the exotic, but not so far away as to make it impossible for people to reach us in time to start their week-long cruise on a Saturday evening. Added to this convenience factor, the magnificent scenery and tranquillity meant that the holiday really began as soon as the guests arrived.

During our first couple of weeks back in the village, we were complimented on how smart the *Glendale* was looking by the locals. Below decks, we still had some painting and varnishing to do before our first cruise. A carpenter from the local boatyard came out and made some impressively swift and skilful adjustments to the woodwork on the seats in the saloon.

The *Glendale* was back where she belonged, afloat and among the waves, but another launch was needed before the Beagle fleet was complete. *Gordon* had been waiting patiently like a faithful dog, tethered to a trailer in the small car park at the head of the pier. Preparations for her launch started there, as I was shown how to ensure that each section of her hull was inflated to the correct pressure.

As the waters rose, and high tide approached, the time came for the Skipper to couple up the trailer to his rusty Volvo, and reverse down the small stone slipway which ran parallel to the pier. The trailer was immersed by the incoming tide, and we climbed into *Gordon*, to set about unfastening ropes and bungee cords. Preparing the engine was hard work, and it took both of us to lower the 55 horsepower outboard into place before bolting it to a wooden board at the stern. Finally, we attached the all-important propeller, which was held in place by a seemingly flimsy split-pin.

By now, the tide was lapping around *Gordon's* inflated orange hull. With the help of the two paddles which were stowed on board as back-up engines, we managed to lever ourselves off the trailer, and found ourselves afloat at last. We donned bulky orange lifejackets, and now it was time for my latest training session; a driving lesson in *Gordon*.

The last time I had been in *Gordon* it was with the old Mate, bombing up and down the straits off Inchmarnock. It had been great fun, but I really had no idea as to whether I would have any aptitude for this, and I guessed that there would be plenty of scope for getting things wrong. We spent the afternoon going through the basics. First, the engine had to be lowered into the water, and a final check made to ensure that the water was deep enough to start her up without damaging the propeller on the rocky sea bed. Then came the trickiest part – starting the engine by quickly pulling a small handle and a cord. The Skipper gave three yanks and the engine roared into life. He then promptly switched it off again. Now it was my turn.

While I was tall, to call me 'wiry' would have been a compliment; 'skinny' was much more of an accurate description. I imagined that a lot of strength would be needed to perform this task, and sure enough, my first few attempts came up short, the cord jamming abruptly each time and seemingly jarring every joint in my limbs. But I persevered, and quickly learned that timing and use of the body, rather than arm strength alone, held the key. At last I was successful, and my reward would be a most exhilarating driving lesson.

It seemed that Gordon had three speeds: astern (still 'backwards' to me), idle and flat-out ahead. We flew across the surface of the Kyle, buffeted slightly by the small waves, travelling at our maximum speed of nearly twenty knots. The throttle also acted as the tiller, so I had to move it away to steer to port, and pull it towards me to go to starboard. It was great fun, dashing to and fro, and getting a feel for how tightly a turn could be made without the engine suddenly growling and losing power. The Skipper explained that this was caused by 'cavitation', when too much air reached the propeller causing a startling growling noise and a loss of propulsion.

The fun part of the lesson was now put on hold, as it was time to learn the routine for taking *Gordon* ashore onto a beach. Again, timing was of the essence. We needed enough momentum to reach the shore, but had to kill the engine and heave the propeller out of the water as we floated in. And again, I had to learn the knack for this task, which involved putting a foot on the board to which the engine was bolted, grabbing a handle, and then leaning back to lift it upwards. We repeated the routine several times, and also tried approaching the shore in shallow water using the paddles and longer oars to help us along.

After about an hour, much to my surprise and delight, I was a fully proficient *Gordon*-handler. I took the helm as we sped back across the Kyle towards the *Glendale* on the pier, and was allowed to bring her alongside, before climbing onto the more solid timbers of the mother ship. The Skipper then had to go up the pier to retrieve his trailer, before we walked into the village to unwind over a pint.

Handling the big boat was a different proposition altogether. I took the helm whenever possible, and getting from a to b was quite straightforward. I would not be allowed to actually dock the boat for some time, but we did practise some of the regular tasks which I would face in the season ahead. We cruised up and down the Kyles, stopping in a small bay off the shore of Bute so the Skipper could show me how to check whether the anchor was secure – he ran the boat gently astern, and I was to hold the anchor rope to make sure that it went taut when the anchor and chain bit into the sea-bed.

Our rather snazzy, hi-tech anchor was stored in a cradle at the bow, behind which was a long length of chain leading back to the original winch from the *Glendale*'s trawling days. In turn, the chain was attached to an enormous length of rope, all the way to the 'bitter end' which was secured to the winch. I had been under the popular misconception that the anchor itself dug into the sea bed, but I learned that the reality was more akin to a plastic weight on a string keeping a helium balloon from floating away. Our flashy anchor was really a piece of over-engineering for our purposes – the length of heavy chain was much more instrumental in keeping us 'anchored'.

*

Now that we were properly based in Tighnabruaich, we were in a position to socialise much more than we had done while staying on Bute. Friday night offered me a chance to join the Skipper for my first big night out on the town.

We started early, and walked a mile along the sea front to take advantage of Happy Hour at the Royal. The Skipper was evidently a popular figure around the village, but one skill in which he was rather lacking was in making introductions. Eventually, I either introduced myself to, or was approached by, a number of his friends. Many of these people had been involved in fitting out the *Glendale*, and still worked up at the boatyard. Others were fish farmers or ran fishing boats, and there was even a submarine officer, who lived in the village when not on duty or working at the base in Rosyth. I had never before been anywhere in which the locals were so inextricably linked with the sea for their livelihoods.

Happy Hour was an almost exclusively male affair, and we stayed in the Royal long after prices reverted to normal at 6pm. The bar was basic, but was obviously a favourite watering hole among the locals, who continued to arrive as the evening wore on. We decided to escape the crush, and moved into the more spacious lounge where we took on some locals at pool. I got to know a lot of people in this way, but I was struggling to remember their names. There were Donalds, Anguses and Ewans, and for the commoner names, the local custom was to use nicknames to distinguish between them. My favourite such nickname was assigned to one of the few remaining Gaelic speakers in the village, a former pier master named Iain. He was known as 'Iain the Pier', although he was quick to point out that this was "On account of my profession, not my bladder control."

We completed our pub crawl by stopping at the Tighnabruaich Hotel en route back towards the boat. This had a more modern, less cosy interior than the Royal, and was panelled with wood which had, apparently, been salvaged from a local wreck. I recognised some of the characters from the Royal, and a few wives and girlfriends were now accompanying their menfolk.

A small, black-haired woman walked in and was warmly greeted by the locals. The Skipper seemed to be delighted to see her, and gave her a warm hug. She noticed me standing nearby, and demanded that the Skipper introduced me. This was Laurie, who had, until recently, been the local district nurse, but who had recently moved to another village a few miles away.

Laurie seemed genuinely pleased to meet me, and was especially pleased that I was a Geordie, as her father had come from the north-east of England. It was the way in which she told me that she loved the Geordie accent that made me start to put my defences up. I was not very accomplished at interpreting the body language and psychology of the opposite sex, but even I could sense that something was stirring here. I enjoyed listening to her tales from her time living in Shetland, and could not fail to be impressed by her superb impressions of a Stonechat's call, but that was definitely as far as I was prepared to take things with Laurie.

It was getting late, and we had a long car journey back down south awaiting us in the morning, so we rounded off the evening's drinking with a couple of malts and walked the half mile back to the pier, where the *Glendale*'s anchor light shone to guide us home. The Skipper took great delight in winding me up about Laurie, telling me that she had a bit of a reputation in these parts as a man-eater, and that he could tell that I was in her sights. I had enjoyed my night out, and the locals had made me feel very welcome. Perhaps too welcome in Laurie's case.

The work had been hard at times, but I felt a real pride and satisfaction that the fruits of our labour were so readily seen by all. Despite all that had been achieved, it was still early March, and there were several weeks to go before the season got underway. The plan was to have a well-earned break for a few days, and then return at the end of the week for a dress rehearsal for the cruises to follow; a 'shakedown' cruise during which invited guests would be our guinea pigs, and I could get a flavour of the season ahead.

Early the next day, we took the *Glendale* over to her mooring near the pier, before leaving Tighnabruaich for a trip back 'down south' to the north-east of England. As we queued for the small, red and white Western Ferry to take us from Hunter's Quay to Gourock, another, much bigger, red and white ferry was dominating the headlines on the car radio. The tragic sinking of Townsend Thoresen's *Herald of Free Enterprise* off Zeebrugge suddenly struck a chord on a number of levels. Firstly, and most obviously, we were about to board a red and white car ferry, but now that I was about to begin a life at sea, the news felt more personally relevant to me. And the fact that I had even travelled on that very ship, on a crossing to France a few years earlier, brought it even closer to home.

Our ferry, *Sound of Shuna*, managed to complete the crossing safely, and we made good progress until we were well on our way down the A74. Snow began to fall as we got into Dumfries and Galloway, and as we approached Beattock (a steady climb), only one lane remained snow-free.

Traffic was now crawling along at 20mph as we made our painstaking progress towards the border. To make matters worse, we were pulled over by a policeman who spent fifteen precious minutes checking whether the rusting Volvo was actually roadworthy.

I became increasingly agitated as the delays began to mount. While I had been working for a little over three weeks, my priorities in the early part of my career had not yet become fully work-focused. I had attended every Newcastle United home match for over two and a half seasons, and one of my biggest concerns in taking my new job had been how I was going to explain to my friends that I wouldn't be able to get home every other Saturday for a pint in the George and Dragon and a trip to stand on the Gallowgate End in the rain. The Skipper's planned trip back to Sedgefield this weekend, combined with the vagaries of the Division One fixture list, meant that I was to have a stay of execution, and would be able to attend the Aston Villa game to maintain my sequence of matches.

Three o'clock, kick-off time, came and went, and we were still on the A69. I could still make it for the second half, I kidded myself. But even this was to be an optimistic aim. As we pulled up outside the Gallowgate End of St James's Park, I heard a loud cheer, and the radio informed us that Peter Beardsley had just put Newcastle 2-1 up. Arriving at the gate, the stewards turned me away, as they would not let me into the ground with my large bag. Still undeterred, I found a friendly burger van owner who allowed me to deposit the bag behind his fat fryer. Returning to the gates, I slipped the steward a genuine Scottish pound note, and sprinted up the steps and onto the terracing. The remaining twenty minutes were played out uneventfully. After the game, I retrieved my bag from the burger van and went home on the bus, surrounded by a slight smell of hot dogs and onions. This marked the end of my sequence of matches. Now I had to face up to the fact that getting to home matches was no longer my top priority in life.

By the time the following Saturday came around, we had travelled north-west again to prepare for our shakedown cruise. To compensate for missing the football for the rest of the season, I decided to try watching a quite different sport.

Tighnabruaich was home to a famous shinty team called Kyles Athletic, who had recently been through a golden age, including a coveted Camanachd Cup title just four years earlier. I vaguely knew about the game – a bit like a cross between hockey and hurling, and a couple of locals suggested that I go along to watch a match that afternoon.

The players used sticks, which at first glance resembled hockey sticks, but further inspection revealed that striking area was triangular in section. Defenders used subtly differently shaped sticks to strikers – a '9-iron' to loft the ball over a longer distance as opposed to the strikers, who used flatter, '1-iron' sticks to make sure their shots did not fly over the bar.

The 'stadium' was on one of the few flat areas at the Kames end of Tighnabruaich. The best vantage point from which to watch a game was from the roadside, which climbed steeply up the hillside along one flank of the pitch. The opposite touchline was a few yards away from the rocky beach. The game which I saw was against Newtonmore from the Highlands; most of the other big clubs in the world of shinty came from the Speyside area.

Shinty players were truly hard men – in fact, I very quickly came to the conclusion that shinty players were the hardest of all sportsmen. The ball, which was smaller than a cricket ball and even denser, would be fired over great distances down the pitch, and then chest-trapped by a defender. I felt sure that if I had tried that, I would have at least cracked my sternum or even been killed by a blow to the heart.

It was a scrappy match, which ended in a 1-1 draw. A more telling statistic from the game I had watched was that there was only one broken nose inflicted. I was asked after the game if I would like to join the club and come along to training. I declined, relieved that I had the ready-made excuse of working most weekends, and failing to mention the fact that I thought that the game looked to be life-threatening. I wondered, in later days, whether I had missed an opportunity in life. Perhaps I could have gone on to play shinty for England one day. If they had a shinty team.

Social life in Tighnabruaich was very much focused on the three hotel pubs (the Tighnabruaich, the Royal, and, if we wanted a really long walk, the Kames). The locals were always keen to add some variety to the routine, and for them, there was nothing better than a good old-fashioned jiggedy-hop to look forward to at the weekend.

A ceilidh had been organised in a barn near Kilfinan, a couple of miles north of Tighnabruaich, and the Skipper was quick to count himself in to attend. I wasn't too keen on dancing in general, and the prospect of traditional Scottish Dancing filled me with some trepidation. The Skipper tried to jolly me along, and I decided to go along to see what it was all about.

The Kyles may not have been a hotbed of fashion, but the current trends followed by the rest of the country had certainly reached the area. There were perms and mullets aplenty, and jumpers were firmly tucked into stone-washed jeans. I was certainly no fashionista, but even I knew that wearing wellies to any party was not really the norm. The Skipper, proud of his new pair of gleaming white wellies, told me that everyone wore them. I had serious reservations, as I pulled on my new green wellies and we headed up the road to the ceilidh.

The party was in full swing when we arrived, and the barn building was jumping with reeling and jigging locals. I was mortified when I immediately realised that the floors were bone-dry, and the company completely devoid of wellies. The Skipper soon got into the groove, introducing his own, bobbing, white-wellied version of traditional dances. I stayed firmly on the fringes and in the shadows, chatting to locals and clutching my can of heavy, hoping that somehow, no-one would notice my footwear.

Back on the *Glendale*, preparations were now complete for the shakedown cruise, with an assortment of friends of the Skipper due to arrive that evening. A couple of his friends had to cancel at short notice, so we were expecting just three guests. Among them was a character with whose reputation I was already familiar, and one who would live up to and exceed expectations.

Jonathan Charles Binge was an entomologist / stand-up comedian who was actually a former Beagle employee, having served as crew on a few cruises in the first season. He applied his insect expertise in his 'proper' career, which was to kill a lot of them on behalf of his employer, Rentokil. Binge supplemented this income by offering his services as a stand-up comedian. His career as an Incredible Hulk-ogram had recently come to a premature end after he was violently mobbed and injured at a hen-party.

I had heard tales of Binge falling off piers while relieving himself, and performing any number of weird shenanigans in odd places. He had evidently taken care to pack only essential items for the cruise, including luminous green contact lenses and an assortment of wigs.

Binge had driven from Teesside with the other two guests; Lizzie was his girlfriend, and they were joined by Susan, a girlfriend of the Skipper.

The objective of the shakedown cruise was primarily to make sure that all systems were fully functioning, but it also served as a valuable training week for me ahead of the season, and gave me an opportunity to get to know some of the locations we would visit during the season that followed. I already knew our first port of call, Tarbert, from my interview.

Tarbert, Loch Fyne was one of a number of Tarberts and Tarbets in the West of Scotland. All of these can be found on narrow isthmuses, which is not a coincidence – any such isthmus over which a Viking crew could drag their longboat would qualify for this Nordic name. Magnus Barefoot, King of Norway, did just that in 1098. Scottish King Edgar decreed that the Norwegians could lay claim to any island around which they could navigate in a boat. Barefoot sat at the helm of his boat as it was pulled across the isthmus, and duly claimed the 'island' of Kintyre for Norway.

Our Tarbert was a cosy little harbour, completely sheltered from the elements no matter what the wind direction. In appearance, the quayside was not unlike that at Tobermory (or Balamory, for that matter), fronted by several brightly-coloured stone buildings nestling under wooded slopes. The waters of the harbour were home to a few Black Guillemots and Grey Seals, including a huge one-eyed bull which would squint at us as we watched it from the pier.

It was getting dark as we tied up alongside another trawler on the crowded fish quay, and we clambered across its decks before going ashore for an evening in the Islay Frigate. So far, the agenda for the evening had been much the same as it had been a few months earlier during my interview, but there would be no frogs' legs tonight – just a bar meal of scampi and chips and a few pints of heavy.

Back on the boat, we made some inroads into the *Glendale*'s stock of drinks. Binge gave us a performance of his Michael Jackson / Incredible Hulk routine, complete with surprisingly scary luminous green contact lenses, whose effect was enhanced as they emerged from the darker recesses of the saloon.

Our sleep was interrupted at dawn, when the fishing boats to which we had tied needed to put out to sea. The Skipper and I got up and re-tied the boat to the quay, before returning to our respective cabins for some more sleep. I woke again in mid-morning to hear voices from the deck above. I was still in my clothes after our disturbance earlier in the morning, so I went up the ladder to see what was happening. The Skipper was up there already, and talking to a ruddy-faced local on the quay. The Skipper greeted him warmly, and shook his hand, and the two seemed to be getting along like long lost friends. This, I learned, was Donald the Water Man. He soon returned, clutching a hose, which we then used to replenish our two water tanks on board. As the tanks overflowed, Donald switched off the tap and took the hose away to tidy it up, before returning and lingering on the quay, obviously waiting for something.

The Skipper went below decks, and returned with four cans of McEwan's Export. Donald took these gratefully, and shuffled off with his payment. The Skipper explained that Donald the Water Man was not employed by the Harbour Master, and that we could have just as easily gone to fetch the water ourselves. Donald had similar arrangements with other boats, however, and used it as a way to keep himself in beer.

We finally left Tarbert after another pub lunch in the Islay Frigate, and our next stop was to my return to the only place in the Clyde which I had visited before joining Beagle Cruises; the Isle of Arran. I had last set foot on Arran just under three years earlier, when I had spent a week based on its south coast for a field course in the first year of my Environmental Studies degree. It was an enjoyable week, and I was looking forward to the chance to go ashore on the island again.

I had never been particularly keen on geology, but soon learned why Arran had been chosen as the destination for our trip. The mountains to the north of the island, which dominated the horizon from almost anywhere in our cruising area, were from the remains of a massive, volcanic upheaval in the area at around the time at which the coasts of Europe and North America were torn apart. The mountains themselves were made of the granite which had surged up into the earth's crust, and all of the rocks which had previously been layered above were now tilted and neatly arranged for examination by students in exposed layers on Arran's north-eastern shore.

I even managed to get some birding in amid the fieldwork, watching Dippers and Grey Wagtails flying past while I waded in Machrie Water, a small river on Arran's west coast. Common Sandpipers and Red-breasted Mergansers appeared at regular intervals around the shore of the island, and further inland, where we saw some very dapper male Whinchats in Glen Rosa.

The undoubted highlight came during a coach trip around the northern end of the island. It wasn't the probable Black Guillemot off Whitefarland, which I could just make out from the coach as a dark, floating object with a big white circular patch. Unfortunately, based on the view I had, I could not completely rule out the possibility of it being an empty can of Tennent's Super. Shortly after that sighting, we passed through the lovely village of Lochranza, and shortly afterwards, I noticed a large bird of prey soaring in front of the hill. I was familiar with Buzzards, several of which had been responsible for false eagle alarms already that week. As I watched, I became more and more convinced that this was the real thing.

Our driver was not the most accommodating type. He was rumoured to have been a Panzer Tank driver during the war, and was not to be trifled with. I walked forward to point out the great bird to some of the lecturers and trip organisers, and the Panzer Tank driver reluctantly pulled the big blue coach into a passing place. The group was able to watch a fine adult Golden Eagle soaring overhead. I could not possibly have foreseen how familiar that place, and very probably that bird, would become just a few years later.

I am not a big believer in fate, but I do like a nice coincidence. At some point during that week, perhaps at Brodick or at Lochranza, or maybe as we drove along the western shore of Arran, I may well have seen a blue and red trawler, with a large orange dinghy in tow. I really don't remember doing so, but if I did, it would have been a nice coincidence.

Now we were approaching Lochranza again, albeit from quite a different angle to the one the coach had done on that sunny May day in 1984. From the north east, Arran's cliffs and rolling, bracken-clad hills offered little indication that a small harbour was just a little further along the coast. Then a space began to appear between two hills, and as we approached, a village began to emerge like a string of beads from behind the headland.

As we rounded the point, the whole of Lochranza Bay spread before us, with the small village huddled along its western shore. The loch and the flat-floored glacial valley behind were flanked on three sides by steep hills which served to frame a ruined, ivy-covered castle behind the bay. This, along with every other ruined castle in the Clyde, was rumoured to have housed the Bruce, and was no doubt the location for his press conference when he named his Scotland team to face England at Bannockburn.

The *Glendale* slowed and glided through the still water. The Skipper explained to me that we would normally spend the night at anchor in the bay, but that the calm conditions gave us a more convenient alternative option. Instead of continuing up and into the bay, the Skipper tentatively approached the near-condemned wooden pier at the mouth of this beautiful bay. The Caledonian MacBrayne ferry had long since switched to using an adjacent concrete slipway to load and offload cars en route to Claonaig on the Kintyre peninsula, and now the old pier was left to the mercy of the elements.

Some of the timber piles at the front of the pier swung loosely as we gently nudged against them, but it felt pretty stable and solid when I went ashore to tie up the ropes. Binge and the ladies joined us as we walked along the quiet road through the village, from where we could see that the castle was actually built on a narrow shingle spit, which snaked out from the near shore but did not quite bisect the loch. The tidal area beyond was much shallower than the main part of the loch, as belied by the presence of wading Herons and Curlews far from the shore.

We carried on along the flat valley floor, with the sun hidden from view by the hills to our right. These hills are responsible for Lochranza's entry in the record books as the least sunny village in the British Isles, as the sun does not break this horizon between November and February.

A hunch-backed hill formed the back wall of Lochranza's glacial amphitheatre, and we made our way along the road on the flat floor of the valley towards it. This was the aptly-named Tor Nead an Eoin, or "Hill of the Bird's Nest" in Gaelic. We stopped at a small, grassy area at the foot of the tor, and started to scan the skies in the hope of glimpsing an eagle. On this day, the search for the Clyde's star bird met with limited success, as we had nothing more than a fleeting glimpse of a magnificent adult. It briefly broke the skyline before retreating out of sight, low over the brow of the hill, but even this fleeting encounter whetted my appetite for a season of eagle-watching ahead. Unlike most birds, which are gone from view over the horizon in an instant, the huge wingspan of the eagle meant that it gradually disappeared feather by feather, leaving a lasting impression on the memory.

The sliver of sunshine was now restricted to the very tops of the hills on the eastern side of the valley, so we decided to make our way back towards the boat. There was still time for my first visit to the very welcoming bar of the Lochranza Hotel, where we made ourselves comfortable and enjoyed a pint. The Skipper introduced me to the landlord, George, and a barman called George who happened to be George's son. George Junior gave us an update on the progress of his new baby, for whom they had chosen the name George.

A friendly, long-furred cat came and joined us, and started to wrap itself around our legs.

"What's the cat's name?" I asked George.

"Seefer," said George.

Perhaps I had been thrown off balance by this unexpected, non-Georgian answer, and I proceeded to fall into the trap.

"Why Seefer?" I asked.

"It's Seefer Cat."

There was another arm to the Beagle Cruises Empire. Carl, with whom the Skipper had dreamed up the whole idea four years earlier, had branched out the previous summer to start a Land Rover-based wildlife safari based in Lochranza. Carl was a big character, with a rock'n'roll background, and had a huge enthusiasm for birds. One of the highlights of his holidays was an exchange, whereby his guests would have a day aboard the *Glendale* and ours were offered the option of spending a day on Arran. This way, Carl could take our group to areas not accessible by boat, and his guests would have a chance to mess around on the water.

Carl met up with us all for another pub meal in the Lochranza Hotel that evening, giving me my first taste of a Beagle 'staff meeting', something which we tried to arrange every week. It was good for me to talk to someone who had been through similar experiences in the past, and the early meetings gave me an idea of what was to follow. I was introduced to some of the parlance on board. At first, I was surprised to hear about the guests being routinely referred to as 'punters'. Surely 'guests' or 'passengers' would be much more appropriate and respectful. But within a couple of weeks, it would seem very natural. Not in a nasty way, but it helped to retain an impression of otherness – they were on holiday and were paying for the privilege, and we had to keep them happy. One golden rule which had to be established from the off was that we NEVER called the punters 'punters' in front of the punters.

Carl shared my passion for birds, but he warned me that the punters rarely shared our level of enthusiasm. All was not lost, though, as he introduced me to the little-known phenomenon of 'Punter Value', or just plain 'PV'. PV seemed to be the best way of quantifying this pizzazz or animal X-factor and was used to describe anything which was known to go down particularly well with the punters, from food and furniture to animals and birds. Some high PV animals and birds were quite obvious. Close-up views of Puffins or Basking Sharks were regular favourites, and Golden Eagles seldom failed to impress. Sometimes it was the little marine critters that went down particularly well. Shore Crabs and Common Starfish scored highly, and we gave the punters an opportunity to see these everyday creatures through new eyes. Carl also pointed out that PV could be delivered by experiences aside from wildlife-viewing, such as a particularly good meal or a spectacular west coast sunset.

It came as a big relief for me to finally find a properly like-minded person, who was on the same wavelength as me when it came to birding. I got on perfectly well with the Skipper, Binge and with most of the people I had met since starting work, but conversations about birds had always been perhaps a little patronising or puzzling. I looked forward to our trips to Lochranza, for encounters with eagles, but also to chat about birds over a pint and a dram with someone who knew where I was coming from.

6. Meeting Morag

The *Glendale* pulled out of Lochranza the following morning with a hung over company and crew on board after another long night in the bar. A course was set to take us southwards down Kilbrannan Sound, the deep channel that separates Arran from Kintyre, for a cruise to Campbeltown. Calculating cruise times was a straightforward affair, as the *Glendale* would bumble along at a steady six knots, and the tides in the Clyde area were not very strong. Today's cruise would be a little over 18 miles, and sure enough, just under three hours later, we were passing under the whitewashed lighthouse on Island Davaar, and entering Campbeltown Loch.

Campbeltown harbour nestled in the far corner of the loch just, below the town itself. We could see three trawlers docked on the outer wall, alongside a busy fish quay where their catch was being unloaded. Lorries waited to take the fish boxes to market, and Herring Gulls shrieked and squabbled over any scraps which came their way. The port presented excellent shelter from the elements, its square of piers being broken in one corner by a small entrance to a large inner harbour. It was a busy day, but we were able to find a stretch of vacant quay between its fleet of trawlers against which to tie up and go ashore.

Campbeltown was the largest town which we visited on a regular basis, and lacked some of the cosiness of the other ports around the Clyde, feeling rather bleaker and more urban than the likes of Tarbert and Tighnabruaich. The greyness of the skies highlighted the austerity of its stone buildings, with its large church providing an imposing sight as its bell tower dominated the town's skyline. The relative peace was shattered by the roar of a huge American military plane overhead, as it made its final approach to the air base at Machrihanish on the other side of the peninsula.

Walking into town involved crossing the only stretch of dual carriageway on the Kintyre peninsula, dodging the suped-up Escort XR3is which roared up and down along its 200 metre length.

What Campbeltown lacked in looks, it more than made up for in convenience and practicality. As well as providing a good harbour and source of supplies, it was a perfect starting point for trips to our two most southerly destinations. The great granite dome of Ailsa Craig, with its huge Gannet colony, would take a little over four hours to reach, but time and a forecast of a brisk south-westerly breeze would prevent us from attempting the rather exposed voyage on this occasion. A lesser-known island, Sanda, which lies about a mile off the southern tip of Kintyre, was about two hours away, and this would be our next destination.

My only previous sighting of Sanda had been from Arran, where the locals knew it as 'Spoon Island' due to its profile from that viewpoint. It was a place that did not look out of the ordinary, either from Arran or from the charts and maps, with no obvious cliffs or other features. But it was a place of which the Skipper and Carl spoke with a real fondness and almost a sense of wonder. Sanda was, in the words of the Skipper, "the jewel in the Clyde."

After such a build-up, I was impatient to get away from Campbeltown the next morning, but I had to learn that we needed to take advantage of our limited opportunities to take fresh supplies on board. I felt like a reluctant kid being dragged around the shops, but there were only so many places in the Clyde where we could buy fresh stilton. I was introduced to the small Galbraith supermarket, as well as local butcher and greengrocer shops.

I was still quite unused to food shopping, especially 'traditional' food shopping. I had no idea about how much anything weighed, so it was a relief to find that, in the greengrocers at least, you could just pick your own. It also helped that I was joined by Lizzie and Susan, who were buying ingredients to make a lamb curry that evening. We struggled back to the pier, laden with provisions, and readied the boat for the next leg of the trip.

It was almost midday by the time we left the shelter of the square harbour, and I took the wheel as we chugged out into Campbeltown Loch. At this point, the Skipper decided to set me a small test. Island Davaar stood at the mouth of the loch, with clear views out to the open sea on both sides. The Skipper asked me which side of Island Davaar we should choose to pass on, as the more direct route appeared to be to its south. I was ahead of the game, however, as I had already noticed from the charts that this channel was something of an illusion. The water here was shallow, and would actually expose a broad isthmus at low tide, an area known as the Dhorlin. So we had to go the 'long' (and only navigable) way around Davaar, passing under the lighthouse on its northern coast.

We rounded Davaar, and turned south to follow the last few miles of Kintyre's east coast. Seabirds became more plentiful as we approached their colonies on the islands to the south. It was still only March, but all of the birds were in smart breeding plumage. Pot-bellied Black Guillemots whirred past, flashing white oval patches on their black wings. Shags, complete with shaggy crests, rested on the surface of the sea around us, some floating with wings outstretched to dry in the breeze.

Sanda then came into view, along with two other islands. Sheep Island appeared flat-topped, almost rectangular, and lay between us and the main island. The island of Glunimore appeared as a pyramid-like pile of rocks off Sanda's east coast. The tide was low, exposing several other rocky, temporary islands which completed the little archipelago.

The approach to Sanda was quite hazardous, with whirlpools and rip-tides off the tip of Sheep Island, and a series of reefs to negotiate before we reached the shallow, sandy area where it was safe to drop anchor. I learned how to find a safe route to the anchorage, by lining up the roof of a farm building with the low point of a saddle on the horizon. The sea suddenly became quite shallow, and depth readings which had shown over ten metres of water beneath us for most of the trip suddenly indicated that the water was now just three metres deep. The Skipper gave me the signal to drop the anchor. I released the brake, and the anchor plunged into the water, followed by its chain and length of rope. I re-applied the brake, and checked that the rope was taut, before signalling back to confirm that the anchor had properly settled into the sandy sea floor.

We all jumped down into *Gordon*, and made the short trip to the shore, where we tied her up to a small stone jetty under a disused and rapidly degenerating farmhouse. The island was uninhabited aside from three lighthouse keepers, whose whitewashed cottages were out of sight on the far side of the island. Even they were due to leave the following year, when plans were in place to automate the lighthouse, and for now, they kept themselves to themselves and left us with a feeling that we were entirely alone on the island.

As soon as we disembarked from *Gordon* and surveyed the scene, I was entranced by the place. *Gordon's* 55 horsepower engine was very noisy, so when it was cut, it took a while for my ears to adjust to the apparent silence. Gradually, I realised that this was not silence at all. I could hear water lapping on the rocks, then sheep bleating on the hillside. Then I began to hear bird calls. The piping of an Oystercatcher, the rich song of a Skylark, and then the agitated calls of the resident Peregrines. Finally, I could hear the 'tseep' of Meadow Pipits and the soft, wheezing twittering of Twites.

The island cried out to be explored. The concrete jetty provided an artificial extension to a rocky headland at the west end of the north-facing bay, giving the harbour added protection against the elements. The farm buildings huddled around the harbour, with a tarmac track snaking away around a corner towards the lighthouse. The scene across the island was dominated by the bulk of a hill which rose a little over 400 feet, and presented a near-sheer face of dappled heather and bracken, interspersed with craggy outcrops of grey rock.

The sheep which dotted the hillsides were owned by a farmer from Southend on the nearby southern tip of Kintyre, who made occasional visits by boat to tend his flock. Among the sheep, a single Guernsey cow stood majestically. Her dark brown coat looked rather lived-in, but her long-lashed eyes were bright and inquisitive as she watched our approach. This was my first meeting with Morag, who would prove a popular attraction for our guests, especially when she stood in Monarch of the Glen pose on the crest of the small hill behind the farmhouse. Morag had a very placid nature, and seemed to look forward to our visits when she would be the focus of attention for a short time.

Far less placid were two of Morag's neighbours, who were another legacy of Sanda's recently departed farmers. Although fully-winged, a pair of Chinese Geese were happy to share the meadow with the sheep and the lochan with the local Mallard flock. They had the waddling, filled-nappy gait of their farmyard cousins, and our appearance provoked a tirade of indignant honking, rather spoiling the tranquillity of the island.

We took a stroll along the shore of the bay, emerging at a headland which overlooked an exposed reef. This was home to a mixed colony of Grey and Common Seals, several of which were hauled out, with flippers waving and occasionally scratching themselves. The Greys could be heard wailing with their siren calls, which were alleged to have been responsible for luring many an old sailor to an untimely end, dashed among the reefs and rocks. I could only think that any sailor who could be attracted by such a discordant sound must have been at sea for an awfully long time.

We retraced our steps past the bay. A Ringed Plover gave a superb performance of its 'broken-wing' distraction behaviour, as it hobbled and fluttered down the beach in an effort to tempt us away from its unseen nest among the pebbles. The mystique of the island was enhanced by an ancient curse on the graveyard of the little ruined chapel, which had been dedicated to St Ninian. Legend had it that the ancient Scottish saint's grave was here, marked by a single rowan tree, and anyone who stepped on it would be dead within a year. But the tree had long since died, and no-one knew exactly where Ninian lay. Even Binge, who was almost a continuous one-man practical joke, gave the chapel a wide berth as we walked by.

Following the road up to the lighthouse, we had our first view of the bizarrely-shaped elephant rock, which did indeed look uncannily like an elephant with the end of its trunk embedded in an adjacent cliff. It was a cool, grey day, but visibility was excellent. The coast of Galloway receded to our south east, and to the south west, we could clearly see the Antrim coast of Northern Ireland, and the shape of Rathlin Island off the north coast of Ulster.

A reef extended away from the cliffs below, on the far edge of which was a large, decaying shipwreck. It was time for a history lesson, as the Skipper recounted a tale which I would need to remember and pass on to guests during future visits. These were the remains of the *Byron Darnton*, a Liberty Ship built in the US during the war which ran aground in 1946.

Prospects had been bleak for the *Byron Darnton's* crew, as she lost power and drifted onto the rocks, and her hull began to break up under the pounding of the waves. But the cliffs on which we stood provided the platform for a remarkable rescue operation, as a line was sent out to the stricken vessel which enabled all aboard, plus the ship's dog, to be safely rescued before the ship succumbed to the waves. All that was left on view now was a stem post and a few exposed bones of the hull, but it was easy to imagine the drama that had played out on that day over 40 years earlier.

Our visit was over all too soon, but I was already captivated by Sanda, and the magic of the island did not diminish on any of my subsequent visits. We returned to the *Glendale*, weighed anchor, and slowly steamed out of the bay and back into the open sea.

The next leg of our trip that day was a long haul from Sanda around the southern coast of Arran, a four-hour cruise which ended in the gathering gloom at the pier of Arran's biggest town, Brodick. A large radar 'target' in Brodick Bay turned out to be a submarine tied to one of two big naval moorings, and we could just make out the shape of the conning tower in front of the streetlights along the shore.

Strong westerly winds were forecast, and Brodick offered us an ideal shelter in its east-facing bay. Unfortunately, on our arrival, the harbour master informed us that Caledonian MacBrayne agreed with our assessment, and had decided to send their ferry, the *Glen Sannox*, there for the evening instead of using the more exposed, regular berth at Ardrossan on the Ayrshire coast. We were therefore instructed to find a space in the tiny inner harbour, which would ensure that we would be out of harm's way before the ferry arrived.

We bobbed slowly into the inner harbour, and the Skipper chose a vacant slot on the wall of the quay, but the ever-strengthening wind meant that getting to our berth was not going to be straightforward. The darkening skies and imminent arrival of the ferry added to the urgency of the situation.

I was given something of a reality check when the Skipper selected Binge rather than me to assist, and I quietly slipped back into spare part mode. The Skipper nudged the *Glendale*'s stern against the end of the pier and Binge scurried up the ladder onto the quay. After a brief battle with the breeze, the Skipper used a heaving line to propel a rope over a seemingly huge void to where Binge stood on the pier. Would I really be up to the challenge in the future when it would be just me as crew?

When we were finally safely tied up, we went ashore to see what nightlife Brodick had to offer. The blustery sea front was completely deserted as we passed some hollow-looking hotel bars and grand houses overlooking the bay. Still, it was a pleasant walk, and a good stretch of the legs after a long afternoon at sea.

We reached the Rosa Burn at the far end of the promenade, and then walked up to the Ormidale Hotel, where we settled around some Arran-shaped wooden tables and enjoyed a couple of pints of 80/-. No sooner had feeling been restored to cold fingers, though, than it was time for us to venture back out into the gloom and retrace our steps back to the pier and to the *Glendale*.

That evening, we broke with tradition and let the guests do the cooking. Binge's girlfriend Lizzie had been practising Indian cooking, and the unfamiliar aromas of cumin and cayenne spilled out of the galley and into the saloon, while Binge regaled us with more of his stand-up routine. His impressions of Mr Rigsby and Regan from the Exorcist were not very convincing, which merely made them funnier, before he brought the small house down with another variation on his luminous contact lens / Incredible Hulk act.

Binge encouraged me to join in. Not with the luminous contact lens wearing activities, but he had noticed that I had quite a flexible voice and could do passable impressions myself. He and Lizzie also decided that I bore a passing resemblance to Anthony Perkins, something which I played along with by occasionally commenting, in an American accent, that my mother would not approve. Binge enjoyed this, and asked if I would consider joining him in an unofficial double act in future, but while I was still unsure which direction my career would take, I was fairly confident that I did not want to be a stand-up comic's mate when I grew up.

The rest of the evening passed in an alcoholic blur, at the end of which, it seems, I got married to Lizzie. In his capacity as skipper, The Skipper performed a simple ceremony, and a three-tier wedding cake was assembled to celebrate. Binge took all of this in good humour, and the stresses of an eventful day at sea were forgotten as we finally made our way back to our respective cabins.

Next morning, we were awoken by the roar of the *Glen Sannox's* engines, as she pushed away from the pier and made her way across to Ardrossan to start her ferrying schedule for the day. She was not due back for two and a half hours, which allowed us plenty of time for breakfast, and we left before the ferry had another chance to entomb us in the inner harbour.

We continued our northward trip towards our base at Tighnabruaich. There was quite a breeze blowing, which led to a change in our plans. We had intended to have lunch in Millport, Great Cumbrae Island's capital town, but its pier was quite exposed to the south-westerly wind. Instead, we made for some sheltered water to the east of Great Cumbrae, where we dropped anchor for a while and had an impromptu soup and sandwich lunch on board.

We were working to a tight schedule, as the plan was for everyone to be back in Tighnabruaich and on the road before dark. Soon it was time to raise the anchor and push on. I was already familiar with the anchor-raising routine. Switch on the engine -> engage hydraulics -> release brake wheel on winch -> push the little lever back to start hauling. All proceeded normally, until I noticed that the winch was beginning to struggle and strain. I called the Skipper forward to see what the problem was, but despite switching hydraulics on and off, he was not able to bring about any improvement to the speed at which the winch was crawling.

I watched over the bow, taking care not to get any of my appendages too close to the frighteningly-taut anchor rope. The chain began to emerge from the dark sea below, but still there was no indication as to what was causing the problem. Eventually, with almost all of the chain on board, I began to get sight of something else rising towards the surface.

We had pulled up a cable from the seabed, which presented us with a headache. As usual, I had not the faintest idea what to do, and even the

Skipper, who was an experienced, resourceful chap, stood for a while scratching his head. He concluded that the cable was probably obsolete, owing to its state of decay and the fact that it was not marked on the charts, nor indicated by a yellow diamond sign on the adjacent shore. Still, we could not take any chances, and it was important that we disentangle ourselves as quickly as possible.

The Skipper gathered his thoughts and had to innovate. He climbed down into *Gordon*, and brought her around to the *Glendale*'s bow. Then he shouted up instructions for me to go and find a short rope. I was just about competent enough to carry out that order, and the next one, which was to tie one end of the rope securely to part of the gantry near the bow. The Skipper then took the other end and tied it to the cable. Then I was asked to slowly let out the anchor a short way, so that the rope, not the anchor, held the weight of the cable.

This was another simple task, but demanded far more concentration than I was used to employing. One mistake or slip could lead to a sudden release of the cable, which could have done untold damage to *Gordon* or even the Skipper. And there remained the possibility that the cable was live.

The Skipper nudged the anchor free, and then pushed himself clear in *Gordon* and shouted an order for me to cut the rope. I hacked away at it with a small knife, and it soon gave way with a twang. The cable whipped downwards, and back into the sea, and was soon out of sight back in the depths, leaving us free to continue on our way.

From Cumbrae, we made our way back up the Kyles to Tighnabruaich, and the shakedown cruise drew quietly to its close. Our guests had enjoyed themselves thoroughly, and we waved our goodbyes at the pier head. I would never see my 'wife' again.

I had enjoyed the shakedown, too. To some extent, my appetite had been whetted for the season ahead, but on the other hand, events had made it startlingly obvious that I was still at the bottom of the steepest learning curve I had faced in my life. I had learned a little about handling the boat and navigation, but I was yet to tackle such basic manoeuvres as docking the boat to a pier. I had also encountered two unplanned tests involving mildly perilous situations within a week, with the tricky docking in a gale at Brodick, and the snagged cable off Cumbrae.

With the shakedown over, we had another two weeks to wait before the season was due to start with the first cruise on 11th April. This gave us time for another trip home, before we returned for another few days' boating skills practise in preparation for the arrival of real paying guests.

One final challenge was planned for me on the evening before the first cruise. This was the 'dinner shakedown', when local guests were invited to come on board and verify that everything in the galley was in full working order. After nearly two months on the *Glendale*, the galley remained a mysterious place to me, and the only full meal that I had prepared there remained the rather austere chops and mash during my interview. The dinner shakedown gave me a chance to learn about cooking a large meal to the exacting standards which were to be expected on Beagle Cruises.

Peter and Jill were invited, as were their neighbours, the Colonel and his wife Sally, who lived even closer to the pier. Our engineer, Tony and his West Country wife completed the guest list of six. Our task was to serve a 'typical' *Glendale* meal, and this time, there was nowhere for me to hide. For the first time, I was to prepare a main course for eight people, and our shakedown guests would act as my guinea pigs.

The starter was one which I would become very familiar over the cruising season ahead. One of Peter's many hidden talents emanated from the home-built smoke-house in his garden. He worked part-time at a local fish farm in nearby Portavadie, and rather than a salary, he was paid in salmon. He took these large fish home with him, where he cleaned and prepared them, setting up a small cottage industry selling fine, smoked salmon.

The source of his smoke was just as enterprising as that for his fish. Peter had researched various types of wood for burning in his smoke-house, and concluded that hickory wood shavings gave a richer flavour than the more traditional oak. As luck would have it, there was a rather unusual craftsman in Tighnabruaich, who was one of only a handful of shinty stick makers in the world. And as it happened, the wood he used for these Highland and Island sporting essentials was hickory. His workshop provided a ready and near limitless supply of hickory shavings, and Peter had struck a deal with him to take them off his hands and transfer them from the workshop floor to the smoke-house.

Beagle Cruises played its part in supporting this local industry, and we bought a side of Peter's salmon ahead of every cruise. As part of my induction, I was given this opportunity to learn the skills needed to carve a side of salmon into thin slivers, and to arrange it on a large platter with slices of lemon and shiny, black lumpfish caviar.

The main course would provide a much bigger test, and preparations for this had started that morning, with trip in *Gordon* to procure our ingredients. The three-mile trip to a fish farm in Loch Riddon also acted as an opportunity for me to get in some more mileage at *Gordon's* tiller, and we dodged in and out of the small natural harbour at Caladh on the way there.

Fish-farming was still a young industry, and provided welcome employment to a lot of local people. The trout farmers at Loch Riddon were happy to show us around, and it was quite a spectacle to see the large, round pens, each stocked with thousands of fish, which leapt and boiled when feeding time arrived. These were rainbow trout, as opposed the more commonly-farmed salmon, and their pearlescent flanks flashed pink and blue as they broke the surface.

The Skipper had a word with a fish farm hand, who used a large net to catch two big, shiny rainbow trout. The fish were transferred into a black bin-liner, and unceremoniously dumped on the metal floor of *Gordon*. I was momentarily taken aback by this lack of compassion, but when I thought about the sheer numbers of fish being processed here, perhaps this matter-of-factness was less than surprising.

Nevertheless, I was not really comfortable with the flapping, wriggling black sack on the floor in *Gordon*, and, as it happened, the Skipper agreed with me. It was at this point that he introduced me to 'the priest'. The priest was a round-headed, wooden mallet, which was used to administer a swift blow to the head, and humanely put the fish out of its misery.

The Skipper showed me how it was done, as he removed a trout from the sack and dealt it a single blow to the head. It was quick and effective, and despite the unchanged expression on the fish's face, it was evidently no longer with us. Now it was my turn.

The first trick was to get a slimy, wriggling trout under control. It was surprisingly strong as I struggled to pin it down, but my initial efforts in wielding the priest proved woefully inadequate. The trout screamed silently in agony and indignation. Another three attempts were needed before I learned that it was accuracy, rather than brute force, which was the key. On the fifth attempt, I hit the target squarely on top of the crown, and the unpleasant deed was done.

The fish went back into the sack, and the killers sped away from the murder scene in *Gordon* on the ten-minute ride back to Tighnabruaich. We climbed back aboard the *Glendale*, with two dead fish in a bag. To me, they looked just like two large trout which you might see in a fish shop, and my naïveté was such that I did not really foresee my next chore.

I was handed the ship's filleting knife. Before we could put the fish into the fridge, their heads and innards had to be removed. This was to be another of the more unpleasant skills which I needed to learn and get used to as the season was upon us. I donned the rubber gloves, and performed the grisly task as instructed.

I crouched down as the Skipper explained how the first incision should be made, just behind the gill and pectoral fin. My knife then met with some resistance as I reached the fish's spine, upon which the corpse twitched quite violently. "It's still alive!" I shrieked, and leapt vertically several feet into the air, before running half the length of the deck.

Although the fish had been dead for half an hour, there was evidently still some nervous activity going on in its spine. The Skipper thoroughly enjoyed my reaction, though, which had evidently made his day.

I finished the second fish, and then blasted the mortuary slab clean with the high-pressure deck-hose, while a few local gulls squabbled over the scraps which had been thrown overboard. I resigned myself to having to repeat this process on a weekly basis, and doubted whether I would ever get used to it. But for now, my focus shifted to an even more chilling prospect.

The two trout would be served as the main course, which was billed as 'trout stuffed with rice and peppers, served with horseradish sauce and baked beef tomato'. To say I was daunted is a major understatement, but the Skipper talked me through it, and broke the tasks down into simple steps. I gradually realised that this might not be as impossible a mission as I had first imagined. I could cook rice, I could chop peppers into small pieces, and I could certainly put a tomato into an oven.

When I realised that baking a trout involved just putting all of this together, wrapping it in foil and putting it in the oven next to the tomatoes, all of a sudden, the fog began to clear. The only element which I was missing was the horseradish sauce. The Skipper demonstrated how a white sauce could be made, and how much horseradish should be added to it.

Our distinguished guests offered words of advice and encouragement, but I felt very much under the spotlight as they sat a few feet away. I crouched over the galley, taking care not to bump my head on the low ceiling. Gradually, though, I began to realise that things were now coming together and were under control. The sauce thickened, the vegetables were drained, and the oven switched off. The final challenge was to break up the fish into portions and make sure that no bones were dished up.

Give or take one or two bones which slipped through, dinner was served as planned, and drew appreciative comments from the critics around the table. My apprenticeship was thus drawn to a successful conclusion. The season would start the following day, and whether I was ready or not, it was time to prepare for our first cruise.

7. The First Cruise

Saturday dawned, and my thoughts turned to embarking on my first cruise. I had little time to dwell on this, though, as I quickly learned that Saturday, while notionally a 'rest' day between cruises, was quite possibly the busiest day of the week. We started by cleaning up from the night before and polishing the extensive wooden surfaces in the saloon and cabins. I was then introduced to the Saturday routine, which started with a trip to Berryburn, a small council estate at the Kames end of Tighnabruaich, affectionately known to at least some of its residents as 'Soweto'.

Berryburn was home to the family of our engineer, Tony, and Beagle Cruises further supplemented the income of his household by paying for his wife, Kat to handle our laundry. They had kept our bedding at their house through the winter, and had given it a final wash and press before the new season. The Skipper talked to Tony about engines and stuff, while I was left to fulfil a more junior role, playing football with the family's two young children.

Next was a stop at the local garage to pick up fuel for *Gordon*. We kept four bright yellow, five-gallon plastic containers lashed to the *Glendale*'s deck, and normally two would have to be filled or topped up at the garage each weekend. The containers just about squeezed into the boot of the Volvo, and then it was back to the pier, where the tide was low, making the task of lowering the fuel back on board quite a tricky one.

Shopping for groceries for a week-long cruise had to be carefully planned. We made a final trip into the village to get fresh bread, eggs and milk. Our fridge didn't have the capacity to hold a week's worth of food, so we would need to call in at butchers, greengrocers and fishmongers at the bigger ports later in the week. For now, it was time to take our provisions back to the boat, get back on board and wait for the guests to arrive.

In later weeks, we often had to hang around on the boat for a long time in the afternoon, as guests could arrive at any time from 3pm onwards. For the first cruise, though, we had a good idea as to when they would arrive. The family who ran the village garage also offered a taxi service, and all of the guests were due to catch the same ferry to Dunoon and then share a cab to Tighnabruaich. I spotted the white Mondeo as it approached along the road from the village, and we walked up to the pier-head to meet our guests.

One of the names on the guest list was familiar to the Skipper. A testimony to the success of the Beagle formula was the number of return bookings we took, and Jack was to be the first returnee of the season. He would be one of three punters for that first cruise. Margaret was quite elderly, and had an interest in nature, especially wild flowers. Jane was a quiet artist from London. And Jack was a paraplegic taxidermist from Reading.

On his previous trip two years earlier, Jack had not mentioned his disability when arranging the holiday, for fear that he would not be allowed to make the booking. He knew that he was more than able to cope, having been on a similar boating holiday in the past, but he preferred not to go through the inconvenience of having to explain himself. When he had appeared on the pier on his crutches, the Skipper and Carl were not quite sure how to react, but he soon put them at their ease, comfortably negotiating ladders using his hugely-strong arms alone.

The Skipper had no such reservations on this occasion, and greeted Jack like a long-lost friend. We helped all of the guests aboard with their bags, and let them choose their cabins. Our three, single guests probably did not realise how lucky they were to have a cabin each. Bags were left on vacant beds, without any need to dismantle the lower bunk in order to access the hollow storage area below.

The kettle piped, and our guests gathered around to listen to a short safety briefing. The Skipper pointed out the three escape routes; the main one through which they had arrived, plus the one via the engine room and our quarters, and a rather improbable one on the ceiling in the corner of the skylight, which was mainly for the sake of meeting safety regulations. The cupboard containing the lifejackets was pointed out, as was the small fire-extinguisher.

For his next trick, the Skipper turned into an air hostess, instructing the punters on how to put on a lifejacket. There were nervous chuckles as he pointed out that the little whistle was highly unlikely to be audible above the engine noise of a rescue helicopter, but he ended by reassuring the punters that no-one had ever fallen overboard after three seasons of cruises.

Then it was on to the 'heads' for the most popular part of the routine. Five pumps, pause, five pumps, pause went the flushing drill. Only 'natural' materials were to be flushed, and the system could easily be blocked if not used properly. The smallest room also doubled up as a 'wet room', so I showed our guests how the shower worked.

I played only a small part in this induction, and it was not something that came as easily to me as it evidently did to the ever-confident, socially adept Skipper. He may have only met one of the guests before, but he had a knack of making them feel at home. Jack may have been treated like a long-lost friend, but the Skipper was just as enthusiastic and attentive to the others, and his blue eyes seemed to take on an extra sparkle from somewhere to make them feel special.

Then it was my job to show the guests where the crockery and cutlery was stowed and invited them to help themselves to tea, coffee and snacks. The mini-bar was also introduced, in which we stored cans of beer, boxes of wine, and a precious cargo of malt whiskies. The latter were secured in a specially-commissioned shelf, with round holes of varying sizes to accommodate long, thin bottles of Laphroaig, and short, chubby bottles of

Bunnahabhainn. There was even a triangular hole made especially for bottles of Glenfiddich.

I was not necessarily shy, as long as the conversation did not stray too far from my favoured topics of football, birds and, perhaps, other aspects of natural history. But I was definitely ill-at-ease when asked to initiate a discussion outside of my comfort zone, even if it was just to point out where the beer was stowed. Still, I managed to get through this latest test, and I was now as impatient as the guests were to get the cruise underway.

Without further ado, the engine coughed into life, and we made our way up the Kyles and Loch Riddon towards our destination for the first night, tied to the end of Ormidale Pier. An hour into my first cruise, it was time for me to lead my first nature walk. The tide was kind to us, lifting the boat to the same level as a pier which didn't have any ladders. I gave Margaret and Jane a helping hand to step onto the grassy pier-top, the Skipper and I gave Jack a guiding shove to get him ashore. Jack brought along his crutches, and it was an easy walk, along a small road which connected the pier and a neighbouring house to the outside world.

The pace of the walk was quite leisurely, as we made our way through the foot of the oak-covered hills. We paused while I set up the ship's telescope on its tripod, and Margaret, Jane and Jack took turns to look at the Oystercatchers, Curlews and mergansers on and around Loch Riddon below. It was a very pleasant stroll, but not quite what I was expecting. Beagle Cruises offered wildlife holidays, so logically, I thought we would have a group of wildlife enthusiasts on board. Instead, our guests took only a mild but polite interest in what I showed them.

Our walk may have been leisurely, but the Skipper had been hard at work while we had been away. The *Glendale*'s saloon had been transformed. I was almost as thrilled as our guests when I saw the full Saturday extravaganza for the first time. The centrepiece was a large platter of Peter's smoked salmon, while ramekins dotted around the table contained shiny, black caviar. Supporting the salmon was smoked salmon pate, home-made by Jill, and a wide selection of salad stuffs. To wash it all down, two chilled bottles of champagne stood on the sideboard, waiting to be drained. This was a real treat, and one which I was to enjoy every Saturday for the rest of the season.

Dishes were quickly washed and stowed, and we ended the evening by enjoying a dram with our guests. The smoky flavours of my Lagavulin were the perfect follow-up to Peter's wonderful smoked salmon. I was beginning to see what Beagle Cruises was really all about; more than a wildlife holiday, this was a miniature luxury cruise, and the Saturday buffet set the standard for the week ahead.

After a brief stop at the fish farm, the following morning was spent cruising down the East Kyle towards Great Cumbrae Island. I was determined to get down to some 'proper' work, as I continued in my attempt to make the transition from bird watcher to ship's ornithologist and guide. This was the central aspect of my job description, but knowing a lot about birds was a very different skill to imparting that knowledge.

To me, even the most apparently mundane birds offered some ornithological talking points for me to pass on to any punters who were willing to listen. The pigeons which nested on the cliffs of the Sanda archipelago were no ordinary pigeons. They sported the pale grey backs, black wing-bars, white underwings and white rumps of the ancestral Rock Dove, small populations of which still persist in remote western islands. While we could never rule out the odd drop of Feral Pigeon DNA, seeing them here gave us a clear indication of how they would have looked and behaved in the days before they were domesticated and colonised every town and city across the globe.

Another common bird with a story to tell was the Hooded Crow. At the time, this was still considered to form part of a single species with the Carrion Crow, but more recently, the scientific community has decreed that they are, in fact, distinct. Our Clyde cruising area formed a large part of the narrow zone in which they interbred. I never did see a Hoodie anywhere near Glasgow, but by the time we arrived in Tighnabruaich, the mix was roughly 50-50, with a variety of shades of grey in between. On Sanda, Hoodies were very much in the majority, and Carrion Crows disappeared completely across the North Channel in Ireland.

While fascinating to me, even I could tell that these facts might not float every punter's boat, so I decided to concentrate on some of the other birds we would meet with, but which ones to choose? It was obvious that they could not expect to remember the finer features of identification of all of the 70-odd species we were likely to encounter during the week, so I thought I would start with the basics. What could be easier than gull identification?

Gulls were almost permanently visible wherever we went around the Clyde, and six species could be seen almost daily. The most obvious ones were Herring Gulls (pink legs and red spot on the bill) and Black-headed (small with chocolate-brown hoods and red legs). Common Gulls (smaller than Herring with no red spot and yellowish legs) were much commoner than they were in summer south of the border, and Lesser Black-backed Gulls (dark grey back, yellow legs, red spot) were present in several colonies. Great Black-backed were much bigger and meaner, and had blacker backs and pink legs. Finally, Kittiwakes were the only true ocean-going 'sea' gull, with delicate black wing-tips and black legs. For the first few days of the cruise, I took every opportunity I could to point all of these features out to Jane, Margaret and Jack, but I quickly began to wonder whether they were taking any of this in.

A walk on the beach at Millport, Great Cumbrae, gave me a chance to demonstrate my knowledge on bird behaviour. As we passed Crocodile Rock (a gaudily-painted, vaguely crocodile-shaped rock on the beach), I noticed a group of a dozen Purple Sandpipers feeding quietly near the sea's edge. Although not uncommon, these birds are particularly unobtrusive, and this was the first time that the species had been met with on a Beagle Cruise. They are lovely little waders, whose tameness has earned the name 'Deefie' in Shetland on account of the fact that they seem oblivious to the noise of approaching people. But I noticed that among them was a Redshank, the notoriously jittery 'warden of the marshes.'

I explained that were it not for the Redshank, we would have had an excellent chance of getting very close to the sandpipers, but that the Redshank would fly off, giving its alarm call, and most likely spook the sandpipers into taking flight. No sooner had I finished my mini-lecture than the sandpipers flew off, and left the Redshank standing alone on the beach, minding its own business. I could obviously not rely on the birds to read bird books and learn how they should be behaving.

As we left Millport and headed south towards Arran, I decided to continue with the gull induction course. Rather than recycling or composting our waste on the boat, we would normally throw it overboard and feed the gulls. As often as not, the birds' mid-morning snack would comprise a combination of unfinished toast and porridge. I was sure that the latter was not very nutritious for the gulls, and worried that it would glue their beaks shut. They did seem surprisingly choosy, though, and would often turn their beaks up at the prospect of porridge for breakfast.

We had attracted a small flock of gulls to our wake, and a couple of Gannets had joined them to check and see what was on offer. Then the Skipper gave me an odd order.

"You can try them with some of the leftover salmon," he suggested. Not one to disobey orders in my first cruise, I dutifully went below deck to the fridge to retrieve the remains of the side of salmon, which had only been half-finished the previous evening. The punters looked a little perplexed as the delicacy was torn into scraps and thrown overboard. Even the Herring Gulls, with their pink legs and red spots on their beaks, were not keen on this unexpected gourmet treat.

I went back into the wheelhouse and told the Skipper that the gulls were not too keen on smoked salmon.

"Salmon!!??" enquired the Skipper.

"Well, you said to try them with some of the leftover salm ..."

It was at this point that I learned that he would routinely interchange the use of the words 'trout' and 'salmon'. I was supposed to have thrown overboard some trout, left over from Friday's shakedown dinner, but instead, half a side of some of Scotland's finest smoked salmon was now on its way to the seabed. I wondered if the prawns down in the deeps would be more appreciative than the gulls had been.

Monday dawned with the *Glendale* tied up to the end of the pier at Brodick. This was a day which I had not been looking forward to – my first day with cooking responsibilities. I had watched intently as the Skipper prepared the porridge on the previous morning, and now the pressure was on me to produce something of similar quality. Three cups of porridge. four cups of milk and two of water were added to the large pan. Then I turned on the gas, and took up the traditional wooden spurtle, and began to stir in an exclusively clockwise direction. The porridge gradually thickened, and after a quick consultation with the Skipper, it was ready to serve.

The gloop was transferred to wooden bowls, from which it was compulsory to eat with cow-horn spoons. By the time it arrived on the table, these bowls of oats, milk and water had acquired a rich seasoning of Scottish tradition and ritual, which made porridge an integral part of the Beagle experience. Later in the season, some Scottish punters would stick to their austere traditions, and insist that only salt could be added. For most, though, there was the opportunity to experiment with Demerara sugar, dark brown sugar, golden syrup or even black treacle. A lump-free serving was safely accomplished, and the empty wooden bowls suggested that I had done well with my first breakfast.

We left Brodick on a four-hour steam south for my first encounter with the great rock at Ailsa Craig. The voyage involved a crossing of the most exposed stretch of sea in our cruising area, so I was a little worried about spending much of the trip below deck, preparing lunch. In the event, it was a calm, hazy day, and my sea legs were sufficiently well-established to allow me to be untroubled by the slight wobbling of the boat.

The sight of the granite edifice on the distant horizon during my field trip to Arran had left quite an impression on me, and I was excited by the prospect of visiting Ailsa. I occasionally popped up to the wheelhouse to see if we were nearly there yet, but the haze restricted visibility to the extent that all we could see was sea. The Skipper had set the radar to its maximum range, so the only sign of Ailsa was a large, bright blob plotted on the screen.

To anyone with an interest in birds, Ailsa Craig meant Gannets. 12% of the world's population of Gannets lived there, which meant that Gannets were everywhere in the Clyde, wandering up the Kyles and occasionally to the very tops of the sea lochs. Sometimes they would hunt alone, monitoring the sea from above, before plunging with their trademark dives from 'up to 100 feet' according to most guidebooks. The majority of their dives were from much lower altitudes, depending on the depth of their quarry, but I was confident that a few of these birds were stooping from higher still.

The sight of a feeding party of Gannets was a highlight of many a cruise, and we had the freedom to divert the boat to go and take a closer look. The Gannets took turns to plunge into the water, setting the surface foaming and splashing, and leaving 'vapour trails' of bubbles in their wake below the water. As they plunged into the clear water, they could sometimes be watched below the surface, propelling themselves along with a flap of their long wings, before bobbing back to the surface. Each time they dived, the birds issued a guttural air-raid warning to others below, leading to gulls scattering in an attempt to avoid being speared.

Gannets could be tempted even closer to the boat when we had some meat or fish scraps to throw overboard. At close quarters, they were even more striking to look at. The subtle yellow covering the head and neck was in contrast to the pale blue horn-rimmed spectacles that surrounded their staring eyes. The grooves and marks in their bluish-horn coloured bills are thought to help them line up their dives as they dart down from their lofty oches.

The radar told us that we only had two miles to go, but the haze remained dense enough to shroud Ailsa from view. Our proximity was eventually betrayed by an ever-increasing volume of Gannet traffic, and when we got to within a mile of our destination, the huge shape of Ailsa Craig loomed out of the haze.

The Skipper slowed the engine to a quiet tick-over, and maintained a course directly towards the foot of the near-vertical, volcanic cliff faces. Gannets criss-crossed the sky above, and we could see that the colony itself was neatly arranged, with ample breathing (and pecking) space for each nest which was marked with a pure white incubating adult.

Several of the Gannets were carrying fronds of seaweed, and it was easy to imagine these as being the Gannet equivalent of bunches of flowers, being delivered to the nest to make up for the days away at sea. A grassy slope attracted slightly less-white, younger birds, and these were packed much more closely together. This slope was nicknamed the 'youth club', where rowdy youngsters could gather without the responsibilities that come with incubating an egg or feeding a chick.

Below the Gannets were ledges, basalt columns and caves packed with Guillemots and Kittiwakes, and below them, some smart, black and white Razorbills. These auks gathered in the water around the boat, giving me another chance to provide an easy lesson in bird identification with some obliging subjects. I fielded the inevitable questions about the relationship (or lack of) between apparently Penguin-like Guillemots and Penguins, but the birds provided the answer themselves, confirming their lack of flippers by taking to the air on whirring wings.

I didn't want to miss any of this spectacle, so I quickly completed preparations for lunch. There was nothing fancy – a salad served with local bread, meats and cheeses, but I was quietly pleased with myself when I stepped back to look at the spread.

It would have been almost criminal to drag our guests below decks while so much was going on outside, so in order not to miss anything, lunch was served on deck. The Skipper and I took turns at the helm while we helped ourselves to the buffet.

After we completed a second circuit of Ailsa, the Skipper pointed the bows north-west again, this time for Campbeltown. I was quickly learning that there was little rest on a cooking day. I had to go below decks again to finish the lunch dishes, and then start preparing my signature dish for the evening – stuffed trout with horseradish sauce. Just three days after first producing this dish with a little help from the Skipper for eight people at the shakedown dinner, this was a solo effort. The fact that it was for three fewer people did not make it any less daunting.

Once again, though, I managed to time the cooking of the vegetables to coincide with the thickening of the sauce and the baking of the fish, and invited everyone to sit down for dinner. True to understated form, they quietly tucked in, and did not volunteer much by way of encouragement. I found that I was already becoming my own worst critic. Perhaps the sauce was slightly too runny and not horseradishy enough, or maybe quality control had allowed too many fish bones to slip through.

Any fears which I may have had were soon put to rest by Jack. He placed his knife and fork together on his plate, and expressed his contentment with two words:

"Proper job!"

Second helpings requested by all at the table. I had negotiated my first cooking day without any disasters in the galley, and, if I dared to allow myself, I had actually enjoyed it.

We never once served a pudding on board, and the evening meal was always followed by cheese and biscuits, or, more specifically, stilton and oatcakes. This was primarily because the main course was such a big undertaking and used up all of the available pans and oven space. No-one ever complained, and stilton and oatcakes at the end of the day became as much a part of the experience as porridge had been at the start. There was usually time for a dram after dinner as a nightcap. This was something I always enjoyed, and despite having only a few months' experience, I was able to offer my advice and expertise on the characteristics of the different varieties of whisky on offer.

On Tuesday the Skipper was 'on' cooking duties again, but even so, I had to turn my thoughts to food once more and gather ingredients for the following day's menu. I was not going to be able to get through a whole year cooking nothing but stuffed trout with a horseradish sauce three times per week. And although nothing had been said following my efforts during my interview, I had a strong feeling that pork chops, mash and mixed veg was not going to become part of the weekly menu.

The Skipper explained to me that the menu for the week, while not rigidly adhered to, did follow a regular pattern. Sunday would be a roast dinner, and Monday would be the day for my newly-established, world-renowned trout dish. The Skipper did a hotpot on Tuesdays and another fish dish on Thursdays, and I would be rounding off the week with a second roast dinner on Friday. This left one night to fill, and unfortunately for me, Wednesday was one of my 'on' days.

I was given a cookbook and asked to find a new recipe for Wednesday's evening meal. My remit was to create something quite hearty but nothing too experimental or spicy, as it would need to be appetising to all on board.

Finally, it could not be anything too similar to what was served on an adjacent evening.

I pored over the book for some time before eventually settling for something which was not too fishy or too spicy or just too difficult. A beef and red pepper casserole, to be served with rice, seemed to fit the bill perfectly. Now I had to note down the ingredients, before heading off on a shopping expedition into Campbeltown.

By now I was quite comfortable to go on shopping errands on my own, but I still struggled to get used to the ways of the local butchers. The Skipper assured me that these were excellent tradesmen, but I was quite unsettled by pallid staff who looked as if they had never seen the light of day. In both Campbeltown and Tarbert, the butchers had the same blood-shot eyes and grey-toothed grins behind their blood-stained aprons. They also shared a habit of using the palms of their hands as miniature mortuary slabs, thrusting a cut of meat towards me and sometimes giving it a pat or a gentle stroke.

I knew what I was looking for, and wanted to get the transaction over with as quickly as possible. The Skipper had told me that I should allow about half a pound of meat per person, so all I needed to do was identify the right cut. The butcher's face cracked into a grey-toothed grin as he found an especially 'nice' bit of stewing steak for me, so I ordered three pounds and hurried back to the boat.

Campbeltown would be our base for two nights on the first cruise, allowing us a leisurely trip to Sanda on the Skipper's cooking day. This was to be the first chance I would have to lead a walk there, and we found the island much milder and more spring-like than when we'd visited just three weeks earlier on the shakedown cruise. Even Morag seemed to have a spring in her step, and a dozen or so Wheatears, recently-arrived from Africa, hopped around in the grassy fields. These new arrivals met a Redwing, which was about to depart for its breeding quarters in Iceland. Jack was able to negotiate the paths and the lighthouse road on his crutches, as we enjoyed a couple of hours exploring the island.

As we cruised back up Kilbrannan Sound on Wednesday, I prepared my experimental casserole. This time, it felt more straightforward than my first attempt at preparing the trout. I browned the beef, threw in onions, carrots and red peppers, plus some rather exotic courgettes. Some stock was added, as was a little Bisto, and then it all went into the oven for a while. I had time to go on deck and throw some off-cuts overboard, so giving the punters an opportunity to do some gull identification revision should they feel so inclined.

I had never cooked a casserole before, and was not entirely confident that what I had produced was a good one, although to my eye, it at least looked like the picture in the book. I was acutely sensitive to the mumblings at the dinner table, but again, plates were cleared, and again, seconds were requested. I could hardly believe what was happening, and my dread of cooking was quickly melting away. In fact, I was almost looking forward to preparing Friday's roast pork. I was certainly some way from reaching perfection, but I now felt happy that I was capable of producing three good meals per week.

There followed a riotous evening in the Lochranza Hotel. Carl had been crew the last time Jack had visited, and the pair got along famously. Jack had us in stitches with a wonderful tale about a visit to a potential girlfriend's house for dinner. He had been quite nervous, but calmed himself by stroking the pet dog under the dining table. His evening was progressing well, until the dog walked in through the kitchen door, and he realised he had his hand on his prospective mother-in-law's thigh. She did not say a word, but Jack blushed deeply on recalling the excruciating embarrassment of the moment.

Carl asked if Jack was still enjoying taxidermy.

"Oh yeah - I like stuffing birds" he said with a heavy Berkshire twang and a mischievous glint in the eye, conjuring images of him in a dark, dusty room surrounded by dead birds and animals.   If I pointed out a living Yellowhammer, I could expect to be informed by Jack of the details of its internal structure and how it could best be mounted.

Mary and Jane seemed to be thoroughly enjoying themselves, in a quiet way, and the Skipper and Carl did a fantastic job in jollying them along. I envied Carl's easy style with the punters, and wondered if this was a skill which could really be acquired or something which came naturally.

As we left the pub, we found that the beer had had a miraculous effect on Jack. He raised his crutches and walked along the road for a few steps, before almost losing his balance and reverting to his steadier mode of transport.

Normally, we were quite disciplined about ensuring that *Gordon* would not be stranded on a falling tide while we were in the pub, especially if there was an onshore breeze as there was this evening. This time, though, we were enjoying ourselves so much that we neglected our duties. By the time we returned to the shore, *Gordon* was high and dry, and a long way from the water.   Carl went back into the pub and called in some reinforcements, and soon a burly, if inebriated, group had assembled on the shore. Between us, we managed to haul the quarter-ton *Gordon* across the gravel and rocks, and made our way back out to the *Glendale* quietly at anchor in the calm bay.

A morning walk at Lochranza brought a momentous event. Carl knew the exact ledge which the eagles had chosen for their eyrie. It was within sight of his hotel, and he spent a lot of his personal time, as well as time with his punters, keeping a watchful eye on the nest site. Jack made easy work of the two-mile walk along the flat valley bottom, and within a couple of minutes of arriving at our stakeout, Carl and I were both intently staring through our telescopes, watching a splendid adult eagle perched on the edge of the eyrie. Then we saw it – a streak of white flying out from an unseen chick on the ledge next to the adult. It was our first evidence that they had indeed been successful this season, and seldom can a flying blob of bird poo have been greeted with such a hearty cheer.

The weather had closed in for the last couple of days of the cruise. We were now back in the northern part of our cruising area, and went ashore at a headland called Rubha Dubh (Black Point) on the eastern shore of Loch Fyne. Jack found the going tough on his crutches as we walked on the wet rocks, which were covered in rain and seaweed, and he cut a sorry sight as he chose a rock on which to sit, insisting that he was happy to stay put while we explored. He later confessed to having feared being frozen to the rock while he waited.

The week was coming to a close. My attempts at teaching the punters about gull identification were showing limited signs of success. On the last day, Margaret called to me to ask for help in identifying a bird. I could see what it was that she was looking at – a Turnstone busily picking its way around on the seaweed next to a pair of Herring Gulls.

"It's over there," she said. "Behind those two ..." (come on Margaret – pink legs and red spot, you can do it ...) "... white birds." I had learned my lesson, and never imposed gull identification on anyone again. I soon found that the punters would find their own level of interest, and some were much keener than others. I would let them decide how much they would like to learn.

Aside from a well-scrutinised navigational chart of the Clyde cruising area, the other reference material pinned to the wall of the saloon was the 'Beagle List'. This comprised the bird species which had been seen on Beagle Cruises by passengers and crew over the three-year history of the boat's operation. The list stood at 120, and was studded with local specialities such as Golden Eagle, Great Northern Diver and Ptarmigan.

There was always scope to add to this list, and a 'Beagle First' would neatly add to the sense of achievement on seeing something a little bit unusual.

On day two of the season's first cruise, a dark phased Arctic Skua overtook the *Glendale* as she steamed down the west coast of Inchmarnock. This was followed by a Great Skua harassing Gannets near Campbeltown, always an impressive sight, and an opportunity to introduce the popular, Shetland name of 'Bonxie' to the punters. On the way back up Kintyre, a stop at Carradale yielded twelve Pale-bellied Brent Geese, stopping over en route from Ireland to the Canadian Arctic. It was cruise number one, and these three, as well as the Purple Sandpipers at Millport, meant that I had already extended the Beagle list by four species.

I successfully negotiated my final cooking duties with roast pork on Friday evening, which was served after we tied up to Tighnabruaich Pier. This still presented some challenges. Never before had I roasted a roastie, nor thickened gravy, but I was quietly pleased with my efforts.

The taxi arrived at 10:00 on Saturday morning and whisked our happy punters away to catch the 11:00 ferry from Dunoon, and then on to carry on with their lives in the real world. The Skipper and I would be heading off later that day too, as we had a two-week gap in our schedule before the next cruise. The boat felt eerily quiet as we cleared up after our guests, and read their comments in the visitors' book. Aside from Jack, they had been an undemonstrative group, but the praise which they entered into the book was quite fulsome.

We could not simply leave the *Glendale* tied to the end of the pier for our fortnight away. This would have broken all boating protocols, being antisocial and denying fellow seafarers access to a prime berth. She would have also been open to any intruders who may have been tempted to help themselves to fittings, or, heaven forbid, our whisky collection.

To solve this problem, the Skipper had laid a private mooring, perhaps two hundred metres east of the pier head, and almost directly opposite Peter and Jill's house. The mooring was marked by a huge orange buoy, alongside which was a white plastic ball. I was sent to the bows, armed with a boat hook which reminded me of a whaling harpoon, while the Skipper edged us towards the buoy. My task was to hook the small ball, and secure the attached rope to the deck.

After a couple of aborted approaches, we finally secured ourselves to the mooring, and went back to the pier in *Gordon*. *Gordon* was anchored off near the steps at the side of the pier, just about accessible on our return, but out of harm's way. Then, after a week of real work, it was time for a fortnight off.

I was eager to catch up with my family and friends, and tell them all about my wonderful adventure. It might have been work, but it might as well have been a holiday for me too, complete with new sights, sounds and stories. I was still buzzing, but I soon found that despite my enthusiasm, eyes soon glazed over when I recounted tales of cruises, punters and places. My friends were doing 'normal' things, like post-grad courses and local council jobs, and they simply could not relate to what I was telling them. I believe Neil Armstrong had a similar problem when he came back from the moon.

8. Meeting the Maids of Bute

After a break of a couple of weeks, we were ready for cruise number two, and it was time for me to meet some Beagle legends. A select few punters had visited in each of the three previous seasons, and many of these were to return for a fourth time in 1987. Most remarkable in their number was a couple who came each year from Iowa. Bill and PJ had stumbled across an ad for Beagle Cruises while planning a Scottish holiday during the *Glendale*'s first season, and were so delighted by the experience that they travelled across the Atlantic each year just for a repeat performance. They were very keen photographers, who loved the West of Scotland, and this year they wasted little time in paying us a visit. Another couple on board that week were also back for their second time, although Bob and Pam had travelled from a slightly less far-flung home in the West Midlands.

Bill and PJ carefully made sure that their camera equipment was transferred on board safely. Formalities over with, we made the already-familiar short trip up to Ormidale for the first evening of the cruise.

Casting off from Tighnabruaich Pier instantly transported all on board into another world. Soon the village shrank away to a thin line of houses along the shore. Mother Nature swiftly asserted herself, and aside from the odd navigation buoy, humans influenced very little of the landscape towards the top of the Kyles.

A more careful scan of the hillside of Bute did reveal one exception, though. A pair of painted rocks appeared as a bright yellow spot among the heather and bracken, and, when magnified using binoculars, they took on a human-like form, with crudely-painted pink faces, bright blue eyes and rosy red cheeks. These were the Maids of Bute.

There were many rumours about who first painted the Maids, and for what purpose. A favourite was the story that they were gazing across the Kyle at some unseen lads, now hidden among the woods behind Caladh, while others swore that they were waiting for their menfolk to sail home up the Kyles. Another story was that they were painted by Para Handy himself for the simple amusement of the 'towerists'. All of our punters had seen the Maids before, but all were keen to spot them again as we passed in the Kyle below.

I led the evening walk by the side of Loch Riddon, while the Skipper prepared the smoked salmon and caviar. We had lost the element of surprise with our returnee complement, but instead of amazed gasps at the sight of the Saturday evening dinner table, there was a satisfying, knowing appreciation that it really was as good as had been remembered. The two couples swapped stories of cruises gone by, and plans were made for the week's itinerary. Bill and PJ produced a photo album, and showed us some excellent, atmospheric scenes from their previous visits.

The routine continued the following morning with a visit to the fish farm, which floated just a couple of hundred metres from Ormidale pier. The Skipper had a long-standing agreement with its owners, who allowed us to land and walk around the floating wooden pontoons, and we made a slow approach in *Gordon*, waiting for one of the farmers to give us the OK to tie up.

We strolled around on the floating walkways between the pens, looking at the masses of fish of varying ages and sizes which were held separately in each one. Slightly less impressive were some of the ingredients being thrown into the sea in large quantities. Living in such close proximity to one another, infections were quickly spread from fish to fish, and several could be seen to be carrying unsightly sores around their fins, tails and eyes. To combat these, large quantities of antibiotics were included in the food pellets. These may have had a short-term benefit for the intended recipients, but the effect on the nature of the sea loch was less easy to gauge.

Several sacks stood on the floating pontoons between the fish food, labelled with the word 'PIGS'. These, it turned out, contained not bacon, but pigment supplements, to ensure that the large trout had the pink flesh preferred by the French customers for whom most of them were destined. Presumably all of the wee crabs and other marine critters which lived nearby also had pink flesh as a result.

The fish farms were, predictably, a magnet for fish-eating wildlife. Herons and Cormorants perched on the pontoons and edges of the nets, but their eyes were bigger than their bellies. Seals, on the other hand, could cause serious and expensive damage. They would break into the nets quite frequently, allowing a mass breakout of fish. Most of the trout were so accustomed to their routine that they would return to the net at feeding time and were easily recaptured. Others were more adventurous, and made a bid for freedom towards the top of the loch, or even up the River Ruel. Opportunist anglers quickly got wind of this, and could be seen along the banks, trying to cash in on this unexpected abundance of big fish.

On noticing that several fish were carrying sores, PJ politely asked one of the fish-farm-hands about the health of the fish.

"Yer fosh uz leyk yer folk," came the local's reply. "Some's a hunnerd 'ercent an some's no'."

"Pardon me?" asked PJ.

After our visit to the fish farm, we chugged down Loch Riddon the short distance to the romantically-named Buttock Point for a walk on the rugged north end of Bute. An oft-repeated anecdote here was passed on by our engineer, who was once asked to ferry a small party here in a small boat for a memorial service, and to scatter the ashes of a loved one. It had been very tense and quiet on board, until one of the mourners broke the silence.

"It's very beautiful here. What's this place called?"

"I'm not sure that I should tell you this, but it's Buttock Point" said Tony.

"Well, he was a bit of a pain in the arse" came an unexpected reply, and the mood of all on board lightened considerably.

Gordon ran us ashore at Buttock Point, and the Skipper returned to the mother ship, leaving me to lead this walk alone for the first time. I had studied the map and listened to instructions carefully, and with the elderly American couple in the party, I knew I could not afford the luxury of unplanned diversions over rough terrain.

After a scramble through a small marsh, we climbed through a sparse oak wood, stopping to watch the comings and goings of Wood Ants on their ant hills, and to have a nibble on the lemony leaf of a wood sorrel. Then it was a yomp across a tussocky area towards higher ground, where a small, olive-brown bird flitted across our path. The view was brief, but long enough for me to identify it as a Grasshopper Warbler, and the punters managed to spot the next one as it repeated the act ahead of us.

Despite their age, Bill and PJ were holding up remarkably well as we reached higher ground. The local Peregrines had noticed us by this stage, and monitored our movements for the rest of the trip, constantly overhead and giving their nerve-jangling alarm calls. This was also a great place to see two other moorland predators. Only the female Hen Harrier was seen on this occasion, but later visits produced displaying pairs of harriers and also Short-eared Owls.

The climax of the walk was at the head of a small valley. The Bull Loch was a small lochan, almost round and apparently lifeless. In its centre, an artificial island was anchored, put in place by the local RSPB group, and each year, a pair of Red-throated Divers (or Loons to our American guests) would choose to nest here. A little hillock by the loch gave us excellent cover behind which to creep up to the loch-side, giving us a great opportunity for close-up views of these bizarre-looking birds. The adults were most striking, with smooth grey heads and fine black and white striping on the nape, and a shocking patch of crimson on the throat. There was one fluffy juvenile this spring, a grey ball of fluff which grew during the year to take on the same, prehistoric-looking form as its parents.

We tried to communicate in whispers, but the silence was punctured by the clicks of PJ's camera, and an exchange between the couple which became a catchphrase for the week:

"Did you gedda shot of that, PJ?"

"I sure did."

We ate our picnic by the loch, sneaking up to the brow of the hill to check on the divers from time to time. Rather than retrace our steps, it was quicker (and kinder to the older punters) for us to descend to a rendezvous with *Gordon* on the west coast of the island. As we walked down the hillside, we glimpsed the Maids again, and little by little, these painted rocks began to set the theme for the rest of the week.

We anchored in Lochranza for the night, and conversation again turned to the Maids. Reference was made to the *Glendale*'s library, which contained both factual and fictional titles. There was one set of novels in particular which we were keen to consult.

We were far from being the first boat to ply these waters for a livelihood, but our most famous forebears were fictional. The *Tales of Para Handy* by Neil Munro told of the adventures of the *Vital Spark*, a Clyde Puffer, and its crew, as they sailed around the West of Scotland. Para Handy took a dim view of tourists. "There iss nothing that the mudges likes to see better than an English towerist with a kilt" was a quote of his with which we would console our guests on days when the midges were particularly vicious.

The Maids appeared to be wearing yellow raincoats to protect themselves from the elements, but reference to Para Handy suggested that this was not how they should have been. In fact, the Maids should have been wearing red and blue dresses. He christened them 'Mary' and 'Elizabeth'. "Mery had a waist ye could get your arm roond, but 'Lizabeth wass a broad, broad gyurl."

This week, a mission was carefully planned as we undertook to right this cultural heresy.

The paint was bought in Campbeltown so as not to raise local suspicion. We then tracked back north a little earlier than usual, and the *Glendale* arrived at Tighnabruaich pier in time for our Friday lunch. Para Handy was consulted one last time, and our landing party was given their brief.

I ran the party across the Kyle to the shore of Bute just below where the Maids stood. I then made my way back to the *Glendale* to prepare dinner, while the Skipper led the party up to the Maids. Mary and Elizabeth were duly identified, and one painted red and the other blue as per the book. The operation took about an hour, and I received a call to go back and collect the triumphant party in *Gordon*.   I looked up to the hillside, and could just pick out the Maids, now resplendent, and correct, in their red and blue dresses. Mission accomplished, there was a real buzz among the punters, and Bill cheerily pointed out that more Americans had walked on the moon than had painted the Maids of Bute.

That night, I pushed my way through the crowd in an attempt to get served at the Royal Hotel. As I carried my drinks away from the bar, I overheard a gruff local voice nearby.

"Some bugger's painted the Maids" he muttered. I put my head down and made a swift exit. News travels fast in a small village.

9. Fledging

After a fairly slow April, things really took off from mid-May onwards. The next set of punters who arrived marked the beginning of a marathon seven-week unbroken sequence of cruises, the longest in the *Glendale*'s history. This group included another pair of *Glendale* addicts, a mother and daughter named Vickie and Winnie. They were back for the fourth time, and on the previous year's cruise, a friend of Vickie's had been so impressed that she went off and married the Mate.

Also on board were a rather older couple from Merseyside. Stan was a sports writer for the Liverpool Echo, and he was joined by his wife, Nora. They were a jolly, enthusiastic couple, and it seemed that they were genuinely excited about the week ahead. Stan professed himself to be especially looking forward to sampling the food on board. "I'll eat anything" he proclaimed when we asked if anyone had any food preferences or dislikes.

Despite his claim, it turned out that Stan was not a fan of smoked salmon, which he pushed around the plate with his fork on the first evening. Roast beef on the second night promised to be a little plainer - surely we couldn't go wrong there. Unfortunately, there was a swell running at our berth on the end of Brodick pier, and Stan was not the only person on board who was looking uncomfortable with the rolling motion. As the dinner was being served, the big Caledonian MacBrayne ferry, *Isle of Arran*, arrived, bringing with it its bow wave and a very lively wake. We were bouncing around like a cork, and it was all too much for Stan, who had to make a leap for the ladder as he went off to find some terra firma and fresh air.

The swell receded during the night, and by morning, all was calm in Brodick Bay. A decision was made over breakfast to sail to Ailsa Craig that day, but we needed to get a few provisions on board before we departed.

The view from the pier reminded me of my introduction to Arran at about this time three years earlier, but my relationship with the island had changed. As a student, I had felt like a visitor, taking a rare chance to explore the island. Now, even though I had only been there half a dozen times, I felt a sense of familiarity and belonging. I knew the skyline well, dominated as it was by the cone of Goat Fell. I knew some of the bars and shops, and understood our relationship with the ferry and other to-ings and fro-ings of the pier. And I knew that if I scanned the bay, I would see a few Eiders, and probably a pair of mergansers patrolling just off the shore.

The shops in Brodick were about a mile from the pier, so the fastest way to get there and back, tide and wind permitting, was to take *Gordon* across the bay and anchor her on the beach. As I untied *Gordon* and looked across the bay I noticed a familiar vehicle parked by the road halfway along the sea front. I approached, both curiously and incredulously, as I realised that this was the same blue coach that had brought me here as a student three years earlier. I cut my journey short, and ran *Gordon* ashore before walking up the beach and putting my head through the open coach door. A former lecturer was dumbfounded, and even the Panzer driver flinched slightly, as I gave an answer to the unsaid question as to what I was doing there. The class of '87 looked on with some bemusement as they watched the mysterious alumnus say his goodbyes and speed off in *Gordon*.

After leaving Brodick, we took a short diversion through Lamlash Harbour, passing between the impressive Holy Island and the town of Lamlash. I spotted wildlife of a kind on Holy Island, and pointed out a herd of Highland Cows to the punters. On leaving Lamlash Harbour, we sailed down past Whiting Bay, before passing the lighthouse on the island of Pladda and heading out into the open sea towards Ailsa Craig.

A Great Northern Diver arrowed its way in the opposite direction, and there was a buzz of excitement when the small fins of a pod of Porpoises broke the surface near the boat.

Ailsa provided its usual seabird spectacular, and we were to take on an unexpected additional passenger as we made our way back to Campbeltown. Seabirds often used the eddies and air currents around the boat to hitch a ride, but while I was at the helm, I noticed a Kittiwake which was much closer and more persistent than usual. As it neared, it seemed intent on landing on one of our tyre fenders near the bow, and after much hovering, it finally settled. Winnie had been watching it for some time, and now crawled along the deck to get a closer look. The Kittiwake seemed unconcerned as Winnie popped her head up from behind the bulwark, just a few inches away, and in that instant another cherished holiday memory was born.

Winnie's enthusiasm and energy seemed to know no bounds, and had she had her own way on the first couple of mornings, we would have been up and about at the crack of dawn every day. A lot of our punters were wildlife enthusiasts, and knew very well that the early hours were often the best time to get out and about. They were therefore disappointed to learn that a Beagle day started with breakfast being prepared from 8:00. Sometimes they would take matters into their own hands, and go for pre-breakfast walks on the first one or two mornings.

Given the opportunity, I would have loved to have risen early, too, but it was simply not practical. The Skipper and I worked what could be described as extremely long hours, from breakfast until bed time, and often had to get up in the middle of the night to adjust ropes or to allow fishing boats to depart before dawn. So we had a strategy. We would make sure that the punters were just as knackered as we were by the end of the first day. Not in a way which constituted cruelty to punters – more a case of giving them a full and active day rather than running them into the ground. It worked, too. By Tuesday, there would seldom be the pitter patter of footsteps on deck early in the morning. They were all content and fast asleep in their coffins. Even Winnie was tired out and happy to fall in with this schedule.

The fruits of the sea provided us with several impromptu lunches. The fishermen of Campbeltown and Tarbert could be persuaded to part with a bucket of prawns for a few quid or a few cans of lager, and marathon prawn-peeling sessions would follow. As well as prawns, we would sometimes be offered a carrier-bag-full of loose fish. This week, during a brief visit to Carradale, a fisherman called me over to hand me a carrier bag containing half a dozen hake. We were about to make the 90-minute crossing to Lochranza, where we planned to have lunch, so this led to a change to the planned menu. I was on cooking duty that day, so I was going to have to deal with them.

Hake have a slightly different anatomy to the other fish I had experience of preparing on the *Glendale*, and the Skipper kindly suggested that I get in some practise in cleaning them ready to be served at lunchtime, so I went off in search of a suitable pair of orange rubber gloves. Finding rubber gloves was seldom a problem, as we kept a stack of them on a shelf in the wheelhouse. Finding a comfortable pair with a dry lining still intact was more of a challenge, as they quickly became cold and dank whenever they were left on a rainy deck, or were inadvertently filled with sea water. I found the least clammy pair available, and chose a metal plate by the winch as a chopping board, before going ahead with my grim task.

The first fish was dealt with painfully slowly, and I tossed the inedible bits into the sea. Unfortunately, what little grip the gloves might have had reduced to almost nothing with the application of a little fish slime and guts, and I also let go of the ship's best filleting knife, which flew overboard with the giblets. I only had half a dozen fish to deal with, but another two knives went the way of the first. Even the gulls and Gannets seemed to be steering clear, presumably reluctant to play the role of knife-thrower's assistant.

We approached Lochranza, and I went below deck to wash the fish and put them into the oven. The end result was quite a tasty lunch, which seemed to be going down well among the punters, including Stan. The Skipper then pushed his plate away, having hardly touched his meal. He claimed not to be feeling hungry, and I was not best pleased having worked harder than usual to get this particular meal onto the table.

After the meal was finished, I called the Skipper into the crew's quarters.

"What was that all about? What are the punters going to think?" I demanded.

"Maggots, mate."

That stopped me in my tracks. As it turned out, rather than undermining me, the Skipper had actually saved my bacon. On cutting his hake open with a knife, he had exposed a swarm of parasitic maggots. Apparently this is not that unusual in certain types of fish, and it had been a stroke of luck that it had not been a punter who had come across this unexpected bonus. Unless, of course, they had unwittingly taken a little extra protein with their meals which had slipped down, unnoticed.

After the narrow escape at lunchtime, I needed to concentrate on preparing the evening meal without any further drama. Stan was proving difficult to please, which was a worry for us as he had hinted that he was going to write an article in his paper about the holiday. Plaice baked in a cheese sauce was turned down on Monday night. Surely a wholesome beef casserole could not cause any offence, but when it was offered, our guest announced that he "could not stand boiled meat." Despite his claim on the first night, Stan only ate two evening meals that week without complaint. Now we began to get paranoid about what he might end up writing about these awful food experiences in his article.

Most of our cruise itineraries were quite improvised, and we seldom had any set appointments or commitments to meet. Some structure was added during our spring cruises, however, by taking part in organised surveys, the majority of which involved collecting census data for bird population studies. A lot of the surveys in the local area were co-ordinated by our cafe owner friend from Tarbert, whom I first met during my interview. He was an active local RSPB member, and was happy to have an extra pair of hands or eight to gather data.

During the shakedown, we had tramped around the wooded hillsides behind Loch Riddon, craning our necks to see which piles of twigs contained active Heron nests. This week we had been set a rather easier, and in many ways more enjoyable task. We were to count the nesting seabirds on a group of small islands in Loch Fyne, almost directly opposite Tarbert.

The islands were small and rocky, like the gently curved summits of rolling, almost submerged hills. They lay not far from the shore of Loch Fyne, but their inaccessibility was enough to make them an attractive home to some of the local seabirds. There were one or two pairs each of Shag, Oystercatcher and Eider on the islands, the latter complete with eider-down linings to their nests. Much larger numbers of nests belonged to a mixed colony of Herring and Lesser Black-backed Gulls.

Despite the excellent camouflage of the chicks and eggs, the nests could be easily counted, and contained eggs and chicks at varying stages of development. The coup-de-grace was the discovery of several eggs in the process of hatching, as the chicks emerged into the world for the first time. It was a privilege to see, and registered unprecedented levels of 'Punter Value', as was duly noted by journalist Stan.

As we made our way back into the Kyles, there was time for one last highlight on this cruise, which awaited us under the waters of Ettrick Bay on Bute's western coast. As well as the more visible wildlife, such as birds, land and marine mammals, a Beagle Cruise would give our punters every chance to see some of the life hidden from view beneath the sea. Each week, we hauled up a fleet of 25 prawn creels, miniature lobster pots which had been baited the previous week with the leftovers from a fish dinner.

The creels were located by a combination of memorising where we had dropped them the previous week, and recognition of our particular orange flotation buoys among all of the other orange flotation buoys that marked other people's creels and pots on the sea bed. While we searched, there was to be another birding highlight.

Two large, dark birds were floating low in the water off to starboard. We changed course and dropped the revs, allowing us all to get the most fantastic views of a pair of Great Northern Divers, in their immaculate, black and white summer dress. Throughout May, these impressive birds would be met with quite regularly in the Clyde, en route towards their Arctic breeding grounds. As a child, I had been gripped by Arthur Ransome's novel, 'Great Northern?' which told of a child's adventure and discovery of a pair of Great Northern Divers nesting on an island off North West Scotland.

I had seen a couple of dowdy immature and winter-plumaged Great Northerns off Northumberland, and sightings on earlier cruises had been limited to brief flight views, or distant moulting birds, so it was a real treat to get close-up views of a pair in full plumage on this calm afternoon in Ettrick Bay. Every one of the intricate white necklace-like stripes could be seen, along with the striking red eyes. We could even see that one of the birds had damaged its bill, perhaps having lost the tip of its lower mandible to one of the crabs on which it was feeding.

We left the divers behind, and eventually found our pots. One buoy was retrieved using a boat hook, and secured to the deck. The guard rails were removed from one side so as not to impede the creels as they came aboard. The final step in getting prepared was to wind the line around a small capstan and make sure that everyone was in position ready to winch the creels up from the sea bed.

During the *Glendale*'s conversion, the Skipper had made a wise decision to retain a lot of the original equipment. Most trawler conversions involve removal of as much clutter as possible, to maximise the deck area on which to perform leisure activities such as strolling around or stretching out. The Skipper had that option available, but had the foresight to realise that the winches, capstans and gantries could be put to alternative use during our holidays.

Getting the creels on deck was quite an interactive experience for the punters, although it was myself and the Skipper who would put our limbs and digits on the line by handling the pots and ropes. Vickie and Winnie knew the drill, and Winnie was given the honour of operating the winch lever. The rest of the punters helped with getting the critters out of the pots. For the strong-stomached, there was the option of wedging lumps of stinking bait between two vertical elasticated strings to attract next week's catch.

Winnie operated the little lever which engaged the winch, while Vickie watched over the stern for a creel to appear. Each time one broke the surface, Vickie gave the signal for the Winnie to slow down or stop, and the Skipper lifted the pot onto the deck so that its contents could be identified and inspected.

Part of the original thinking when the creels were first purchased was that they could be a way of supplementing our food supplies with fresh seafood, especially prawns. In reality, we never caught more than half a dozen prawns, and a typical catch only contained two or three among our 25 creels. These were large Dublin Bay Prawns, aka Norway Lobsters, aka Scampi, aka *nephrops norvegicus*. They were striking little beasts, with attractive orange shells and long, dark orange pincers. And they tasted good with a fresh salad and some garlic mayonnaise.

Much more common were crabs, and we regularly caught up to four species. As well as the familiar Shore Crabs, we caught Velvet Swimming Crabs, which seemed to be covered in dark red crushed velvet and had little paddles for back legs to help them swim. Edible Crabs were also familiar, and these had formidable pincers with which they often chained themselves to the netting of the creels as a protest against being dragged up from their seabed homes. The fourth species was the Spider Crab, with its pointed shell and long, spindly legs. Crabs were always popular, and closer inspection allowed males and females to be identified, the latter often carrying large egg masses under their tails.

The final crustacean which we brought in on a regular basis was the Squat Lobster, which, as the name suggests, had short, round bodies, but hugely long arms tipped with pincers. In the eighties, these were quite obscure little creatures, but the ever-increasing demand for seafood has since seen them adding supermarket freezer cabinets to their range of habitats.

Other 'stars' of the show, pun fully intended, were the starfish, which came in an even greater variety than the crabs. The Common Starfish was well known to everyone, but less familiar was the Spiny Starfish, whose arms were armed with sharp little spikes. Sun Stars bucked the five-armed trend, with a dozen or so short arms. Even more striking were the Cushion Stars, with their stubby arms and vivid orange or crimson colouring making them firm favourites with the punters. Brittle Stars were often abundant, and had a rather startling habit of writhing and shedding their arms on the deck as an instinctive escape reaction.

The odd Sea Urchin also managed to wander into the creels over the course of a week. Closer examination of these revealed them to be surprisingly similar in a lot of ways to the Starfish, with food being passed via tube-like suckers towards their mouths, the main difference being that the main five arms had been fused together and hardened to form a shell.

Different groups of punters had differing approaches to the creel sessions. All were fascinated by the whole experience, which was a bit like opening 25 Christmas presents and waiting with bated (and baited) breath to see what was in the next parcel. Some studiously logged the contents of the pots, before popping the beasts back into the sea. During other weeks, we would have a microscope session below deck to take a closer look at what had been caught. And if people were feeling especially peckish, we might eat the odd specimen.

'Shooting' the creels, or returning them to the sea bed, was quite a risky undertaking, and we made sure that all of the punters were well clear of any of the lines and ropes. The Skipper and I alternated roles from week to week – one of us would take the wheel and move the boat forward in a gentle arc to starboard, while the other let the rope run out and threw the pots back into the sea one at a time. Any snagged line or misplaced foot could have been disastrous, as the combined weight of ropes and pots could easily drag an unwary crewman overboard, and this really did happen, as I would learn during my time on the *Glendale*, sometimes uncomfortably close to home.

Vickie and Winnie were great Beagle fans, and liked nothing better than to sit around the table in the saloon recalling their own experiences and listening to some of the long list of well-told anecdotes in the Skipper's repertoire.

These anecdotes never faded in their brightness and fondness of recall. There was the one about a formidable pair of ladies, nicknamed Himmler and Goering, who had repelled boarders as a fishing boat tied up to the *Glendale* at Tarbert. "This is private property!" they bellowed, which was not good PR with the local community. Another favourite tale was about punters on the very first Beagle Cruise, who had disembarked from a cruise aboard the QEII and travelled all the way from Southampton that very day.

I guessed that the Skipper was prone to embellishing the facts, something which was confirmed after a few weeks when I realised that I had been present when some of the alleged incidents had happened. We engaged in some whisky-fuelled debates back in the blunt end after the punters had turned in for the night. The Skipper always argued that there was no harm in stretching the truth, while I was adamant that the truth was quite

111

entertaining enough in itself. Either way, the punters seemed to enjoy it, so really it mattered little.

There always seemed to be an element of tension among the punters on board, presumably due to sharpened senses in an unfamiliar environment. The sound of any movement on deck was hugely amplified when heard from below. Herring Gulls sounded as if they were wearing hob-nail boots, and they were regular visitors early in the morning. They would attack the black sacks on deck with unerring accuracy, snipping them open at precisely the spot behind which there was a tasty bit of bacon rind or fish carcase. Even tiny birds such as Rock Pipits could be heard loud and clear, scratching and pattering along the boards above.

Being tied up to wooden piers in a wooden boat on a breezy evening inevitably meant that there were other, almost innumerable mysterious bumps in the night. Water slapped against the hull, often surprising punters by its proximity to their heads as they rested in their bunks. Timbers flexed and groaned and ropes creaked loudly as they tightened around the cleats which were on deck, just above their heads. "What's that noise?!" was a common exclamation in the early stages of many a cruise.

"I don't want to scare anyone, but it's probably the ship's ghost," said the Skipper, as eyes widened and jaws slackened. Vickie and Winnie knew what was to follow, but this only seemed to add to their enjoyment of the Skipper's performance.

Our ghost, who went by the name of Llewelyn, was reputed to be a hapless fisherman who had lost his head in a terrible accident with winches and nets. He was Welsh purely because the *Glendale*'s last registered port as a fishing vessel had been Conwy in North Wales. His presence would be announced by the bumps and scrapes of netting and chains being dragged across the deck, accompanied by the faint whiff of herring. The punters would be transfixed to the Skipper's tale, and contributed to the proceedings with occasional yelps of nervous laughter, despite the fact that it was delivered in the most appalling Welsh accent. It was a complete pack of lies, of course.

We were safe, snug and warm in the saloon, but life on board was an ongoing battle to keep the interior of the boat dry. The constant motion and flexing of the boat in rough seas meant that leaks regularly sprang. We were under attack from three sides, with water seeping into the keel below, forcing its way between the planking of the hull in rough seas, and finding cracks in the surface of the deck or edges of windows above the saloon. A quick application of tar to the deck or sealant to the skylights above the saloon kept the leaks from above at bay, but only temporarily. It was a battle that we would never win.

Even more worrying than the annoyance of a dripping deck was the continuing necessity to employ automatic bilge pumps to keep ourselves afloat. These used small windscreen-wiper motors, activated by float-switches, whose rhythmic, wheezing beat could be heard throughout the boat, especially at night. This would often keep the punters awake for the first few nights of a cruise, especially as they strained to hear the tell-tale sound of dragging chains which would announce a visit by Llewellyn. We tried to put the punters at ease with our answers to the inevitable questions about the unfamiliar noise, but far from reassuring them, the thought of taking on water only served to bring to mind the possibility of their coffin-like beds turning into watery graves.

I was more worried when I didn't hear the pumps, or if I could tell that they were straining more than usual. A legacy of the extensive refurbishment to the boat was a large quantity of wood shavings which had been dropped into the bilges, and these would sometimes clog up the pumps. When this happened, it was another of my not-so-glamorous tasks to stick an arm through the cold, oily water, and remove any obstruction that could be detected by touch alone.

All boats leak to some degree, but the *Glendale* was perhaps more leaky than most. Her keel and lower planking had suffered from an infestation of gribble worms, otherwise known as keel worms, several years earlier. The result was a network of tiny tunnels which these little crustaceans had dug. By and large, though, the bilge pumps did their job, ever since they had been reinforced after an especially alarming incident in a previous season when punters were awoken with water on their cabin floor, and carpet tiles floating away.

Another visit from Vickie and Winnie was drawing to a close. Meanwhile, back in the blunt end, our whisky drinking became more copious, and was beginning to become a problem. We kept a bottle of malt for staff consumption between our bunks, and took turns to pour a tot over which to wind down and mull over the day's events. We referred to these drams by an acronym for one of Peter's expressions when offering hospitality.

"W – woo – woo – would you care for a f***ing big wh – whisky?" Hence the expression, FBW. The ritual began to transform into a competition, as each of us tried to outdo the other in generosity when pouring the evening's FBW. The routine's success proved to be its own downfall when, after a few weeks of this escalation, the size of the measures meant that it took so long to drink them that we were not getting enough sleep, and the increasing hangovers were making it harder to get out of the bunk to prepare porridge in the mornings. Eventually we declared a truce, and the FBW was consigned to history.

Another week was over, and Vickie and Winnie's enthusiasm remained undimmed. As with Bill and PJ the week before, we said our goodbyes at the pier head, but we knew that they would be back. Stan, meanwhile, made tracks for Liverpool, his journalist's mind already engaged in planning his newspaper article.

*

Despite our proximity, there really was no competition between our *Glendale* holidays and Carl's Arran holidays, and in most cases, potential customers were quite clear about what they wanted – either a week on a boat or a week on the island. But on one occasion, a couple called Jack and Mina had decided to spend a fortnight on a Beagle double-bill. The first week of their fortnight was to be spent on the *Glendale*, but things did not start too well, and for a while, I feared that they might become my first dissatisfied customers.

Despite the best efforts of the brochures, expectations of the punters varied wildly when they arrived for their holiday. On one occasion in a previous year, a couple had turned around and abandoned their holiday, after presumably having arrived with the impression that a 52-foot trawler was something a little bigger than what they saw. On the other hand, there were a few guests who were thrilled by the *Glendale*'s cosiness, and one or two punters even bought into the idea that the accommodation was indeed palatial.

Jack's main problem was that he could not adapt to life in a confined space with low beams. There was one in particular which would get him every time, and his mood darkened with every thump of scalp on oak. On the first night, he asked me if we had any cold beer on board. When I said that we did, he barked an order at me to go and fetch him one. I was quite taken aback, although it was difficult to take him seriously, as he was already sporting a comedy crossed sticking plaster on his balding forehead.

As the week went on, Jack slowly adapted to the crouching posture needed to avoid collisions with beams, and his mood improved enormously. He turned out to have had an interesting life, and had even had a spell on the playing staff at Newcastle United, although he never made it as far as the first team. Recently, he had bumped into the great Jackie Milburn.

"Hello there Jackie, remember me? I'm Jack – we were at Newcastle together in the fifties."

"No" was the great man's reply.

*

During another of our 'staff meetings' at the Lochranza Hotel that week, Carl had some hot bird news for us. For the first time in many years, Corncrakes had returned to Arran, and two or three were to be heard 'crekking' their presence on farmland at Shiskine on the west coast. It was too far and too late to drive from Lochranza that night, so we made plans for a mission the following evening to track them down.

Corncrakes are most active at dusk, and the clear, calm evening that followed would present us with perfect conditions to listen for them. We anchored off Blackwaterfoot, some distance off the shallowly sloping shore, and made our way in *Gordon*, towards the little harbour. Dusk was gathering, and visibility deteriorating rapidly, but we could see enough to safely tie up to the quay. Carl picked us up in his Land Rover, and we took the short drive to Shiskine. As soon as the Land Rover doors were opened, the crekking call of the Corncrakes could be heard, loud and clear in the still evening air.

We stood and listened. At least two birds were calling from a nearby field. Occasionally we heard a third, but we eventually dismissed this as an echo from a nearby building on the edge of the village. We strained our eyes through the darkening dusk to try to glimpse the birds, which sometimes seemed to be almost at our feet, but even with the aid of a powerful torch, the chances of a sighting were nearly zero.

It was after midnight when we got back to Blackwaterfoot, but we safely navigated our way out of the harbour, and made for the anchor light of the otherwise dark *Glendale*. After our successful mission, we set off for a short night-cruise under the stars across Kilbrannan Sound to Campbeltown.

The evening had given Jack and Nina a foretaste of what was to follow during the second week of their Beagle double-bill with Carl on Arran. They had considered leaving the car at Tighnabruaich for the fortnight, but instead opted to spend their Saturday on a drive around Loch Fyne and take the small ferry from Claonaig to Lochranza, where they joined Carl for another week of Beagle adventures.

10. Tricky Punters

The vast majority of our punters were very likeable, and they were appreciative of our efforts in providing holidays which were hopefully memorable ones for them. Most were easy-going, and presumably quite like-minded, having seen fit to buy into the Beagle experience. Eventually, though, we had a group who bucked that trend.

We had a booking for two entrepreneurs from northern Scotland with their wives. They had made their fortunes from fishing boats, and later, support for the oil industry. The first signs were apparent as early as the Saturday evening, when they became the only set of punters to refuse to help tidy up the dishes. Of course, they had every right to refuse, having paid good money for their holiday. But for the first time, the Skipper and I were made to feel truly subservient to our guests.

To make things more irritating, the weather that week was glorious. We had just come through a wet spell, and it seemed profoundly unfair that this had broken for such unappreciative punters.

"It's the weather that makes it," Sheena said to me.

"No it's not," I thought. "It's the wildlife, the history, the scenery and the adventure." "Yes," I replied.

We stopped at the end of the Kyles for some mackerel fishing, and again, their luck was in, as several fish quickly came up over the side. Seeing them left floundering in a bucket, I went to put them out of their misery.

"What you doing that for?" asked Alex. Fish, like crew, had no rights in the eyes of these punters, and should be left to die a slow death.

I was constantly on the lookout for something which would interest the punters. Seals were OK, but the novelty tended to recede after the first couple of days. Among the seabirds, skuas were sufficiently scarce and dashing to attract some interest, but the ever-popular Puffin was always a must-see bird.

Fortunately, for the weeks in which we visited Sanda, there was ample opportunity to watch Puffins at close quarters. More often, though, Puffins appeared as distant, rugby-ball shaped dots flying low over the waves, usually in the whirring-winged company of the slightly more elongated dots of their larger cousins, Razorbills and Guillemots. I soon learned that it was sometimes best to let these pass, and not waste energy and emotional stress on pointing them out.

"A Puffin?! Where? Where?"

"Well, you see those little dots flying over the waves about a mile away?"

"Err, no."

"Well the Puffin is the fourteenth from the left."

"Oh."

Most punters were happy to trust my eyesight and expertise and believed what they were told, even if they could not really recognise these distant birds for themselves. I could have all-too-easily made things up, but I resisted that particular temptation, and there was quite enough to keep people's interest without going to such dishonest lengths. Sheena, though, was having none of it.

"I defy you to tell me, hand on heart, that that wee dot over there is a Puffin." She was challenging not only my expertise but also my professionalism and integrity, and I was not used to being doubted in this way. I did my best not to snap back, but explained, rather defensively, that it was a skill which had been developed over many years, and that I did in fact know what I was talking about.

The Skipper was just as uncomfortable with this group of punters as I was. For him, things came to a head when he was approached by Martin in the wheelhouse.

"How old are you, son?" asked Martin.

"Twenty-six," replied the Skipper.

"And are ye married?"

At first, the Skipper was confused, but then it dawned on him that Martin was making enquiries on behalf of his daughter. The Skipper was a good businessman and entrepreneur, like Martin, so he would obviously make an acceptable son-in-law. Marrying into this family was not something which appealed to the Skipper, and he asked me to take the helm while he went down to the galley. I was not too disappointed when Martin also wandered off – presumably a mere Ship's Ornithologist was not of suitable stock and breeding to be considered worthy of his daughter's hand.

On another sunny, calm day off the north-east coast of Arran, I spied a nuclear submarine steaming down the Clyde towards us from its base up-river at Faslane. They were quite a common sight in the area, as they engaged in exercises in the deep waters, and we would often see them disappear below the surface as they dived. When they were on the surface as this one was, they would push along a huge bow-wave as they ploughed up the surface of the sea.

Our smug punters were relaxing on deck, sunbathing with cups of tea at their sides. Lying down, they were unable to see anything of the sea over the bulwarks which were offering shelter from what little breeze there was. I changed course, and made towards the oncoming sub.

Normally when approaching a large wave or wake such as this, the effects could be stifled by 'shoulder-barging' the wave at an angle of about 30°. As the sub steamed past, I turned the wheel again, so that I could be parallel to the wave. This meant that we were beam-on to the waves and troughs.

The wave hit, and our ten tonnes of ballast quickly took effect. The boat then fell into the trough behind the first wave, and we began to roll violently from side to side. There was pandemonium on deck, with tea cups falling over and rolling around, and punters rudely shaken from their slumber. After a thorough shaking, the punters eventually managed to get to their feet and saw the cause of the 'accident' as it steamed away from us.

"Sorry," I said.

The Skipper, who had been below deck, popped up through the hatch and asked what was happening. I explained the situation, and he returned below decks with a knowing grin.

Our faith in the Beagle formula was reinstated when we arranged our punter exchange that week. Jack and Nina were joined us for half a day on the *Glendale*, and they looked thrilled when they came back on board. We had a gentle cruise around the coast of Arran, and dropped them off back at Lochranza. As they disembarked, I heard Joe muttering again under his breath.

"I never thought I'd miss that bloody boat" he said. It was a genuinely satisfying experience to have won over this punter so completely, and after our experiences with that week's complement, it went some way to reassuring us that we were doing something right after all.

Saturday morning soon followed, and now it was time for us to force one last smile as we waved our most challenging punters off. The Skipper and I went straight up to the Hamilton's to fetch mail and salmon, and had a chat over a cup of tea. Peter had evidently recently emerged from the bath, and came downstairs wrapped in a towel.

"Do – doo – do come in and take your clothes off, otherwise I shall have to go and put some on," was Peter's typically eccentric invitation for us to come in.

The Skipper suspected that Peter and Martin may have crossed paths during their time while working on boats in Aberdeen, and he asked Peter if this was the case. Peter immediately reacted on hearing the name.

"Know him!" he boomed. "Bastard!"

*

Joining us the following week as an extra crew-member-cum-guest entomologist was Jonny Binge. He had stayed nearby on the Friday night, and came aboard to help with our Saturday changeover routine. The decision to have Binge along was not as foolhardy as it might have first appeared, as his role extended beyond that of an entertainer. In fact, he was one of the few people to have actually crewed for the *Glendale* during her first season, when he had stood in for Carl for a few weeks. As well as supplying laughs, his entomological expertise would give us a new, microscopic view of the wildlife to be met with during our cruise.

Our new punters all arrived together later in the afternoon. This was to be my first experience of a full block-booking, as three school-teacher couples had taken all of the available berths. They evidently knew each other and got on very well together, and there was a thoroughly relaxed atmosphere on board from the moment they stepped on board.

I had recently taken to sleeping on the bench seat under my bunk, but the crew's quarters were suddenly very crowded, so I retreated to my recessed bunk for the week. Binge brought his sleeping bag, and found space on the seat beneath the Skipper's bunk to call a bed.

After half a dozen cruises, I now felt much more at ease in the galley, but I quickly learned that I would have to extend my repertoire beyond my three tried and tested dishes. One of our couples, Jim and Carolyn, had let us know when they made their booking that they were fish-eating vegetarians. It was a concept which I found a little difficult to grasp, as I had always categorised fish as animals rather than vegetables, but at least I would only need to re-think menus for two of my evening meals, as we could go ahead with the usual trout on Monday.

Smoked salmon was dispatched on the first evening with minimal fuss and appreciative comments from all. We followed our regular Sunday morning routine, too, with our weekly visit to the fish farm. As usual, I took the two large trout to one side on deck, and set about cleaning them, ready to serve the following evening. A few minutes later, Jim appeared next to me in the wheelhouse. He spoke on behalf of himself and his wife.

"You know how I said that we eat fish?"

"Yes?" I replied, sensing what might be coming next.

"Well, we don't eat fish anymore," he informed me.

The grisly reality had finally dawned on them that fish had blood and guts just like any other animal. I needed to consult the Skipper for advice as to what options I had to change the menu at such short notice, and once more, I found myself in the galley preparing an unfamiliar dish. Now, though, a new dish was much less of a leap into the unknown than it had been a few weeks earlier. Now I had some experience, I was more able to improvise and adapt. Instead of trout, I stuffed a pair of red peppers with the same ingredients, and an item was added to the menu with a minimum of fuss.

We stopped for a walk at Skipness, opposite the north end of Arran, where Loch Fyne meets the rest of the Firth of Clyde. The walk there was undemanding but rewarding, with families of breeding birds seen in the hedges, and graceful Arctic Terns patrolling the unspoilt beaches on which they were nesting. Dominating the headland was the ruin of an old castle and chapel, and in its grounds were a number of ancient slab gravestones, some of which were protected by wooden boxes to help preserve the detail on the stones. These archaeological treasures depicted relief carvings of knights in armour, with detailed knotting designs and weapons at their sides.

None of this was sacred to Jim, however, who climbed into one of the wooden boxes while Carolyn wasn't looking. Not to be left out of a practical joke, Binge called Carolyn over to see this particular grave. With perfect timing, Jim threw back the 'coffin lid', which successfully scared his wife out of her wits.

We made our way down to Campbeltown, in time for dinner, and as dusk was falling, we could see the lights of a fair which was in full swing. This fair provided our entertainment for the evening, and having won an armful of coconuts, we made our way across a football pitch back towards the harbour. I dropped a coconut to the floor and dribbled towards goal.

"On me head!" called Binge. I lobbed the coconut, fully expecting him to feign a header and catch it at the last moment. Instead, there was a sickening crack, as he met it with the meat of his forehead like a true centre half, and Binge reeled from the impact. It was clear that this had not just been done for effect, as he had blood running from his head, and showed some signs of concussion. Still, he had got a laugh, which was the main thing, and there was no lasting damage done.

The weather stayed calm and sunny, and we were able to fit in visits to both Sanda and Ailsa Craig. It was en route from the latter to Brodick that a calm afternoon became an unforgettable evening. We noticed a feeding frenzy among the local Gannets, which were diving to pierce the glassy surface of the sea not far away, and took the boat in for a closer look. The Skipper flicked on the sonar 'fish-finder', and several fishy targets immediately materialised onto the plotter. We were obviously over some fairly sizeable shoals.

We dusted off some old hand-lines and attached bits of Kit-Kat wrapper to the rusty hooks as shiny lures for mackerel. Within minutes, we were bringing them in almost constantly, with some lines snaring fish on all six of their hooks. We very quickly had enough for a substantial meal, and only about ten minutes after the first line went over the side, we were ready to continue towards Brodick, having caught more than enough to feed all on board.

Some of the less squeamish punters volunteered to help clean the fish, so I gave out some filleting knives, and gave a quick demonstration to show how it was done. Within a couple of minutes, we had hordes of squabbling gulls and Gannets following on behind to feast on mackerel heads and giblets.

It was a wonderful sight, with sea and sky a clear, pale blue, and the white seabirds tinted golden by the late afternoon sun. To a bystander on the shore, the *Glendale* must have looked like a real trawler, making her way towards port on a sunny evening being followed by a flock of gulls.

Our evening meal plans were shelved. Tonight, we would have fresh mackerel, barbecued on the beach. We loaded *Gordon*, and sped across to a quiet, sandy corner of Brodick Bay. The Skipper gathered some large, flat stones, and began work on constructing a small hearth. I joined the punters and Binge in a search for fuel, and soon we had gathered enough dry seaweed for kindling and driftwood to build a decent-sized fire.

The fish were soon sizzling on hot, flat stones, and the delicious smells that drifted around the beach were enough to persuade Jim and Carolyn to make one further exception to their newly-established abstention from eating fish. Soon we were sitting on the sand, feasting on the most scrumptious fresh mackerel, which we washed down with white wine. Our party's chat and munching was all that broke the silence of a calm, balmy evening, as the mid-summer sky above failed to achieve total darkness.

It was well after midnight by the time we climbed back into *Gordon*, and the return journey provided us with yet another highlight on a wonderful evening. The outline of Goat Fell loomed large to our north, and above it, some high-atmosphere clouds glinted, pearlescent, reflecting light from the unseen sun beyond the horizon. Better still was the scene below us. On this evening, the luminescence was spectacular. *Gordon*'s wake almost shone with a green glow, and the bow was flashing in a shower of sparks. Deeper in the water were more lights, as individual fish and larger shoals could clearly be seen darting around under the boat. I leaned out over the side of *Gordon*'s rubber hull, watching the show and looking out for the next shoal of fish. It was an almost surreal experience, but a wonderful one which would be remembered by all of those who were present.

11. Luminescence

On calm nights, the deep, clear waters of the Clyde are among the best in Britain to see the magical natural phenomenon of luminescence. Male punters would often wonder what they had actually been drinking when they attempted to quietly avoid the rigours of the pump-action toilet, as the splashing water would come alive with bright green flashes. These marine glow-worms were, in fact, bioluminescent dinoflagellates, microscopic plankton that would produce a vivid green spark when disturbed.

We headed from Brodick to Tighnabruaich earlier than usual to on Friday morning, and went for a walk behind the village after lunch. Binge had brought some of his insect-trapping gear along, and captured some odd-looking mini-beasts, most impressive of which was a near-microscopic Pseudoscorpion. So microscopic it was that we took it back to the boat to examine under a microscope, which allowed us to clearly see its miniature pincers. Binge's expertise and entomological knowledge had opened up a whole new dimension to our wildlife holiday offering, and the microscope session kept the punters as enthralled as any other spectacle which we had shown them during the week.

We had a good night in the local pubs, and Binge's entomological exploits were not over yet. While we were in the Royal, a scream came from the direction of the pool table, where a large moth had been attracted to the light. Into this limelight stepped the expert, and shot out a hand to capture the beast. Within a few seconds, a spellbound audience was appreciating the feathery antennae and finer anatomical points of a male Drinker Moth.

That evening marked our first visit to the recently re-opened bar at the Chalet Hotel. This was located at the pier end of town, a long way from the other pubs, and getting there involved a climb up a small brae behind the houses. The hotel had been closed for a number of years, and its re-opening had generated a lot of interest in the town. The bar was buzzing, and there were some unfamiliar faces among the crowd.

A rather smart, elderly lady who had been a former resident of Tighnabruaich was paying a visit to the village, and had decided to try out the re-vamped Chalet. She knew the Skipper, and started to chat to him in her soft, west coast accent (or should I say westCOAST accent), in which she continually emphasised the most unexpected syllable in a sentence, making it almost sound as if she was being tickled while she was talking.

She sang her way through some funny anecdotes, and told us about her journey on the train from Glasgow to Gourock that afternoon. She recalled that western ports were named, quite understandably, Port this and Port that. For example, the proper name for our part of Tighnabruaich was Port Driseach, and nearby was Portavadie, while Islay boasted Port Charlotte and Port Ellen.

The lady recounted how she had passed through Port Glasgow, which stirred memories of some of these wonderful places. But then one station name drifted past the window of the train which she did not recognise. A wee place called Port Akabin, with the emphasis on the first 'A' in 'Akabin' (PortAAakabin).

We awoke nursing some severe hangovers, and there was no sign of urgency when it came to our punters disembarking on Saturday morning. Almost invariably, our punters would set out early on a Saturday morning to embark on their long journeys south. This week, though, only Binge departed, while the rest had decided to stay in a bed and breakfast in Tighnabruaich on the Saturday evening. This meant that not only were they very slow in leaving, but the Skipper and I felt obliged to join them for lunch after they had 'left'.

We traipsed back up the brae to the Chalet to see what lunches were on offer. Beer inevitably accompanied the cheeseburgers, and our busy Saturday routine was pushed further and further behind schedule.

Suitably inebriated, we finally said our goodbyes and turned our attention to the next set of punters. Normally, our threshold for breaking even would be three paying guests, but early in the season, we ran a few cruises for couples, primarily in an attempt to give me as much work experience as possible. Today, only two were expected, meaning that our preparation of the boat would be mercifully quicker than it had been for six. To complicate matters slightly, one of the new guests would be the Skipper's former maths teacher from school.

Lunchtime hair of the dog had not been effective, but by late afternoon, I had pulled myself together. The Skipper, on the other hand, was still suffering, and decided that drastic medication would be needed if he was to appear sober in front of his old teacher. The instructions on his box of energising tablets clearly said 'Do not take with alcohol or excessive caffeine,' and 'Do not exceed the maximum dose of two tablets.' So the Skipper took four and washed them down with a strong cup of coffee.

There followed a surreal first evening with our new punters. They were a very pleasant couple, and it had come as a surprise to them to discover that the Skipper was a former pupil. Despite their shared profession, the contrast in personalities on board the previous week could not have been greater with our latest teacher, who was a calm, quietly spoken gentleman.

The Skipper's attempts at being on best behaviour through the use of energy tablets left him sitting, almost lost for words, with eyes wide open like saucers. He was normally a master of such a situation, jollying the punters along and preparing them for the delights of the week ahead. I wondered what our esteemed guests made of the rather strained atmosphere, and I did my best to retrieve the situation, keeping the conversation going as best I could. At least the Skipper managed to stay awake.

I needn't have worried though, as all turned out well, and we had a very enjoyable cruise that week. The teacher's wife was quite badly arthritic, but with a little persuasion and cajoling, I managed to get her ashore and complete some fairly lengthy walks at Lochranza and Carradale. This was a rewarding aspect of my new job, and added a sense of achievement to the guests' enjoyment of their holidays.

Carradale Bay was a particularly productive stretch of sand for a gentle spot of beach-combing, and usually yielded 'mermaid's purses' (the egg-cases of dogfish), and the egg-masses of whelks, or 'buckies' as they were known locally. A favourite, almost mythical animal could sometimes be found in the shallows, a peculiar, furry wee beastie which would apparently run in and out with the waves. I would get a lot of disbelieving looks when I informed the punters that this animal was in fact known as a 'sea-mouse', but it was true. However, it was no rodent, actually being a large member of the polychaete worm family.

Behind the beach was some rough heathland, which hosted several of the flower species which were typical of the area. By now, we had had several flora enthusiasts on board, and I had learned to identify a handful of species. There was bog asphodel, sea campion and marsh orchid alongside familiar species such as yellow flag iris and birds-foot trefoil. On the drier areas, heather grew in profusion, and I was able to point out the differences between ling, cross-leaved heath and bell heather.

I had begun to learn a little about the butterflies which we met with, and Carradale seemed to have a particularly good variety. Small Coppers flashed among the low flowers, but my powers of identification were not enough to confirm which types of blue butterflies we saw. Much easier to identify were the spectacular Golden-ringed Dragonflies, which glided around on gossamer wings.

There was a bird highlight that week, too. On a foggy day, we were making our way up Loch Fyne towards Tarbert. Looking out of the wheelhouse door, I noticed four dark seabirds loafing a little distance away in the mist. Suspecting that they were skuas, I asked the Skipper to change course to intercept. We would see skuas on most of our cruises, but normally in ones and twos of either Arctic or Great Skuas. On approaching the four in Loch Fyne, I realised that they were neither, and their long, spoon-like tail extensions quickly identified them as Pomarine.

Small numbers of Pomarine Skuas regularly pass Britain's shores as they migrate to and from their Arctic breeding grounds. I had only ever seen a couple before on the Northumberland coast, but here we were, in among a flock of four. Two of the birds appeared to be younger, with stubbier tails, while the other two were pristine adults. By rights, they should have been over a thousand miles away on the Arctic tundra. I tried to lure them closer still by throwing some bread overboard, but these mean pirates would have been happier chewing on something meatier; some fish or perhaps a Common Gull.

My lucky visit to the wheelhouse to spot the 'Poms' came during one of my cooking days, and I had to return to the galley as soon as the birds had drifted off. Breakfast was always porridge, but our other meals were much more varied, especially lunches. This was the most flexible meal of the day, and we had a number of options available depending on the weather and the day's itinerary. Sometimes we would take a picnic lunch ashore and factor in a stop to eat on the planned walk. We would often eat on deck at sea if the weather was good. Loch Fyne kippers tasted particularly good that way.

On a cold, damp, misty day such as this one, the option of a hearty, warming soup was very appealing. The Skipper had taught me a few tricks for making thick broths in quick time. Any soup involving potatoes, pearl barley and lentils would surely have to be prepared well in advance, but with the aid of a pressure cooker, and by grating a potato, the end result could be ready in under an hour.

And for a really tasty stock, we used the carcases of smoked chickens, which had, needless to say, been provided fresh from Peter's garden smoke-house. Smoked chicken featured on the lunchtime menu on a regular basis, until we had a batch of chickens which smelled a bit off. On learning of this, Peter apologised profusely, and, never one to do things by halves, cancelled his regular order with the local butcher and buried his remaining stock in his garden.

The *Glendale* was embraced by the local fishing community, and while that brought some perks such as bags of prawns or spare fish, there were some drawbacks. There was no space available at the quay in Tarbert, so we tied up outside two docked trawlers when we arrived in the evening. The next morning, the entire fleet of Tarbert trawlers would leave the quay well before dawn, which at this latitude and time of year meant 3am.

We were awoken by the sound of heavy boots on deck, and the curious rushing sound of nearby propellers from trawlers outside. The fishermen would have no qualms about leaving us drifting in the harbour, and it was up to us to get up and re-secure ourselves to the quay after the real trawlers had gone.

We were back in our bunks by 3:30, and able to catch some more sleep before the alarm went at 8. The Skipper was on porridge duty, so I stole another few minutes in my sleeping bag.

We spent the next evening in Lochranza, and arranged another 'staff meeting' up at the hotel. This time, it was calm enough to tie the boat up to the dilapidated pier, and walk to the pub, leaving the couple for a quiet evening to themselves on board. I was looking forward to telling Carl about our latest bird sightings, but knew that he might not take my latest news very well. He had a near-blind eye, a result of an operation on a 'lazy eye' early in life, and it seemed that this blind eye was always turned every time a skua flew past the boat. In his three years on board, he had never seen one, yet I was almost tripping over them nearly every week. News of the four Pomarines in Loch Fyne had made even his bad eye green with envy.

The following morning, we had a punter exchange, and our couple went off in Carl's Land Rover to explore Arran, while we took a family of five of Carl's punters for a half day on the boat. We were treated to a rare and wonderful wildlife spectacle off the north-east coast of Arran.

We were cruising along the coast next to the evocatively-named villages of Sannox and Corrie. I noticed a flock of Gannets diving about a mile away. This was always a signal to take a closer look, as there would sometimes be other birds attracted to the frenzy, such as skuas, shearwaters, or tiny Storm Petrels. Suddenly, a big fin came to the surface, and then another one. Thinking that they could be Killer Whales, I frantically took the wheel from the Skipper and steered towards the spot. No-one else could see anything, and people were beginning to look at me as if I was suffering from a delusion. The fins appeared again – too small and curved for Killer Whales, and most likely some large type of dolphin, but still no-one else could see what I could see.

All of a sudden, finding them again was not a problem at all, as the four dolphins decided to come and see us. We spent the next half-hour in their company, as they surfed in our, rather pedestrian, bow-wave. It was a thrilling experience for everyone on board, except for the father of the family, who insisted on pointing out some rather mundane seabirds to his sons.

"Look at that, kids, the closest we've been to a Fulmar all week," he said. But the kids did not give a fish about the Fulmar. They were transfixed by the sight of four fantastic dolphins playing in the surf below.

The dolphins seemed to be attracted to the sound of our 'fish-finder' sonar. When the Skipper happened to turn this off, they began to swim away, but immediately returned when he switched it back on again. They were beautifully marked with cloudy grey stripes and patches, and had short, white beaks. They would spend a lot of their time swimming on their sides, apparently looking back up at us as we stood in the prow of the *Glendale*.

Across on the far side of the Sound, we could see another holiday boat, a Clyde Puffer named *Vic 32,* which was steaming on a parallel course about a mile away. The Skipper hailed her on the radio, and invited her across to come and share the fun. Soon the Vic's steam enthusiast punters were enjoying a superb dolphin experience, as our new friends left our bows for a short while to join the Vic, before returning to us one last time. I don't think that we would ever have tired of this wonderful spectacle, but after about half an hour, the dolphins decided they had had enough, and went off in search of a faster boat to play with. We watched as their fins broke the surface ever more distantly, until they were finally lost to view completely.

It was not until some time later that I was able to identify them. Field guides to cetaceans were not widely available then, and the only reference book to which I had access was at Peter and Jill's house. In it, there was an incorrectly-labelled picture of our beasts. 'Risso's Dolphin' said the caption. But their true identity had a clue in the name – these were, in fact, White-beaked Dolphins.

I was sorry that the teacher and his wife had missed the dolphins, but they were truly appreciative at the end of their week. In the guests' logbook, they mentioned the skuas, but paid a further, and quite unexpected compliment. In addition to my bird knowledge, they praised my 'expertise on wild flowers'. In reality, I knew only about fifteen of the local species, so I felt like a bit of a fraud, but I was secretly pleased, and felt that this was another sign that I was quickly establishing myself in my job.

*

Now I was a veteran of half a dozen cruises, and I was beginning to tick off the boxes which had been listed in the original job description. I had navigated the waters of the Clyde's sea lochs and sounds, seen eagles and Peregrines, added Beagle Firsts, shot the creels and cooked fine dinners. I felt more confident to engage in boat-related chat with new punters and passers-by, who tended to ask a standard set of questions for which I now had all of the answers:

Passer-by: "When was the boat built?"

Me: "1947, but there is no record of where she was built – perhaps in the North East of Scotland."

Passer-by: "What kind of wood was she built from?"

Me: "She's larch (planking) on oak (frame and beams)."

Passer-by: (a frequent question from local trawlermen): "What kind of engine has she got?"

Me: "A Gardner 5L3, with 96 horsepower."

One part of Beagle folklore which I was still yet to experience at first hand involved some serious climbing and hillwalking. Arran boasted a skyline containing a string of distinctive peaks, and these were objects of desire for hillwalkers. During the preceding season, a group had set themselves a challenge which was to become known as the 'Transarran walk', an epic journey which started in Lochranza and took the party along the ridges of the 'Sleeping Warrior', up and down the precipitous 'Witch's Step', and on down Glen Rosa and into Brodick. They successfully re-joined the *Glendale* at Brodick pier twelve hours later after a twelve-mile hike.

I was young, reasonably fit, and could be described as an outdoor type, but I did not have much of a track record when it came to hillwalking. A climb of the Old Man of Coniston in ill-fitting walking boots was probably the most significant hike I had managed, so talk of a Transarran filled my mind with images of painful blisters.

A new set of punters arrived for the next cruise. There were two couples in their fifties, including a pair of returnees; a jovial birder and Para Handy fan called Alastair and his wife Maggie. The couples did not know one another, but it very quickly transpired that they had much in common, and all four happened to be keen hillwalkers. Maps were unfurled and ideas floated on the first evening, with the focus turning to Arran's mountains, but thankfully there was no talk of a Transarran. Instead two hikes were mapped out, both on northern Arran, between which we would take a trip down Kilbrannan Sound to Sanda. North Arran meant more time with eagles, and I was more than happy to go along with the proposed itinerary.

As it happened, both walks were on my non-cooking days, and for the first walk, the Skipper dropped us off in *Gordon* on the beach of the distinctive little village of Catacol on the north-west shore of Arran. This was an attractive starting point for the first walk, featuring a row of twelve identical, whitewashed cottages on the roadside facing the bay. Rumour had it that there were once thirteen, but such were the superstitions of the locals that no-one would move into number thirteen, so it had to be demolished.

The climb behind Catacol was steep, but not too difficult. I left it to one of the punters to read the map while I just concentrated on keeping my bearings to ensure that we were walking in roughly the right direction. Soon we were up on a ridge which took us all the way to the hills behind Lochranza. All of a sudden, I began to recognise landmarks, albeit from a different outlook to the one I already knew well. We were now looking down on the eagles' tor. I quickly found the grassy ledge which contained the eyrie, and we watched as a large, white eaglet shuffled about, with one of its parents standing guard nearby. The walk was put on hold as we took turns to look at the eaglet through the telescope, and the punters mumbled appreciatively as they leaned over the tripod, thrilled to behold such a rare sight. This encounter rivalled the experiences earlier in the season with hatching seabird eggs as a high accumulator of Punter Value. With hindsight, I do not understand how we did not see the second chick, which was to fledge at the same time as the first. Perhaps it had nestled deeper into the nest and was having a nap, or maybe it was just shy.

We continued along the ridge and descended into the glen, then out onto the flat valley floor behind the village. It had not been too strenuous at all, and a check of the map revealed that we had completed a walk of about six miles. Perhaps I had less reason to be cautious about hillwalking than I had thought.

During the afternoon, we cruised down Kilbrannan Sound. The punters would not be allowed into the galley during the preparation of meals, but they often helped out, particularly when we were underway, by making teas and coffees. Perhaps it was because they all wanted to have a turn with the bagpiping kettle.

Maggie brought up a welcome cup of tea and I was chatting to Alastair, when I noticed a bird which I had been looking forward to meeting with, but which I knew would be tricky to point out to the punters. A tiny, black seabird, with a white rump, was flitting along just above the surface of the sea off our port bow. I managed to get Alastair onto it, before it flitted away, like a marine House Martin, and was lost to view. This was the first Storm Petrel, or 'Stormie', of the year.

En route to Sanda the following day, we met with a second Stormie — clearly the Stormie season was now getting underway. There was a lot of breeding bird activity on Sanda, with chicks having replaced the eggs in the auk colonies. Willow Warblers and Pied Wagtails busily fed their nestfuls. Morag watched on with the wisdom of a cow who had seen many springs come and go on the island.

We made our way back north, ready for our second walk on Arran, via an overnight stop in Brodick. This time, we landed on the northern tip of the island, on the unfortunately-named Cock of Arran. As on the earlier walk, our destination was to be Lochranza, but the angle of the light and the new viewing aspects gave us a very different perspective.

This new view of Lochranza Bay from the hills to the east was superb, with the massive Paps of Jura thrusting skywards to dominate the view out to the west. The bay itself looked dark blue, with the shallows around the curving shingle spit on which the castle stood an almost tropical-looking turquoise. And completing this magical picture, giving a neat, understated focal point in the middle of this vista, was the blue and red *Glendale*, at anchor in the centre of the bay.

We came down along a trail which would lead us back into Lochranza. Two large raptors appeared overhead, but it was not until they were joined by two smaller birds that I was able to get a sense of the size of what we were looking at. It was obvious that the smaller birds were 'mobbing' the larger, predatory ones, a common behaviour used to try to intimidate or irritate the raptor into moving away from their home territories.

The first bird looked tiny – a lark mobbing a Buzzard perhaps? No, the small bird was in fact a Kestrel, and it was truly dwarfed by the huge bulk of a pair of adult Golden Eagles. The second bird to arrive was another raptor, slender but bigger than the Kestrel. This was a male Hen Harrier. The combat continued above us for a few minutes, but it appeared to be a futile exercise on the part of the mobbers. Their size meant that they were mere irritants, and the fact that their entire territories were well and truly within the eagles' home range meant that they would be back as soon as the mood took them. I have never heard of an eagle striking back at its assailants, but other raptors have been known to kill their attackers in similar circumstances.

Our group was transfixed and stopped in its tracks, gazing up as the drama unfolded almost directly overhead. Eventually, whether or not influenced by the attentions of the other birds, the eagles majestically glided back towards their eyrie, while the Kestrel and the harrier returned to their hillsides, congratulating themselves on a bit of mobbing well done.

We descended into the village after a thoroughly fulfilling afternoon's hillwalking, and stopped for a well-earned, refreshing pint in the Lochranza Hotel. Walking had been the focus for the week, but we still had a couple of days left, and no real plans in place as to how we would fill them. It was Alastair who came up with one further request before the holiday was to end. He had heard about a ghost town which overlooked Loch Fyne, and he was keen to investigate and explore.

During most of our cruises, we shunned civilisation and instead sought out some of the wildest places in the area. There were constant reminders that we were on a frontier between wilderness and modern society, though. Our peace was regularly shattered by the sound of Phantom and Buccaneer jets, which roared up and down Kilbrannan Sound at what seemed to be no more than the height of our mast above the water. Glasgow's conurbation had outposts in Largs and Gourock, while Ardrossan, Irvine and Stevenston were satellite towns which extended the big city's reach further still.

The Kyles and Loch Fyne were still virtually unspoilt, but at Polphail, near Portavadie, there was a reminder that this remoteness was a fragile thing not to be taken for granted. During the boom of the Seventies, Scotland saw its future in oil, and poured vast amounts of money into rig construction. Mercifully, the Clyde was nowhere near any oilfields, but its other resources did not pass unnoticed by the industry's researchers. There may have been no oil, but Loch Fyne offered deep water close to shore, and a ready workforce was at hand for building and testing rigs.

In the early Seventies, work commenced on a new deep-water dock at Portavadie, specifically built for rig construction, on the east shore of Loch Fyne almost directly opposite Tarbert. An ultra-modern village was built to house and serve the port's workforce. Then, just before the first workers were due to arrive, it was realised that the whole business case was deeply flawed. The dock was never developed, and the new village was abandoned before anyone could move in.

The port at Portavadie was not completely wasted, and gave shelter to one of the biggest salmon farms in the area. The village, though, was left to nature. We ran *Gordon* ashore in a small, wooded bay, just below the village, and walked up into the ghost town. It really was quite surreal, strolling through deserted streets, and walking in and out of the empty buildings, most of which were in good condition and apparently ready for occupation.   Nature had begun to encroach, though, with oak and hawthorn saplings sprouting around the buildings, and ivy creeping up the walls.

The silence was perhaps the most striking feature of the place, giving it a profound sense of loneliness. The Seventies architecture which generated these huge concrete blocks had now produced a modern-day Easter Island, with hulking, hollow-eyed edifices silently gazing out to sea, awaiting the return of creators who would never come back.

*

Our marathon spell of forty-nine days at work without a break had come to an end at last, and at the start of July, it was finally time for us to have a week off. For the first Saturday in eight weeks, we could go for a night on the town, and having been used to English opening hours in the 1980s, it was a refreshing change to have the option of staying in the pub until after 11pm in Scotland. There was a notional closing time of 11:30, but this would be regularly waived for 'special' occasions, such as Saturdays.

The pub finally began preparations to close at 2:30am, but we were still part of a large and lively group. The *Glendale* had a reputation for throwing impromptu parties, and on our rare punter-free weekends we would often invite people back to the boat for a get-together. There was a regular crowd of friends of the *Glendale*, largely made up of the many local craftsmen and service providers who had been involved in her conversion. And an honorary member of this in-crowd was the former district nurse, Laurie.

Walking back to the pier with the dawn already well underway was an enjoyable new experience for me. The glow in the northern skies behind the village seemed to reinvigorate our group, and contributed to everyone's feeling that the night was still young.

As we made our merry way back along the sea front towards the pier, I noticed a small gap which seemed to have recently been torn in the railings which separated the road from the sea wall. This gap was opposite the end of a small road, which was effectively a back lane leading up the brae. I joked that a car must have driven through it, but sure enough, when we reached the spot, there was a Renault 5, parked neatly on the beach below the sea wall. There was no sign of an owner. It was as if they had found a parking space on the beach and just walked off to the pub. There was little we could do about its predicament so we carried on down to the pier.

Now Tighnabruaich was not a place to go out on the town and expect to pull (not that I particularly expected to pull in any other town). There were only three girls of a certain age in the whole village, and each of them had a well-established boyfriend plus a waiting-list of several more as backup. On top of this, the punters tended to cramp our style – it would not have been the done thing for a responsible crew member to abandon them and go off chasing women. I was about to learn that despite this lack of opportunity, strange things could happen in a small village.

Back on the boat, the Skipper's generosity knew no bounds as the drink flowed freely from the *Glendale*'s bar. Everyone seemed to be in a good mood, but I soon realised that one person seemed in a better mood than the rest. Laurie was paying me an uncomfortable amount of attention, and became increasingly predatory, circling her quarry and trying to isolate me from the crowd.

Sensing my unease, the Skipper did not help matters by his admittedly effective wind-up techniques, as well as none-too-subtle attempts to engineer situations for me and Laurie to spend some quality time together on deck. My resistance weakened slightly when she started to serenade me with those wonderful Stonechat impressions again, but I pulled myself together and kept my defences intact.

I was twice Laurie's height, and she was almost exactly twice my age. The Skipper had informed me that she had a son, who was the same age as me. I was no expert on women; to me they were as mysterious as any uncharted stretch of sea, but even I could tell that this one had more than just bird impressions on her mind.

I was stuck on a boat, and wanted to run a mile, but the best I could do was make sure that I wasn't left alone with her, sticking close to others, including the Skipper. Laurie could finally sense my deep unease, and gave up the chase, putting the blame squarely (and fairly) on the Skipper for her failure to land her catch. The situation was eventually eased significantly a few weeks later, when Laurie found another boyfriend, who was, coincidentally, 22. I no longer had to live in fear of spotting her blue VW Polo when we arrived in Tighnabruaich on a Friday night.

Eventually things began to quieten down, and people drifted off back up the pier. There were still several people on board, but I decided to turn in and tucked myself away in my bunk for the night. Within a couple of minutes, though, I was awoken by a loud crashing, as someone opened the engine room door and stumbled into the cabin. I could just about make out two figures in the dim dawn light, and could see that it was two of the party who were visitors to town. One was a tall girl, apparently a niece of a shopkeeper in the village, and the other was a young man to whom I'd been introduced earlier who went by the name of Tommy.

I pretended that I wasn't there, but I was soon subjected to an uninvited assault on the senses. I tried to sleep, but I was far too preoccupied with what was going on on the bench right outside my bunk between wee Tommy and partner.

I desperately waited for sleep to take me away from all of this, but the harder I tried, the more impossible it became. I was well and truly trapped

– there was no way I could get out of my bunk without stepping on the writhing couple. In the end, I buried my head under the pillow, and waited for it all to end.

Suddenly, the cabin light came on, as the Skipper came through from the saloon. The couple quickly got to their feet, quite unabashed as they straightened themselves out. Wee Tommy was apologising profusely to his new acquaintance.

"I'm really, really sorry," said wee Tommy. "Really, that's never happened to me before." I didn't ask, but the Skipper and I tried our level best not to add to his embarrassment by attempting to suppress our snorts of laughter.

Several of our guests were to be found, strewn around the cabins and saloon the next morning. I had the most acute hangover I had ever experienced. Headaches I had known in the past were usually triggered by standing up or loud noises, but this time, the merest turn of the head had me in agony. I swore never again to mix beer, whisky, white wine, more beer, red wine, port and more whisky.

Squinting out into the mid-morning light, I watched as a salvage operation was underway to winch the Renault 5 from the beach and back up onto the road.

*

After a few days of civilisation and sleeping in proper beds, it was time to re-acclimatise to the less-than-salubrious conditions of the crew's quarters. Our cabin was always a complete disaster area, and definitely out of bounds to the punters. Its shape was dictated by the tapering of the hull towards the stern of the boat, and the bunks and benches curved to leave only the narrowest area of floor space at the far end. This space was always occupied by the 'fet bag', a black bin-liner which ingested our dirty socks and boggers and became fatter as the week progressed. It was with some embarrassment that we delivered the finished article to our laundering friends each Saturday, when the fet bag was exchanged for a bin-liner full of neat, ironed washing, and the weekly cycle started again.

Neither I nor the Skipper were tidy people, and it was a challenge to find enough space on the floor on which to lay a foot en route to our recessed beds. There were spells during which the little hole in the wall became just too claustrophobic for me, and I moved my sleeping bag out onto the bench below (having knocked everything previously stored on this bench onto the floor first, obviously). This was very narrow, but at least gave me enough room to breathe and wiggle my toes.

Somewhere down by my feet, the ship's stilton was left to ripen, perhaps enriched by a blend of its own fungus and the spores from my socks. A piece of cheese had been broken loose, and was found some time later among the mess on the floor. It had seemingly taken on a life of its own, and had engulfed a 2p piece in an apparent attempt to absorb it, amoeba-like. I rescued the coin, and found that the 'grazed' area was now shining and tarnish-free. What was all of this stilton doing to our innards?

It was not just our cabin which was fetid. The area off the North-east coast of Arran received regular visits from a pair of large, grey sister ships, which came down from the upper reaches of the Clyde to do their business. One was named *Garroch Head*, which was very relevant geographically, but did a disservice to the nearby, scenic headland on Bute of the same name. Quite what the small town of Dalmarnock, some 100 miles away on the banks of the Tay, had done to deserve its name being given to the second ship, I do not know. These ships were full of raw sewage. They emerged from behind Garroch Head at Bute's southern tip, and after a furtive look around, deposited their cargo in the deep waters, before returning up the Clyde to pick up their next payload.

We pointed out *Garroch Head* and *Dalmarnock* to the punters when we saw them, usually in the distance, and the punters regarded them with a mild, but amused curiosity. Our relationship with the ships changed for the worse on a sunny, calm morning when we had an unprecedented fourteen people on board; our full complement of six punters, plus five from Carl's holiday, and one past and two present crew members. Our punters had decided not to take up Carl's offer of a day on Arran, so he was free to join us for the trip. I was at the wheel, and noticed one of the big grey ships dumping its load a mile or so away. As it departed, I watched as a gathering of birds, mostly gulls, was assembling in the waters which the ship had just left. Perhaps they would attract a passing skua or Storm Petrel.

I turned towards the flock of seabirds. All was calm on deck as we approached the gull flock, and I asked the Skipper to take over at the helm in anticipation of having some spotting to do for the punters. Within a few seconds, there was pandemonium. The boat was overwhelmed by an unseen cloud of the most foul-smelling gas. The punters rushed about, vainly trying to escape the stench, grabbing towels and cloths to cover their noses. We had entered the slick at full speed, so we decided to plough on rather than spend time trying to turn and escape. Fortunately, the Skipper remained conscious, with the help of a tea-towel stuffed up both nostrils, and we somehow found enough breathable air to support life for long enough to see us through. The unseen, putrid cloud seemed to be dense enough to exert its own gravitational force to hold it together, so our emergence into fresh air was just as abrupt as our entry into the cloud. Never had fresh air smelled so sweet.

There were no unusual birds after all, but presumably, far below us, the fish and prawns were tucking into a feast.

12. Rescuing a Celebrity (almost)

The *Glendale* flew a flag from her mast, tattered and frayed by the elements, which indicated our status as an auxiliary coastguard. This meant that the land-based Clyde Coastguard could call upon us to assist if anyone was reported to be in difficulty nearby. For our part, we would log our route plan with the coastguard over the radio, and one of my jobs was to make this call on most of our trips.

First, I had to make sure that the radio was tuned to Channel 16 before hailing the Coastguard.

"Clyde Coastguard, Clyde Coastguard, this is *Glendale*, *Glendale*, over" (you had to repeat the names on the first call in case of unclear transmission). I was then asked to change to a working channel, from where I was to provide the route plan, which always followed the same pattern:

"Clyde, this is *Glendale*, we have just left Tarbert for Lochranza, with eight persons on board. Estimated time of arrival at Lochranza is 11:30." On the vast majority of occasions, the radio remained unused for the rest of the voyage, until a further call to sign out and confirm that we were about to arrive at our destination.

Calling the coastguard every day served several purposes. First and foremost, it reassured the punters that if we went missing, the search and rescue team would have a decent idea where to look for the wreck and bodies (or 'life-rafts and survivors' as we told the punters). The other main objective was to let the coastguard know where its auxiliary coastguard colleague was in case we were needed to help someone in trouble.

The only time I was ever hailed by the coastguard was in very odd circumstances, on 4th July 1987.

On the face of it, the coastguard's request for details of our current position was a fairly standard question, but what followed was completely bizarre. We were vaguely aware that Richard Branson had been attempting a transatlantic hot-air balloon trip. Apparently his balloon had just crash-landed on Rathlin Island off Northern Ireland, and bounced off back into the sea. Branson and his crew had scrambled out of the capsule before it was carried off to sea again on the wind.

Confusion reigned as the balloon crew had been asked how many people had been on board, and a rumour had started that someone was still missing. We had been down at Sanda, within sight of Rathlin, a day or so earlier, but by now we were up in Lochranza, much too far away to be of any help. We gathered around the radio to listen as the drama unfolded. The boats which were at the scene were out of reach as far as our radio's reception was concerned, so we had to piece together the story based on the Coastguard's side of the conversation. Eventually, the Coastguard was assured that there were, in fact, no missing persons, and soon, normal service was resumed.

It was a pity that we didn't get involved in a rescue attempt, as it was later rumoured that Branson had donated £25,000 to the Rathlin lifeboat for their part in the search and rescue operation, a sum which could have kept Beagle Cruises afloat for several years to come, and could have even led to an increase in my wages.

Aside from logging our movements and earwigging on Richard Branson rescues, our main use of the ship's radio was to keep the mother ship in contact with our shore parties, especially when it came to arrangements for being picked up in *Gordon*. Strictly-speaking, this was a misuse of a ship to ship radio, but in a world without mobile phones, it was the only option for keeping in touch.

A typical example of day-to-day use of the radio came later that afternoon. I was on cooking duty at anchor in Lochranza, while the Skipper was leading a walk with the punters. Dinner was ready on schedule, and contact from the shore party was now well overdue. I had seen them from the deck approaching the bay some time earlier, and had worked out exactly where they were, although I couldn't really blame them for deciding to slake their thirst in the pub after a walk on a sunny day. Still, enough was enough, so I called the Skipper on the radio.

"*Gordon, Gordon*, this is *Glendale, Glendale*, over."

"*Glendale*, this is *Gordon*, go ahead" (muffled chortles in the background).

"*Gordon*, this is *Glendale*. What is your current position, over?"

"*Glendale*, this is *Gordon*, please stand by." (roars of pub laughter in the background). I saw the Skipper bolt from the front door of the pub, radio in hand, and a couple of minutes later, miraculously, the party was ready at the shore for me to collect them.

*

Throughout the year, I was gradually trained up in the handling of the boat and learned the 'Rules of the Road' at sea. The aim was for me to take an exam at the end of the year, and apply for a Boatman's Licence. I was amazed to learn that no qualifications were actually needed in order to take charge of a boat, especially one taking out passengers on a regular basis. The licence was primarily for insurance purposes should I need to take over as skipper, but it was also a nice qualification to have in its own right, as it enabled its holder to take up to 110 passengers on a vessel in the Firth of Clyde. The *Glendale* would have probably sunk if we ever managed to get that many people on board.

'Driving' the boat, to use the nautical term, was quite straightforward. There were three gears, controlled by a big metal wheel on the wheelhouse wall, at right-angles to and adjacent to the main ship's wheel. Ahead, neutral and astern – nice and easy to remember, and neutral 'felt' different, since it offered less resistance in turning the wheel. The throttle was controlled by a small lever, just behind the gear wheel – push back for more power, and push forward to reduce to idle.

In the early days of the Beagle venture, there had been a big, very characterful ship's wheel, which controlled the rudder via a series of chains. Unfortunately, this proved to be unreliable, and downright dangerous, as the chains became jammed, so the Skipper had arranged the installation of a more modern hydraulic system with a smallish, varnished, light wooden wheel.

I quickly learned the basics of navigation. Rule number one was to drive on the right, and let oncoming boats pass on your port side. Other than that, it was really just a case of keeping a straight wake and avoiding shallow water or bumping into land. For the latter, I had to overcome my instincts, which told me to take the shortest route possible when passing around points and headlands. I soon learned that staying out in the open water was safer, as it not only reduced the chances of meeting with unexpected shallows, but it also bought time when any unforeseen problems or distractions arose.

The next trick was for me to remember my port from my starboard. A nice aide memoire for this was 'port left in red can', but you had to bear in mind that this only applied to navigation buoys when entering a harbour (the 'in' part of the phrase). The port buoy was flat (or 'can' shaped) and needed to be passed on the left-hand side. The green buoy to starboard was always triangular-shaped, so that its silhouette could be distinguished from the can-shaped port buoys in poor light.

Revision for the exam was somewhat tedious, and I had to spend my spare time poring over a 'Rules of the Road' textbook. The Skipper tried to enliven my revision by introducing a novel way of instruction through bodily functions to replicate the signals of the ship's horn. One short blast = 'Alter course to starboard'. Two short blasts = 'Alter course to port'.

More worryingly, three short blasts = 'I am operating astern propulsion', and five or more short blasts indicated that something had gone badly wrong.

As early as cruise number three, I had been entrusted with bringing the *Glendale* onto a pier. It was a sunny afternoon in Inveraray, with no other boats around and a good-sized pier to aim at. The idea was to lower the engine revs, and then approach the face of the pier in neutral, at an angle of about 20°. Then it was a case of choosing the right moment to swing the bow to starboard, and put the engine full astern, at the same time spinning the wheel to a full left lock. To start with, it seemed that three hands were needed, as all three controls (wheel, gear wheel and throttle) had to be moved simultaneously.

The first time I tried, I came to a halt a few yards off the end of the pier, just too far to get a rope or a crew member ashore, so I had to go around and try again. On my second attempt, the angles were all correct, and I had a huge sense of satisfaction as the boat glided gracefully to a halt, the tyre fenders gently bumping against the pier. From this point onwards for a few weeks, I would take the helm when we were approaching any pier, so that I could gain some experience and hone some skills.

Despite the fact that I had made a good deal of progress, I had never been fully in charge of the boat. The Skipper handed over control of the helm with the words "You have the con", or "It's all yours, number one", but he was always at hand to step in should anything untoward seem likely to happen. During a week off in August, though, just for an evening, I made a small step towards being trusted to take command of the *Glendale*.

I had used my week off for a kind of busman's holiday. My Dad was also quite a keen birder, while my Mam was more than happy to spend time out and about in scenic countryside, and she was interested in birds to a point. I wanted to show them the boat, so we planned a whirlwind tour of Scotland, beginning with a drive up the A9 all the way to Kingussie near

Aviemore, where we would stay for two nights before returning down the west coast to Tighnabruaich. It was a bit of a trip down memory lane, as we had taken a family holiday in Aviemore when I was seven.

That holiday gave me some of my very first birding memories, and I can still clearly remember the white breast of a Dipper on the banks of the Spey, and looking down on my first Buzzard from the peak of Ord Ban. Less fond was my first memory of Pied Wagtails. The village green in Tomintoul was alive with them, running in all directions and darting after unseen insects. Meanwhile, I was hunched on a bench, my face as green as the green, attracting attention of well-wishers who had witnessed my being violently 'bus sick' throughout our winding coach journey from Aviemore.

We had an enjoyable couple of days going back to the forests and glens, and seeing my first-ever Crested Tits was a big highlight. Ospreys put on some fine displays, including one raiding a trout hatchery, while we had great views of males of both Hen and Marsh Harriers over the reeds at Insh Marshes. Afterwards we retired to the hotel bar, which was extremely well stocked with well over a hundred different malts.

On leaving Speyside, we drove down the west coast, through what to me was the uncharted territory of Fort William and Oban. Our arrival at Inveraray marked a return to my 'home patch', and we finally rolled into Tighnabruaich late in the afternoon. The Skipper would not return until the following day, and I was keen to show my parents my new-found boating skills. The *Glendale* was out on her mooring, and while I was notionally in charge, the Skipper had been in touch with instructions to stay out there for the night because of a windy weather forecast.

As soon as I reached the pier, though, I hit a snag. *Gordon*, which we had had left anchored off but tied up to the steps at the base of the pier, had vanished. Losing *Gordon* was not a situation I was prepared for, but fortunately, the owner of the house at the end of the pier soon appeared. He explained that *Gordon* had been obstructing a yacht which wanted to use the steps during the week, and someone had come and taken her off to a mooring off the boatyard. Sure enough, in the distant corner of the bay, I could see our orange inflatable bobbing around and looking rather forlorn.

I approached the office at the boatyard, and one of the lads working there pointed me in the direction of a small rowing boat. Now I was really shown up. I had rowed *Gordon* over short distances, and had rowed on boating lakes as a child, but I did not feel confident enough to make this journey single-handed, less still to somehow tie the two boats together and safely return the rowing boat back to the boatyard. Sensing my unease, the lad offered to take me out to *Gordon*. I felt a bit silly, sat there like a spare part while this lad took the strain, but I was glad to get into *Gordon* and start her engine at the second attempt.

I had sent my parents back to the pier to wait for me, and they had come to the steps with their overnight bag. Unfortunately, the tide was low, and the green, slimy, wooden steps were unfeasibly slippery. Hanging on gingerly to the hand-rail, my Mam came down first, her feet giving way a couple of times before she mustered the courage to step onto *Gordon's* inflated sides. My Dad carefully passed his bags down, and I was relieved to get everyone safely off the slippery steps and ferried them across to the mooring.

I didn't really relish the idea of returning to the pier that evening, but fortunately, we had some food on board, so I was able to treat them to some Beagle hospitality and some more malt whisky. My Dad, especially, was apprehensive about spending time on board, as his track record in retaining his stomach contents on boats was not good, and the breeze was starting to blow up as had been forecast. In fact, it made me wonder how I had made it this far through the season without being seasick myself, especially now that my Tomintoul travel traumas had been brought to mind

Suitably anaesthetised by whisky and a small glass of sherry, my folks retired to the big cabin in the pointy end, while I took the opportunity to escape the squalor that was the crew's quarters to sleep in a guest's cabin for the night. I could hear the wind blowing through our rigging, but the breeze actually helped us through a quiet night, swinging us on our mooring rope to face directly into the small waves and keeping the boat on an even keel.

The morning dawned as windy as had been forecast, but the supremely sheltered waters of the Kyles meant that barely a ripple had disturbed us. After a Beagle breakfast of porridge, it was time to head back. I got my Dad to help release us from the mooring, and we made the short trip back to the pier. With hindsight, I wish I had taken them for a quick spin, even if it was only to the Maids and back, but perhaps time was short, and perhaps I was a little anxious about getting them ashore in one piece on my own, so I decided just to go straight back.

The wind was blowing offshore, so I could see that this was going to be a tricky docking manoeuvre. I planned to send my Dad up the ladder and throw a rope to him to start getting us tied up, but my approach left us a yard or two short, and we were getting blown, inch by inch, away from the pier. Fortunately, a tourist appeared at the end of the pier, and I was able to step out of the wheelhouse and hurl a rope over to him on the second attempt.

My folks got ashore safely, and we said our goodbyes. They still seemed a little bewildered by the utterly different context in which they were now seeing their son, but I hoped that they could see how much I was enjoying my new life. Secretly, though, I was a little disappointed that my display of boat handling had not gone as smoothly as I'd have liked.

13. Man Overboard

After my parents left, I got on with the Saturday routine, as The Skipper wouldn't arrive until early afternoon. We had to get ready for another full boatload arriving later in the day, and all but one were to be first-time Beaglers.

The group for the week was younger than average, with Andrew being the only returnee among them. He was a quiet but keenly curious, intelligent chap, with a slightly bird-like sharpness to his movements. There was an engaged couple from Birmingham; Dave, who had a phobia about sharks, and his fiancée, Yvonne, who was a keen club runner and was to go out for early morning jogs with the Skipper. We also had a squaddie on board; Mark was posted in Northern Ireland, and bore an uncanny resemblance to a young Norman Wisdom. In fact, he was a big fan, and would give regular, quite convincing impressions during the week. Boosting the average age were Glenn and Pauline, a smartly turned-out, recently retired couple, who gave off the wealthy glow of success in business.

While being the quietest of the group, Andrew had a slightly Messianic air about him, and often it seemed that the rest of the group would follow him anywhere. He was a keen botanist, and this week, he had taken it upon himself to address the finer points of thistle identification. We all soon learned how to identify the low-growing Creeping and the tall, typically Scottish Spear Thistle. Andrew set us on a mission to identify an in-between variety known as the Welted Thistle, and soon the whole group was engaged in a search of boggy, weedy fields to find examples of this species.

One of my regular training exercises on board was a man-overboard drill, which we carried out during most of our cruises. The routine involved the Skipper throwing one of the life-belts over the side, and shouting 'Man overboard!' I had to take a quick note of my bearing, then swing the boat

45° to port, and get someone (normally the Skipper but sometimes a volunteer punter) to point towards the stricken 'man' in the water. After a short while, I swung around hard to starboard, and if things went to plan, I could return on a reciprocal bearing to the spot where the victim was floating. In practice, compass readings were never needed, as we always managed to keep the lifebelt in sight. The final manoeuvre, bringing the boat to a standstill alongside the lifebelt, was the trickiest part, as obviously we were aiming to avoid running it over. The Skipper completed the exercise by fishing the soggy victim out of the water, using a long boat-hook, and announcing how long the exercise had taken. Normally we took about two or three minutes, sufficiently quick to prevent the lifebelt from suffering from hypothermia.

While it gave some entertainment to the punters, this was a drill which had become something of a routine, even a chore for me. On this August cruise, we were making our way up Kilbrannan Sound, along the west coast of Arran, when the familiar 'Man overboard!' shout went up again. I swung the boat around as usual, but rather than the expected lifebelt, I was confronted by the sight of Andrew, happily bobbing about in a bright orange lifejacket and green oilskins. This had obviously been planned with the Skipper's consent, as there was to be a further change to the regular routine.

The Skipper had 'invented' some life-saving equipment, which had been dangling over the side of the boat, unused, for several cruising seasons. This comprised a long pole (a broomstick handle in a former life), and a cargo net, which was lashed up into place against the starboard side. Now, at long last, he had a chance to put his creation to good use. Using some of the old pulleys and a gantry which had been retained from the *Glendale*'s trawling days, the broomstick was lowered to water-level.

Now the instructions became a little bit jumbled. I had to bring the boat alongside Andrew in such a way that he floated into the cargo net, but this was much easier said than done. We shouted to Andrew to get him to swim into the apparatus, as he was considerably more manoeuvrable than a 52-foot trawler, although it was doubtful whether a genuine victim of an accident would have been capable of this. Even when he did finally reach the net, he was hampered by his life-jacket and clothing, as the net was floating on the surface.

Finally, after much laughing and bobbing about, Andrew managed to get himself into position for his life to be saved. The Skipper, who had evidently been dreaming of this moment since the day of his invention several years ago, gave a swift yank on the rope.

The broomstick immediately snapped in half. Andrew, more helpless than ever, was now almost paralysed with laughter. Eventually, the Skipper had to admit defeat, and conceded that his invention was not going to work. Crestfallen, he resorted to getting into *Gordon*, and hauling Andrew from the water in a most undignified manner.

The whole exercise had taken over five minutes, but we could, at a push, claim that we had saved a life. A number of conclusions were drawn from the exercise. The first was that the apparatus was completely useless. Secondly, it confirmed that a real person in the water is a dead weight very difficult to lift from the surface, and, from now on, we should use *Gordon* to fish out any unfortunate who fell overboard.

The waters into which Andrew had fallen were truly shark-infested. Basking Sharks arrived in the Clyde from early July onwards, and we saw them regularly on our trips, particularly on calm days when the plankton rose to the surface. A big, triangular dorsal fin was always the first thing to be spotted, and on closer inspection, the top of the tail was usually visible above the surface, swishing from side to side. The nose could sometimes be seen breaking the surface as well, which helped form an impression of the size of the beast hidden below. A close approach on a calm day allowed a glimpse of the bright white insides of the shark's gaping, toothless mouth. Most of the sharks we saw were around fifteen feet in length, but occasionally we would come across a real big basker. They could grow up to forty feet long, and we saw several which must have been around thirty.

Much to shark-phobic Dave's alarm, Kilbrannan Sound was positively teeming with sharks, but Andrew had not been in any danger, aside from the off-chance of an accidental collision or a gumming to death. Our drill on spotting a shark was to change course to intercept, and then drop the engine revs and let the boat drift towards it. Sometimes the shark would turn onto a collision course, and we were able to clearly see the whites of its gums before it gave a flick and a twist of the tail to dive, disappearing from view for a few seconds and resurfacing a short distance away.

Our cruise up Kilbrannan Sound ended at Lochranza, where we anchored for the evening. Standing on the old pier there, a scan of the sea through binoculars revealed several glinting shark fins offshore in the low evening sun. It was an amazing sight, with perhaps ten in view at any one time, and a fine way to end what had been a very eventful day.

On the morning after our shark-fest, attention was switched to that other, apparently never-disappointing deliverer of punter value, the Golden Eagle. I had made a picnic, mainly bread rolls with various fillings, which we took up to the eagle stake-out at the top of the valley. We made ourselves comfortable and waited for the eagles to appear. The young had recently fledged, and it had been a good year, with two eaglets being successfully reared, but on this sunny day, none of the four deigned to put in an appearance for our audience.

Finding eagles was something of an inexact science. They could frequently be picked out soaring as we made our way along the road towards the tor, and there were even occasions when I had seen them from the deck of the *Glendale* while at anchor in the bay. But as time ticked by when they weren't so obliging, I always felt under increasing pressure to come up with the goods.

I knew that the best chance of a sighting was always when the birds were on the wing. I constantly monitored the ridges which surrounded Lochranza on three sides, and the skies over the Glens which flanked the tor. If the birds decided to rest, to quietly digest a hare, perhaps, then I had to work a lot harder. Carl, who had been eagle watching for four seasons, had given me some tips, especially about scanning the horizon. Unfortunately, our birds did not have any particular favourite rocky perch, so it was a matter of scanning the skyline and looking for the bulky, regal profile which would give away its position.

This approach was time-consuming, and almost always fruitless. Punters often joined in the search, which helped to build a sense of suspense and anticipation, but no punter was ever successful in actually picking out an eagle. More often, it resulted in me having to gently let them down by breaking the news that their bird was, in fact, a crow or an oddly-shaped rock.

To keep things ticking over, I was always on the lookout for other wildlife to help the time pass. Sometimes it would be the flora. As well as Welted Thistles, Arran was a particularly good location to see Sundew, both the long and round-leaved varieties, and we often found a specimen or two with semi-digested insect remains stuck fast to their 'dew-drops'. On the fauna front, Red Deer were usually visible after a short scan, either grazing on a hillside or trekking across the horizon.

Andrew had found a plump toad hiding under a rock next to our chosen picnic site. The toad posed for the cameras, and became the focus of attention for the group. I had to admit that the toad was a bit of a looker, but I soon got back to the 'real' work of searching for eagles.

Almost inevitably, while all other eyes in the group were down, the eagles chose this moment for the show to start. An adult and one of the fledged eaglets swooped overhead and perched on a ledge above us, while the other parent circled nearby. By this time, I could tell the parents apart.

The female was bigger, which could only be discerned when the pair were together, and the male was missing a couple of flight feathers which made him easy to pick out.

I invited the punters to come and take a look through the scope, but to my dismay, they were still crowded around the toad.

"Come and see the eagles. There are three of them together up there!" I implored.

"Hold on a minute, I'm changing the film in my camera," came Andrew's reply.

For most of the season, I'd found that nothing could beat the spectacle of a soaring eagle, but now, it appeared, for this group of punters at least, a toad could provide some real competition. I was dumbfounded, but this episode served to prove that perhaps I was still not in tune with their priorities and expectations, even after more than half a season of cruises.

It was Friday and time to head back to base. Yvonne came and joined me in the wheelhouse as we made our way up the Kyles. Being at the helm was often quite a solitary pastime, so I was always glad of some company, and there was easily enough room for two people to sit on the black, fake leather cushion behind the wheel.

For the umpteenth time in the year, I introduced a female punter to some birding parlance, whereby the observer 'has' birds rather than 'sees' them, hence we had had three eagles earlier in the day. And hence Yvonne and I had just had a Shag on a seaweed-covered rock. And like umpteen punters before, Yvonne laughed politely at my puerile play on words.

She then went below decks to fetch something, and returned a few minutes later with a small bag which she handed to me. By now, I was quite used to receiving tips on the final days of cruises, and I usually amassed a total of around fifteen pounds in a week. Yvonne explained that she did not like to give cash tips, and had instead brought me a small gift. I opened the bag and found a rather nice t-shirt, and I was surprised and touched that someone would go to the trouble of buying me a present.

It was a happy group of punters who made their way up to the Royal on the last night of the week, but there was no way in which I could have anticipated the events that were about to unfold. I spent some time chatting to Yvonne, when she suddenly asked me to step a little closer. I couldn't make out the next question when she first asked it, and when I did hear it, I was not sure that I fully understood the implications. She asked if she could write to me. My initial reaction was one of puzzlement, especially as her fiancé was standing just a few yards away, but she assured me that all would become clearer in due course.

Maybe I had missed some signs earlier in the day when Yvonne and I had had that Shag on a seaweed-covered rock, but I had very good reason to assume that she was not available. Even more puzzling to me was the fact that she had a choice of five compatibly-aged men that week, or six if it turned out that she was a marriage-breaking gold-digger and went for Glenn. My reading of the situation and the personalities involved had been so wide of the mark that even this idea seemed just as realistic a possibility as what seemed to be unfolding.

Putting the marriage-breaking, gold-digging theory to one side, I reflected on the remaining four potential suitors. Dave was obviously in pole position, what with actually being engaged to her, but now it began to dawn on me that the couple had not been exactly inseparable during the week. Mark was perhaps second favourite, and he had actually flirted with Yvonne from time to time during the cruise. Maybe she was one of those girls who had a thing about squaddies. The Skipper had spent a lot of time with her, and there was a chance that he could have begun to form a bond, and perhaps spark some chemistry, during their early morning jogs. And of course, who could rule out the Messianic Andrew, especially after he revealed his hidden daring side by fearlessly leaping into the shark-infested ocean?

All four of my 'rivals' seemed to me to be surely better potential suitors than the fifth; the geeky, angular bird man who was earning thirty-eight quid per week. What I failed to realise at the time was that despite what I felt inside, to the outside world, in Yvonne's eyes at least, I had seemingly been reinvented. Now I was living the life of Reilly, bobbing around in this other-worldly Scottish paradise, and what was more, I was now quite independent, and could cook fine food. I was oblivious to it at the time, but apparently the tall young ship's mate on that trawler had somehow been transformed into something of a catch.

For someone to whom girls tended to be as elusive as a skulking Corncrake, this was difficult to comprehend. The Skipper, who was much more tuned in to this type of thing, sensed that something was afoot, and he expertly engineered a situation whereby he and all of the other punters returned to the boat. Yvonne and I were left to walk and talk alone.

Dawn broke and Saturday morning was uneventful, if slightly awkward. I began to wonder whether I had imagined the previous evening's conversation, or if it had all been a drunken miscalculation. We said our goodbyes, and I was left none-the-wiser. I was going to have to wait for the postman to arrive the following Friday to see if Yvonne would keep her word.

*

By this time, in August, I was already a veteran of 15 cruises, and the next one was also a memorable one, but in a completely different way. Our normal capacity on our cruises was six passengers, but for block bookings, we would consider taking eight. The extra two people were accommodated in the saloon, where the seating could be used to provide temporary, rather narrow, beds. This week, we had a large, extended family on board, comprising a patriarchal doctor and his wife, their children (aged 13 – 32) and assorted girlfriends and boyfriends.

A group booking made for an entirely different atmosphere on board. Overall, the mood was much more relaxed from day one, with the teenage daughter allowed to play her 'Dirty Dancing' cassette all day long, without fear of annoying other guests unduly. Breakfast was prepared while beds in the saloon were being either slept in or tidied up. Evenings were spent having far too much to drink and engaging in highly entertaining conversation.

The eldest of the sons was also in the medical profession but his chosen speciality was gynaecology. Strictly-speaking, he did respect client confidentiality in that no clients were actually referred to by name, but his anecdotes were thoroughly hilarious, if, on occasion, very inappropriate.

Our bar made a large amount of money that week, as we sampled several of the malt whiskies on board, and made inroads into our wine and beer supplies. We operated an 'honesty bar', whereby a pricelist was pinned to the inside of the door of the drinks cupboard, and punters would fill in little chits to say what they had taken. The Saturday morning routine included some time spent dividing up the chits and settling up, giving the punters a chance to offload some Scottish notes before heading south for the border.

This group had a great time, but they were almost completely indifferent about the wildlife aspect of the holiday. They did appreciate some speedy rides in *Gordon*, which served to blow away cobwebs and hangovers. We also went ashore for a number of short walks to clear people's heads and offer a change of scene while we killed the time ahead of the next drinking session.

Inchmarnock was an ideal destination for one of these gentle walks. As usual, we had some fun in *Gordon* before going ashore, dashing up and down the strait between the smaller island and Bute. We had spotted a large Basking Shark during our approach, and soon we were drifting alongside it in *Gordon* in silence, with our engine cut. This was one of the largest sharks we ever met with, and must have exceeded thirty feet in length. Sitting in eighteen-foot *Gordon* and floating alongside such a monstrous creature was another unforgettable experience for the nine people on board, and even our wildlife agnostics couldn't fail to be impressed with this close encounter.

The island's charm owed much to the fact that it was uninhabited, which gave a sense of enchantment and adventure, and added a slightly mysterious atmosphere to the place. I ran *Gordon* ashore on a little sandy beach below the deserted Mid Park Farm, and then led a gentle walk of a couple of miles. The island had been abandoned quite recently, and the buildings at Mid Park were still in good, habitable condition.

We walked up the island to the rather more dilapidated North Park Farm, and came across a tame, apparently dazed creature. It was fully albino, with white fur and pink eyes, and was slowly stumbling around one of the farm buildings. At first, I took it to be one of the large local population of feral mink, but on reflection, it seems more likely that this was, in fact, a ferret, either escaped from or abandoned by its owners who had since left the island. There was certainly enough food on the island to sustain a ferret, although the rabbit population was in the midst of an outbreak of myxomatosis.

North Park was in a rapidly advancing state of disrepair. Ceilings were giving way and roofs collapsing throughout the buildings. In one room, we found a remarkable collection of bills dating from the 60s which had recently tumbled down from the loft. Some of these were apparently unpaid or overdue, for farm supplies and machinery from 'mainland' Bute. It seemed that there were advantages in the isolation offered by island life.

We left Inchmarnock and headed south, our ultimate destination being that other other-worldly uninhabited island, Sanda, where I was to be presented with a new challenge. A circumnavigation was a big highlight of any trip to this archipelago, and I had watched the Skipper and navigated for him on several previous occasions. I had learned some of the hazards on the route, particularly the locations of submerged rocks and reefs, and now I had to put that experience into practice, as it was my turn to take the helm for a trip around the islands.

We left the *Glendale* at anchor in the bay, and set off in a heavily-laden *Gordon* towards Sheep Island (for some reason, the trip was exclusively executed in a clockwise direction). We headed through a deep channel of clear water between reefs extending from Sheep Island to port and a rocky spit off Sanda to starboard. On a calm day, it felt as if we were floating through a woodland glade at canopy level, as forests of kelp gently swayed on either side of us. As we slowly made our way along this channel, Puffins could be seen among the boulders of Sheep Island, while to starboard, a colony of Common Seals was hauled out on a rocky spit on Sanda. Atop Sheep Island, fittingly, was a flock of Soay Sheep, which we could see engaging in fierce courtship fights, the rams butting one another with shuddering force.

Leaving Sheep Island behind us, we were soon approaching the rocky islet of Glunimore, accompanied by curious Grey Seals, which bobbed to the surface nearby. We cut *Gordon's* engine and drifted onto the rocks, allowing us to enjoy more of the multi-sensory experience that is a visit to a seabird colony. As well as the sights, we could enjoy a sound track which was dominated by the kittiwaking of Kittiwakes and odd, guttural grunting calls of Guillemots. Our nostrils caught the whiff of guano as it wafted in our direction on the breeze.

The remainder of the trip was conducted at high speed, starting with a sprint down Sanda's east coast, with birds scattering in all directions ahead of us. A Puffin was spotted, so I changed course to intercept, keeping pace with it as its orange feet pattered across the surface. Eventually its whirring wings generated enough speed and lift for it to gradually pull away from us.

The distinctive shape of Elephant Rock then appeared, with its 'trunk' buried in the rock face below the lighthouse. At this point, we had to give the island a wide berth, as the exposed bones of the wrecked Liberty Ship reminded us that Sanda's south-western shores were surrounded by an extensive system of dangerous reefs.

The west side of the island was more featureless, but here, the highlight was the sense of being in the open sea in a small boat. To our port side, the North Channel stretched unhindered between the Mull of Kintyre and Rathlin Island, and into the North Atlantic. There was nothing else to bump into for thousands of miles until North America. No matter how hard we strained, though, the Mull of Kintyre lighthouse was not in our line of sight, and I'm sure that some of the punters were secretly disappointed not to be able to see one of the few famous local landmarks.

The tour ended as we rounded a rocky headland and re-entered the bay. Another group of exhilarated, spray-soaked punters then boarded the *Glendale* using a little wooden ladder slung over her side. A familiar face appeared nearby – a curious Grey Seal which had been watching us as we climbed into *Gordon* at the start of the trip. Surely it hadn't followed us all the way around the island?

As we chugged back northwards towards Tighnabruaich Pier, my mind was again filled with intrigue about the previous Friday, and what might await me in our pile of mail at the Hamiltons'. The Skipper normally did the mail run, but this time I volunteered, and was off up the ladder before the ropes had been fully secured. The mail was always left in a little pile on a chair inside the ever-unlocked front door. And in the pile on this day was a small, unassuming letter with a Birmingham post-mark.

I took the letter back to the boat and found a quiet moment to go down to the blunt end to read it. It turned out that last Saturday morning's appearances of normality had been deceptive, and the drama had continued on the train back to Birmingham. Yvonne had called off the engagement during this journey. My immediate feeling was of guilt, and sympathy for Dave, but the letter went on to attempt to justify the act, with a claim that the holiday had just meant that the inevitable had happened a little sooner than expected.

There was a phone number in the letter. The Skipper pointed out that here was a potential returnee punter. I agreed that I had no choice but to gather my courage and give Yvonne a call, as an exercise in Beagle public relations if nothing else.

Another Saturday dawned, and another boatful of punters was about to go home happy but not before one last piece of mischief by our gynaecologist. Entries in the guests' logbook were made by most of the visitors before they went home. We would wave them off at the pier head, and then return to the boat to read what they had said about us. Every week it would be complimentary, sometimes with illustrations or lists of highlights from the week. This time, there was one entry which bucked the trend.

"Dear Captain Codpiece. Thank you for a delicious evening in the wheelhouse. You discovered parts of my body I never knew existed. All my love, Frank (not his real name)". For the first and only time, censorship was applied to the logbook using a black marker-pen.

14. Highland Games

The Skipper didn't look as if he was really built for speed, but his jowly features and stocky build belied a mean turn of pace. So quick had he been in his prime that he had actually been a champion in the 100m handicap race at a local Highland Games event a few years earlier. Since then, he had endured a back operation and a loss of fitness, but he had decided that this was the year that he would try to regain his crown.

The Skipper would disappear for runs with increasing frequency as the games approached, interspersing jogs with sprints in an attempt to recapture his champion's speed. Throughout the season, on the way back to the boat from the pub in Tighnabruaich, he and I would have a race, normally the 'two-lamppost dash'. I was never much of a sprinter myself, but I could give the Skipper a decent run for his money early in the season. On one famous occasion, I actually beat him convincingly, and on a couple of others, I would have done so had he not cheated by starting too soon (on the second 'y' in 'ready, steady, go'), or by pulling me back. But as the season progressed, he gradually became quicker, until I was unable to keep up with his now-blistering pace.

The day of the games would be in August, during one of our cruises. On board for the week we had an elderly, moustachioed Scotsman named Angus, along with a young family of four, including an unfeasibly cute four-year old girl who insisted on us calling her 'Sproglet'. As a special treat, we proposed a visit to the 1987 Dunoon and Cowal Highland Games as part of the itinerary for the week. Fortunately, our punters were happy to go along with this plan.

The father of the family had recently undergone a routine operation to prevent his family from growing any further. Each mealtime would be accompanied by the sound of his whimpers, as he squeezed his way around the dining table, which was at exactly the wrong height for his tender post-operative scars. His wife had terrible back problems. And Angus had angina. Perhaps it would do everyone good to go and watch some healthy people participating in an athletics event.

We arrived in Dunoon on the evening before the games. A large section of the pier was reserved for regular use by the CalMac ferry which ran over to Gourock. On this evening, the only available berth was occupied by a black-and-cream-coloured naval auxiliary boat, so we tied up alongside it for the night. We were informed by the naval crew that they would be leaving at some unearthly hour the next morning. This could interfere with the Skipper's restorative sleep before his big day. Being a dutiful first mate, I agreed to set the alarm and 'do the ropes' in the morning.

With military precision, the naval vessel slipped its berth right on time at six the next morning. I started the *Glendale*'s engine, and swung her in on the single rope which still attached us to the pier. I would have to attach another rope at the pointy end, too. Unfortunately, the tide was very low indeed, so I had to stand on the guard rail to reach the ladder and climb up onto the pier to secure the extra rope. Descending the ladder was even more hazardous than going up. As I leapt from the bottom rung of the ladder, I caught a foot on the guard-rail, and was catapulted head-first towards the deck. Fortunately, I somehow managed to break my fall and escape injury, and no-one was awoken by the clatter onto the deck. Mission had been accomplished, and the Skipper was still sound asleep.

Breakfast that morning was a quiet, contemplative affair, save for the whimpers of our post-operative punter. In between stirs of the porridge spurtle, I prepared some coffee in our big, brown coffee pot. In the absence of a plunger, I would sprinkle cold water on the surface of the coffee to make the granules sink to the bottom.

"Why is Steve washing his hands in the coffee pot?" Sproglet asked her dad, giving us all a laugh to relieve some of the tension around the table.

The Skipper put his faith in his regular Beagle breakfast of porridge and black treacle as part of his pre-race preparations. The time soon arrived for us to disembark, and we made our way up the pier and through the streets of Dunoon towards the stadium.

The Skipper went off to find the players' entrance, while I led the punters to find a group of seats together towards the back of the small, wooden stand. A horde of pipers descended a grassy bank and into the arena, and then the games commenced. Cabers were tossed and old-fashioned hammers chucked. The Skipper had entered both 100 and 200 metre sprints. These were handicap events, so depending on age and form, each athlete would be given a head start in order to ensure an even race and a close finish.

For the 100 metres, the Skipper's past form as an ex-champion had counted against him when it came to the handicap distance allocations. Prolonged lobbying on the grounds of his back operation had fallen on deaf ears, and his three-metre start left him second last from the outset as the athletes took to their blocks. The gun was fired, and the Skipper was soon into his running, but he could only make up a single place before they reached the tape. There was no glory, but he had acquitted himself reasonably well. In hindsight, I wished that there was a high-definition super-slow-mo replay, as I am sure that the sight of his jowls in full flow would have been spectacular.

He had not been looking forward to the 200 metres, where he was hindered from the start by a similarly harsh handicap as he had been for the 100. Before the race, he had told me that if he thought he was coming in last, he would feign a pulled hamstring and limp off to save some of his dignity. The gun was fired, and the Skipper ran a good bend, making up a couple of places against his rivals. As he came off the bend, he 'opened his legs and showed his class' in the words of David Coleman. But then things went horribly wrong, and he suddenly pulled up. This was no fake hamstring strain. My diagnosis from the stands drew some puzzled looks from the spectators around me, as I burst out with laughter, cheered and shouted "Groin strain!" The Skipper hobbled off the track, his Highland Games career having come to a premature end.

*

After a busy period, we now had a couple of weeks off in early September. The Skipper went back to Sedgefield to nurse his groin strain, but I had little time to rest. After a short stay in Newcastle, I went off on a Beagle Customer Relations trip to Birmingham to spend some time with Yvonne. I then had to return to the boat, as the time had come to sit my exam.

We were now entering the latter stages of the season. I had several hundred nautical miles of helmsmanship behind me, and had encountered a wide range of scenarios at sea. I had also studied my Rules of the Road book, and was quite familiar with most of the main principles of not bumping into other boats or running aground. An examiner was to travel out from Glasgow and meet us in Rothesay one evening, to see if I was made of the right stuff to qualify for a Boatman's Licence.

I sat down with the examiner in the saloon, and he tried to put me at my ease. It quickly became apparent that he was not familiar with any of the ports which we frequented, and I didn't know any of those which he knew on the Ayrshire coast. The Skipper instructed me not to mention the fact that we made the longer sea-crossing to Ailsa Craig (we were not allowed to stray more than four miles from land, so should really have made the journey via Ayrshire rather than Brodick or Campbeltown). Fortunately the examiner allowed me to steer the conversation to describe the few navigational hazards to be encountered in the northern and western reaches of the Firth of Clyde.

My revision of the Rules of the Road soon paid off, when I was tested with a lot of pictures of patterns of light, and I remembered the fine details, such as the limit of 22.5 degrees abaft the beam through which the coloured steaming lights would be visible. After a short, tense pause, I was informed that I had qualified to skipper any vessel carrying up to 110 passengers within the Firth of Clyde. I was now the proud owner of a Boatman's Licence, a full two years before I took the landlubber's test to drive a car.

Refreshed after our two-week break, and with a confidence boost from my successful exam, we were ready for the arrival of our next set of punters. This time, we had another couple from the West Midlands, and a striking-looking girl; an acquaintance of the Skipper's, who had recently studied marine biology. The Skipper had his eye on her, although he claimed that this was purely in the context of a potential crew member.

The cruise started with an ominous weather forecast, which predicted storm-force winds on Saturday night. We headed up to Ormidale, and put out some additional ropes to brace ourselves for the onslaught. But the morning dawned calm, and a peep out of the hatch revealed that the storm had failed to materialise.

During our morning walk on Bute, the wind began to blow up, and soon we were steaming into choppy waves in the West Kyle en route to Tarbert. As we approached the end of the Kyle, I noticed an unfamiliar silhouette of a seabird flying straight towards us. As it approached, it banked sharply, gliding first towards us, and then sweeping away up the Kyle. Although I had never seen a Leach's Petrel before, I instantly knew that this was what I was looking at. Much bigger and longer-winged than the Stormies which I'd got to know during the season, this bird also had subtly different wing markings and a distinctly forked tail. The encounter was over within a few seconds, but as ever, I was secretly thrilled to have seen a new bird, even though I had not been able to share it with anyone.

Spirits remained high for the week, but this was my first experience of a cruise which was so severely hampered by the weather. Still, we found more than enough to do in the upper reaches of the Clyde, and visited the sheltered waters of several sea lochs which were new to me.

The following Saturday, we were back in Tighnabruaich, and I was carrying out a few chores on board. After my encounter with the Leach's Petrel and the persistence of the windy weather, I was still on the lookout for more storm-driven seabirds among the regular local flocks. As I walked across the deck, I noticed an odd-looking gull among the Herring Gulls at the end of the pier. It seemed paler than the others, but lacked the paleness I would expect of an Iceland or Glaucous Gull. It started to fly away before I had a chance to get a proper look, so with a bit of quick thinking, I emptied the stale bread from the bread-bin overboard to tempt it back.

I was successful, and the bird returned, soon settling on the water behind the boat. It was quite plain, and digestive biscuit-coloured, being a little darker on the wingtips and tail, although the underwings appeared paler. I was very familiar with Iceland Gulls, which were regular visitors to my local North Shields fish quay. I knew that they could vary a lot in tone, so I had to put this bird down as bit of an unsatisfactory and exceptionally dark juvenile Iceland Gull.

The mystery of its identification was not resolved until three years later when I visited Vancouver, where I found several, near-identical mystery gulls. These were Thayer's Gulls, a close relative of the Iceland Gull which breeds in northern Canada and winters in the northern Pacific. And sometimes, evidently, in the Kyles of Bute. Thayer's Gull was unrecorded in Britain at the time, but they are still notoriously tricky to identify positively, so even now, I have to put it down as a 'probable Thayer's Gull'. What was probably the rarest bird I ever encountered on the *Glendale* would never be enshrined as a Beagle First.

15. A Triumph

There then followed what would turn out to be the best of cruises and the worst of cruises. The Hollicks were already part of the fabric of Beagle Cruises, having spent their holidays on board for the past three summers. Al (yes, Al Hollick) was a large Lichfield lad whose jovial face was framed by thick, dark brown hair and a bushy beard. His wife, Jill, was somewhat smaller, and lacked the beard. Both were self-confessed *Glendale* nuts, and Al frequently sported his favourite fisherman's hat, a black affair with 'TARBERT' emblazoned in knitted white capitals across the front.

Al and Jill were joined on board by four punters, each of whom was travelling alone. The eldest was Mary, a sturdy lady fond of long, brisk walks. Then came Nigel, a quiet chap in his sixties who had a habit of making unexpected and irrelevant contributions to the conversation. Emma was a strident journalist who made freelance contributions to magazines. Last to make his way along the pier, in a pair of very fetching white wellies, was George, a very camp West End theatre producer.

The Hollicks took the 'honeymoon suite' in the bows. Mary and Emma took the port cabin, and Nigel and George the starboard, before they decided among themselves who would sleep on top and who underneath. All settled in quickly and without a fuss, and we were off on an epic voyage. Things started well for Al and George, both of whom were keener birders than the average punter, as we met with a Hen Harrier over Inchmarnock and a Bonxie en route to Arran.

In a change to our normal agenda, we landed in a bay near Garroch Head at the southern end of Bute. We had a pleasant walk through low, rocky hills, up to a small lochan, with Mary striding off ahead and setting a brisk pace for the group. The rest of us struggled to keep up, and Nigel's legs went from under him on a couple of occasions, much to the amusement of Mary.

"Little Willie's fallen over again!" she chirped, and a rather unfortunate nickname was born.

We met Carl on Arran and went for a soggy walk up the glen behind the eagles' eyrie site. The cloud was quite low, and our star birds were not their usual obliging selves. Eventually, the unmistakable, huge silhouette of the adult male emerged over the hilltop, and it glided effortlessly across the valley overhead. It was a brief show, but George in particular was thrilled by the encounter.

We stayed the night at anchor in Lochranza, and had a lively evening in the bar of the Lochranza Hotel. No doubt we were well over the *Gordon*-drink-drive limit, but we managed to successfully dodge a few yachts and safely locate the dark shape of the *Glendale* courtesy of torchlight and some good luck.

The next day saw us cruising down Kilbrannan Sound to Campbeltown, where Emma the journalist went for a short walk and came back with a description of a bird which, after reference to the ship's library of bird books, could 'only be a Terek Sandpiper'. I decided to congratulate her on her good fortune (a Terek Sandpiper is an extremely rare shorebird from Asia, closely related to the much commoner Redshank), rather than point out that there was a very strong chance that she had actually seen a Redshank. I did not feel a desperate urge to drop everything and go and relocate the bird. Obviously it COULD have been a Terek Sandpiper, and who was I to say that she was wrong?

We left for Sanda the following lunchtime, and arrived there early in the afternoon. The path to the lighthouse was alive with small birds, mostly common ones, and many of them migrants. This was my favourite kind of birding; to me, it was like Christmas come early, as anticipation grew as to what would be revealed each time another bird emerged from its cover.

There were Whinchats, Whitethroats, Wheatears and Willow Warblers, and a tiny Goldcrest hopped around in the little front garden outside the old farmhouse. Then an odd-looking bird flew along the path ahead of us and landed at a strange angle on a fence post. It looked like a cross between a thrush and a woodpecker, which could only mean one thing. It was a Wryneck. This was only my second-ever, and the only one to be recorded in the whole of Argyll in 1987. It gave us great views of its cryptic markings, and stayed in view to allow everyone to get a good look. Al and George were particularly pleased, as this was a new bird, or 'tick' for both of them.

We carried on along the track to the Lighthouse, stopping frequently to check each of the multitude of migrants as they flitted across our path. Mary was beginning to get frustrated by our slow progress, and eventually struck out alone at the front of the group. There would be no further surprise finds, but we did spend some more time marvelling at the Wryneck before climbing back into *Gordon* at the jetty and saying farewell to Sanda for another week.

Back on board, we took a trip to Campbeltown for the night. I prepared my trout special, while the group sat around the table exchanging stories, jokes and anecdotes.

"I once saw a French film where a condom blew into the sea" was Nigel's typically irrelevant contribution to the conversation.

The group had gelled superbly, perhaps a little too well at times. I was becoming very concerned about George, who seemed to be taking a shine to me. My fears were confirmed by Emma, with whom he had already begun to engage in regular, girly chats. He had sought her opinion as early as the second evening on the cruise, when he was concerned that he might have already spoiled his chances and 'blown his cover.' It seemed that my new-found magnetism, which had surfaced a couple of weeks earlier, had carried on into this cruise. Maybe there was something in the porridge.

Dinner was served, and was a great success, leaving George unable to contain himself. He cleared his plate and placed his knife and fork down in as camp a way as it was possible to put down any cutlery.

"That was a triumph, darling," said George.

"Don't call me darling at the dinner table," I growled in reply. I think that my coyness only served to encourage him further.

Most of the next day was spent at sea. We headed down to Ailsa Craig and then north to Brodick. Nigel had not looked too good for most of the voyage, as there was a bit of a swell running, and eventually he lost his lunch overboard.

"That's the first hot meal those gulls have had for weeks," joked the Skipper, not for the first time. And not for the first time, the joke went down very well with everyone, except for Nigel.

It was on long cruises such as this that I looked for a chance to have a rare wash. Showering for the crew was a bit of a sporadic event. For the most part, I was just too busy either cooking, tidying, driving the boat or leading a walk. Our notional time off on Saturdays was normally far too busy to indulge in ablutions, as we had so much work to get through to ready the boat for the next set of punters. A dash through the engine room and then dodging a saloon full of punters wrapped in a towel was never particularly appealing either, especially with George on the prowl. And if any of the six punters, quite reasonably, wanted a shower themselves, then they had to take priority. While we had two large water tanks on board, I always had to be mindful that water was not in limitless supply.

One shower per week was about the norm for me. Now I was on my way to achieving a personal best, with a gap of thirteen days, at the end of which I was completely covered in a layer of salt and diesel particles.

A visit the shower-room always carried an element of trepidation for the Skipper and me, and not just because of the towel-clad dash through the saloon. It was effectively a 'wet bathroom', which was also home to the dreaded heads. By now, I had first-hand experience of dealing with some of the less pleasant aspects of life on board which had been foretold in the job description. We told the punters that they should not hesitate in asking the crew to assist in the event of any problems in the heads, but little did they know that they were potentially loading the gun in a tense game of Russian roulette for the crew. Each time a punter reported a problem, the Skipper and I took it in turns to attend the scene of the incident.

The Skipper often told a horror-story from his early days on board, when he had tackled a particularly stubborn blockage in the pump-action toilet. He tried to use brute force in an attempt to pump the problem away, but only succeeded in building up more and more pressure behind the little hatch which housed a simple valve mechanism. He needed a hammer to prise open the hatch door, and the resulting small explosion left him looking like a mud-wrestler, and smelling an awful lot worse. This was in the days before a shower was installed on board, so the white boiler suit had to go into the bin. As for his hair, the story goes that he waited for it to dry before he could comb it out.

I seemed to be leading a charmed life, as every time it was my turn, I would be able to pump just a little harder and clear the problem, but this week my luck was to run out on a choppy day off Kintyre. My standard pumping techniques were futile. Mindful of the legend, I did not want to build up too much pressure, but the hatch was jammed. I was left with no choice but to fetch a hammer to deal with the hatch door.

The hatch came loose, and to my enormous relief, there was no explosion. But I had to go in there to find where the problem lay. From the slurry, a red object emerged – it was a small condom-like affair which had become tangled in the valves. I had to untangle it and re-assemble the hatch, but how on earth was I going to tactfully ask the unidentified punter not to repeat the offence? In the end I opted not to say anything – the excruciating embarrassment would have been even more unpleasant than a repeat performance. I was lucky, and was never called to the heads again that week. And even after thirteen days without a shower, I counted myself fortunate never to have needed one as desperately as the Skipper had on that legendary occasion.

*

As far as possible, we let Al and Jill have a big say in setting the week's agenda, as we treated them as honoured guests. They had not been to Brodick Castle before, and Jill was keen to visit, having read about the gardens there. Their wish was our command, and we found ourselves speeding across the bay in *Gordon* towards the castle.

As we enjoyed our stroll around the gardens, Emma raced over to tell us she had seen a 'huge hawk', but on this occasion, I had seen the bird, which was, in fact, a Mistle Thrush. With her talent for exaggeration, I was beginning to see just why Emma had chosen to be a journalist, and made a mental note to take any articles written by her with a large pinch of salt.

From Brodick, we made our way towards Millport on Great Cumbrae. We steamed between Little Cumbrae and the ominous nuclear power station at Hunterston. Unlike its larger neighbour, which was readily accessible to the public, Little Cumbrae was a bit of a mystery, being privately owned and with no public access. There were rumours that Irish Wolfhounds guarded the little jetty there to prevent intruders from landing. All of this secrecy gave us licence to let our imaginations run free.

Suddenly, it became obvious to Al and me that the island's location opposite the nuclear power station was no coincidence. There must be an undersea tunnel linking the two, providing the shady owners of Little Cumbrae with boundless supplies of energy. And those Shags on the rocks near the jetty were actually killer androids, armed to the beaks. The greatest threat to world peace was here on Little Cumbrae, where the madman landlord wanted nothing less than world domination.

Having safely slipped past the lair of the tyrant and his army of android Shags, we arrived in Millport, another place which was new to Al and Jill.

We tied up to the quay there, and spent an enjoyable evening in the George Hotel at the head of the pier, where there was a particularly generous quiz machine which provided funds for an extra round of drinks.

Millport was always a pleasant port of call, which offered two regular activities on a day's agenda. One was a walk around the bay to a little research station on the headland, where there was an aquarium housing a collection of the marine life which could be found in local waters. It gave the punters another chance to get a close-up look at some of the animals they had seen during the creel sessions, as well as fish, crustaceans and anemones. The octopus tank proved especially popular, and always prompted comments and surprise about the fact that such creatures abounded in Scottish waters.

The highlight of a trip to Millport was a ride around the island on a hired bike or tandem. The hire shop had even acquired a couple of snazzy, red Sinclair C5s, already obsolete less than three years after their initial launch. We never did persuade any of our punters to hire a C5.

George was inexplicably enthusiastic about hiring a tandem. Specifically, he wanted to share a tandem with me. Even more specifically, he wanted to take the rear seat on a tandem behind me. Eventually we set out with a mixed fleet of tandems and bicycles, Famous Five-like, along the 10-mile road that runs around the perimeter of the island. George had been unable to secure a berth on a tandem with anyone, and had to be content with a bicycle of his own.

It was a bright and breezy day, and we cycled around the bay, past Crocodile Rock and the research station, then up the east coast and past the landing slip for the ferries from Largs. Around the northern and western coasts, there were crystal-clear views up the Clyde and across to Bute and the sun-lit mountains of Arran. We stopped occasionally to take in the view and let stragglers catch up.

After about an hour of pedalling, we freewheeled back down into Millport and to the hire shop. George dismounted his bike gingerly, and straightened himself out.

"Ooh! Me legs are like jelly and I feel like the whole Royal Navy's been through me!" he proclaimed.

A few weeks after the cruise, I received a letter from George. It was really very pleasant, and in it, he thanked me for three things:

1. The eagle at Lochranza. It was not the greatest view, but he had always wanted to see an eagle, and the surroundings, atmosphere and company had combined to make for a great experience.

2. The Wryneck on Sanda. It was a great birdwatching moment, again made all the more enjoyable by the island surroundings.

3. Me. (At this point I cringed).

He enclosed a very generous cheque for £25 as a token of his appreciation, adding that nothing could ever repay me for the knowledge I had imparted. I never did reply, probably through a mixture of embarrassment and sheer laziness, but also because I was worried that any reply might be taken the wrong way. I had no such problems in cashing the cheque, though, meaning that for the only time in my *Glendale* career, tips had exceeded wages for the week.

The holiday was now drawing to a close for George and the others, and Friday afternoon arrived all-too-soon. It was turning into a pleasant evening by the time we approached Tighnabruaich Pier after an enjoyable and very memorable cruise. Peter stood on the pier to welcome us. This was quite unusual, although he would sometimes pop down to help with the ropes if he had spotted us approaching up the Kyles. But his white-faced expression told us that something was seriously wrong.

We tied up the boat, and then Peter quietly invited the Skipper back to his house. I stayed on board to prepare dinner, and did my best not to speculate about what could be happening just up the road. An hour or so had passed, before we heard the Skipper stepping back onto the deck above. He called down the hatch and asked me to go to our cabin.

The news that Peter had broken was that the Skipper's father had suffered a massive heart attack earlier that day and died, aged 65. The Skipper was distraught. I had no experience of dealing with such a traumatic loss, but did my best to offer my condolences, although I could not begin to imagine the pain he was going through. He and his dad had been very close, and although I had only met him on one occasion, I knew that he had been a larger-than-life character without whom the whole Beagle enterprise would never have been possible.

I had to go back through the saloon and break the news to the punters. What had previously been the jolliest and most enjoyable of cruises had ended on a tragic note. Things would never be quite the same again.

16. Becoming Skipper

The Skipper rose the following morning and made the long drive back to County Durham alone. He had a huge amount on his mind, and a difficult few weeks ahead of him. He was suddenly the only man in the family, and had to help his mother and sister through funeral preparations and sending out the terrible news. The fact that his father had been a prominent and active doctor meant that this was a long and drawn-out process, with calls continuing to come in regularly from patients who were due for appointments over the following weeks.

Back on the *Glendale*, I had to deal with a crisis of a somewhat different nature. We had another cruise planned to start that very evening, and it was much too late for any thoughts of cancelling the holiday. The five punters were probably already on their respective ways, including a lady from Hong Kong and a couple from Germany. A Scottish journalist and a returning photographer made up the complement for the week. Just a couple of weeks after qualifying for my Boatman's Licence, I was going to have to step up and be Skipper for a week. And I was going to have to find a crew.

Peter was more than happy to step in, but he had a prior arrangement which meant that he would not be able to join us until the Sunday evening. He had already made enquiries on our behalf around the village, and had found someone who could cover for the first night and day. Ian knew boats well, and probably had as much experience and knowledge of the waters around the Kyles as I did. I was confident that he could do a good job, but what were the punters going to make of a twelve-year-old crew member?

I was worried how the youngster would interact with our guests. The *Glendale* was very much part of the community in Tighnabruaich, and villagers would occasionally pay us a visit even when we had punters on board. The only time that Ian had visited, he'd popped down the hatch and was surprised to see a saloon full of holidaymakers tucking into their evening meals. Ian sat down on the stairs, a little lost for words.

"Are these your punters then?" he asked the Skipper.

We NEVER called the punters 'punters' in front of the punters. For all the fact that as crew of the *Glendale* we had become part of Tighnabruaich life, I got the impression that punters remained a bit of a mystery to the locals.

The punters arrived, and we welcomed them on board. I had been through a lot during the season, but I had never been so nervous, and felt that I would be unable to create the relaxed, welcoming atmosphere as the Skipper would have done. Walter the German approached me.

"He is very young, yes?" he asked, or rather, stated. I did my best to explain that Ian spent a lot of time on boats, and he went some way to backing up my comment with some confident rope-handling as we left the pier. But I could not really argue with Walter's statement.

We took the regular first-evening cruise up to Loch Riddon, and Ian accompanied the punters for a walk while I prepared the usual first-evening spread. We were making the most of a difficult situation, and the smoked salmon, caviar and champagne went some way to reassuring the guests that they were in good hands.

The following morning, breakfast was a rather subdued affair. Walter did not help matters by studiously examining the milk carton to check its use-by date. The plan was to return to Tighnabruaich Pier to change the crew late in the afternoon, so we could not go too far afield in the morning. A visit to the fish farm was followed by a steam down the Kyles to Inchmarnock. It was a fine, calm afternoon, and we took a stroll on the little island before heading back up the Kyle.

A slight breeze had blown up while we were on Inchmarnock, and a few ripples appeared on the sea's surface as we emerged from the shelter of the island. It was still a force 3 at the very worst, and the bow gently bumped into the ripples as we headed north.

"Is this rough?" came a question from the open wheelhouse window. It was Walter, who seemed to have brought rather unrealistic expectations about the conditions we could expect to encounter on the ocean waves. At first I thought he might be joking, but then I saw from the expression on his face that he was, in fact, deadly serious.

This left me in an awkward position. If I laughed, it would seem to be disrespectful. If I agreed, then I would be lying. The worst sea-state I ever came across was high. Then came very rough, down through moderate to what this was – somewhere between calm and slight. I could see that I was going to have problems with Walter, and reassured him again that this was nothing to worry about.

I left Ian at the helm, and went below deck to start preparing the evening meal. It was soon time to say goodbye to Ian, and thank him for a job well done. Now it was time for us to pick up my new first mate. Replacing the twelve-year old lad was one-time Naval Frigate Commander, SBS veteran and global circumnavigator, Peter.

Peter was an instant hit with the punters when he joined us. I left the helm in his hugely capable hands and completed the preparation of our Sunday Roast. Peter called for me as we approached Tarbert, and I took the wheel as we navigated the narrow harbour entrance. As we did so, a young Glaucous Gull, an Arctic wanderer, flapped by off to starboard.

"Glaucous Gull!" I called, as I kept one eye on the channel ahead.

"Good lord, so it is!" exclaimed Peter.

We settled down for our first evening meal. Peter went around each person at the table and tried to get to know them individually. He came to Walter and his wife, Helga.

"W – w - wh – where whereabouts in Germany do you come from?" he asked with his characteristic, booming stammer. He recognised the town that they mentioned. There then followed a 'don't mention the war' moment. "Oh, I swam across the Rhine there during the war." The slight unease that followed was soon dispelled, as Peter went on with his tale.

He told how, during the Allied advance, he had been dropped from a glider into Holland under the cover of darkness. He made his rendezvous, and was taken across the country to the banks of the Rhine. His task was to swim to the far shore (with no light to guide the way) and establish whether the bank was mined. This would be done using nothing more than a hand knife being poked into the sand. Presumably if the answer was that they were mined, he would have lost an arm, or even his life. Fortunately, he concluded that it was clear and jumped back into the Rhine to return and pass on the news.

This time, he missed his target pick-up boat, and found himself being swept along in the strong current. Eventually, he scrambled ashore, but he was exhausted and disorientated, and had no way of knowing whether he was in allied or enemy territory. He found a road, and caught some sleep in an adjacent ditch.

At first light, he was awoken by the sound of an approaching motorcycle. He had to think quickly. Should he risk being seen in order to get a look at the motorcyclist? Instead he decided that more drastic action was needed, and leapt from the ditch into the path of the oncoming bike, which then careered off the road into the ditch. A voice emerged from the ditch, and Peter quickly established that the cyclist could swear perfectly in English. His final challenge was to persuade his disgruntled compatriot that he was on the same side.

Sanying from Hong Kong carried on the Germanic theme with a most enthusiastic account of a visit to the Mercedes factory in Stuttgart. It turned out that she was mid-way through a European tour, and it was rather flattering to think that a week on the *Glendale* would form part of that same tour itinerary. Peter did not warm to the journalist though – he was under the impression that Bob was a bit of a freeloader, and with hindsight, he was probably not wrong. The fifth punter, Les, was a quiet chap who brought along some photos and told us some stories about his previous week on board the *Glendale*.

The next morning, I was keen to press on southwards, as we were effectively a day behind schedule following our crew changes. The forecast for the end of the week was for strong gales, so if we were to get to Sanda it would have to be sooner rather than later. I made a decision to sail straight from Tarbert to Campbeltown in a day, which was much further than we would normally go, but would give us the maximum opportunity to visit sites in the south of the cruising area.

We made a routine approach up Campbeltown Loch and into the square harbour, but it was particularly crowded with trawlers and yachts on this day. I chose a fishing boat against which to tie up, and made my usual slow approach. But when I asked the engine for some astern propulsion, I could not get a response. Instead, we gently drifted straight towards the tied-up trawler. The kick of astern propulsion was crucial to getting the bow to swing away from the other boat, so I could only look on helplessly as the bow continued on a collision course.

There was a sickening crunch as the bow ran into the bulwark of the trawler. The impact was enough to slow our progress sufficiently to stop and swing alongside. While I was concentrating on getting us into position to tie up, I thought I could feel dozens of eyes on me as the noise drew attention of passers-by, and punters watched to see if I had things under control.

I checked for damage, and mercifully, there was no visible effect on either the *Glendale* or on the other trawler. My embarrassment was the biggest problem, as I was concerned that I would have lost some of the hard-won confidence of the punters. More importantly, I was genuinely worried that we might have a real problem with the engine or the gearbox.

As soon as we were safely tied up, I left Peter cooking a cottage pie in the galley, and went to find a functioning phone-box. I blurted out the details of the crisis to the Skipper and waited for his prognosis and advice on how to fix the problem. The advice turned out to be far simpler than I could have imagined. The Skipper told me to go back to the boat and see if there was anything on the shelf next to the fridge.

The 'mechanical failure' had been caused by a wine-box. It had been left next to a lever by the fridge, which moved when the gear wheel was turned up in the wheelhouse, forwards for ahead or backwards for astern. The wine-box had prevented the lever from giving us anything more than the gentlest astern power. I was still learning the basics, and was relieved that the solution turned out to be such a simple one.

The following morning, a southerly breeze had sprung up, but it was still only force four or five, and certainly nothing to be worried about. The sea state had increased from slight to moderate, but as usual, Campbeltown Loch was nearly flat-calm. We rounded Davaar, and made our way south, but it was not until we rounded the headland at Ru Stafnish and Sanda came into view that we encountered some waves.

This was still very comfortably within the limits of our endurance, and only the occasional wave slapped into our bows with sufficient force to splash the decks. Again, I had a visit from Walter.

"We would like to get off," he told me. Not turn back to Campbeltown, just to go ashore here and now and wait for us to pick them up on the way back.

A quick look at the shore was sufficient to explain why this was a very bad idea indeed. We were travelling past low cliffs at the southern end of Kintyre, the foot of which were strewn with boulders, and these were being splashed and broken on by waves driven by the onshore wind. Any attempt to get ashore would have been dangerous, and once more, Peter and I had to persuade Walter that he was in no danger whatsoever.

As a compromise, I agreed to put Walter and Helga ashore as soon as we reached Sanda. To be fair, it was quite choppy, and there was a slightly scary moment as we boarded *Gordon* in the normally sheltered harbour. *Gordon* got caught under our little boarding ladder which was slung over the side of the *Glendale*, lifting it away, and giving Helga a bit of a fright, but soon, the couple were settled on the harbour wall, tucking in to the packed lunch I had provided for them. The rest of us were able to join them after we had eaten on board with minimal discomfort.

After a typically peaceful and pleasant walk on Sanda, there was a perceptible change in the atmosphere on board. Perhaps it was the fact that we had following seas for the remainder of the week, or that there was a sense that we would be returning to calmer waters to the north, but Walter visibly relaxed and became more involved in the general bonhomie among the punters.

Peter had taken it upon himself to do all of the cooking for the remainder of the week, leaving me to decide the itinerary and take the punters ashore for walks. This led to a fairly stark departure from the regular *Glendale* menu. On our second evening in Campbeltown, he concocted a fried rice dish, and was thrilled to be complimented on this by our Chinese guest.

The wind had strengthened further the following morning. It was now a south-westerly force five to seven, which would have prevented a trip to Sanda had we arrived a day later. We headed north, and got as far as Carradale where we stopped for lunch and a walk across the isthmus to the broad bay, and explored the scrubby heath behind the beach. Stonechats gave their pebble-rapping calls from atop the gorse, and a Peregrine powered its way through the air along the rocky peninsula that flanked the bay.

By late afternoon, we were ready to go again. A curving pier sheltered the narrow, shallow harbour at Carradale, and it often proved a difficult place to get into and out of. A three-point turn was out of the question, and the only manoeuvre which could safely get us out to sea was to go out backwards. Once clear of the pier, a full left wheel lock was needed to send us around in a 180° arc astern, before switching to forward propulsion and getting underway with the wind at our backs towards the sheltered haven of Lochranza. Peter had been tidying the ropes during this procedure, when I noticed him standing in the swinging bows with a big grin on his face. He was clearly relishing his time back on the open sea.

When the wind was in the right direction, there were few better anchorages than Lochranza. Wild waves could be seen running at right-angles across the mouth of the bay, but in the lea of the hills, there was scarcely a ripple to disturb us. We went ashore for the evening to meet up with Carl, and another good night out at the Lochranza Hotel was to follow. Tonight's sport was a game of "Get the non-Scottish person to ask for a difficult-to-say malt whisky", the highlight of which was Sanying's game attempt at getting in a round of Bunnahabhainns. She was successful, and we were soon sipping our tumblers of this nectar from Islay.

Friday dawned with a storm brewing, but we remained safe and snug in Lochranza Bay. Peter ferried us in *Gordon* across to the shingle spit under the castle, and I took the party for a walk up the valley. Eagles like windy weather, and this week, we were treated to the sight of three soaring together over the tor. Despite the westerly winds, there were thousands of migrant thrushes on the island, with swirling flocks of Redwings and Fieldfares freshly arrived from Scandinavia.

I called Peter on the hand-held radio to let him know that we would shortly be ready to be picked up. This was more easily said than done, as Peter was profoundly deaf in one ear (due to a near miss with an exploding World War II shell), and his hearing was not much better in the other one.

To my relief, we saw Peter emerge from the wheelhouse and descend into *Gordon*. There then followed another tense moment as the white-haired figure in a blue boiler-suit and wellies tried repeatedly to start *Gordon's* engine. This was never an easy task, more a question of timing than of brute strength, and we could just about make out mutterings and the odd sweary-word drifting across the loch as Peter struggled.

After a quick breather, Peter had success, and Gordon's engine roared into life. He came across to the shore where we were waiting and a few moments later we were back on the *Glendale* with warm cooking smells emerging from the galley.

"What's for lunch?" I asked.

"Soup," came the reply.

"What kind of soup?" I asked.

"Brown," came the reply. The brown soup primarily comprised the watered-down remains of left-overs, the main ingredient being a two-day-old cottage pie. It was perhaps not the most sophisticated dish to be served on the *Glendale*, but it was politely wolfed down by the punters, who were grateful for its warmth, if perhaps not its flavour.

We weighed anchor, but I was to be set one final challenge in my first week as Skipper. The anchor seemed heavier than usual, and the winch strained as it struggled to raise it. This reminded me of my experience on the shakedown cruise when the anchor had snagged on a cable, and now I half-expected another length of cable to break the surface. This time, though, the culprit was a huge, old anchor, which judging by the thickness of accretions and rust had not seen the light of day for quite some time.

I racked my brains to remember how the Skipper had dealt with the cable five months earlier. I had to act quickly, though. The cable, while much heavier and more awkward to handle, had at least ensured that we stayed anchored in one spot. Now there was a strong breeze, which was blowing us towards the reef on the eastern side of the loch at an alarming speed.

I needed to find a way of securing the snagged anchor to the Glendale in a way which would allow me to release the tension on our anchor. I found a suitable length of rope with which to perform the task ahead, and asked Peter to man the winch while I hopped into *Gordon*. I tied one end of the rope to the offending, barnacle-encrusted anchor, while Peter secured the other end to the *Glendale*'s bulwark. Then I asked Peter to lower our anchor a little.

The next step would be crucial, as I had to stand in *Gordon* and push our anchor clear. Should our hastily-rigged up rope not be sufficient to hold the weight of the old anchor, it could easily crash into *Gordon*, or even into me. It was a huge relief when I gave our anchor a shove, and it immediately swung free. The rusty old anchor now dangled on its short length of rope, and slammed into the hull. I made sure that *Gordon* was clear before cutting through the rope, and with a huge splash, the relic returned to the depths.

"Why did you do that?" asked Peter, as the huge old anchor sank out of sight. He evidently had designs on the object as a garden ornament or a useful mooring. In truth, salvaging the antique had never crossed my mind, and I was just glad to be able to get underway again.

Leaving the calm of the bay, we were soon swept along with a following force seven, with some decent-sized waves nudging against the stern. It was quite exhilarating – Peter was again in his marine element, and even Walter was enjoying the ride. The clouds over Kintyre gradually transformed until they were aflame with a crimson glow from the setting sun. The wind followed us all the way to the Kyles, where we found ourselves back in calm waters and heading safely back to Tighnabruaich.

Saturday was bright and breezy as we said our farewells to our guests. A cruise that had had the makings of a disaster had been turned into a great success. I walked up with Peter to his house afterwards to pick up another letter from Yvonne. Jill was on the phone to relatives in Kent and seemed to be almost dumbstruck by what she was hearing. When the call was over, she told us about fallen trees and airborne garden benches, and something about a hurricane that had hit the south-east of England during the night. We had escaped with nothing more than a cheerful breeze. After a quick cup of tea, I had to go straight back to the boat, where young Ian was due to re-join as crew for the weekend.

17. Fushunchups

The vast majority of our custom came from the regular wildlife holidays, but we were occasionally asked to take on other kinds of work. I was below decks tidying the boat, when a young chap called to me from the end of the pier.

"Do you do fushunchups?" he asked.

"Pardon?" I asked.

"Do you do fushunchups?" he asked again. I was confused. Surely the fame of the *Glendale*'s cuisine had not spread sufficiently that people would come to us specifically for meals.

"No," I replied, "but the cafe in the village has just opened a fish and chip takeaway."

"No, no, no," said the lad. "Fushun chups, no fushunchups." It was obvious now. He actually wanted to go on a chup on the boat to catch some fush.

We did occasionally do fishing trips, and in the continuing absence of the Skipper, I was going to have to be in charge for my first. Ian arrived promptly, and we headed around the Kyles to start a two-day fishing charter from Rothesay. We had arranged a rendezvous with another chartered trawler, the *Terranova*, in the bay off Rothesay Harbour, and twelve hopeful fishermen transferred their rods and themselves onto the *Glendale*.

Being a complete angling novice, I had taken some advice before the trip from the skipper of another converted trawler which operated out of Tighnabruaich. *Green Pastures* was much smaller than the *Glendale*, and ran regular fishing charters from the pier. We knew Andy, her skipper well, and he often approached us to see if we could help out on the occasions when he was fully-booked.

We often called Andy on the ship's radio if we saw him during the week, and it always seemed as if fish were constantly leaping from the water onto his decks if his conversation was to be believed. "There's another one coming over the now!" was a well-used catch-phrase of his, but he was also generous with his advice. I learned the locations of a couple of reefs and hotspots, such as the Ascog patches near Rothesay, and the rumoured location of the wreck of a Wellington bomber in the Kyles. Ian also knew a few local spots, but I was not expecting a fishing frenzy.

Our first stop was near the eastern shore of Bute at Ardmaleish. The rods went over the side, but for a long time, nothing at all happened. The fishing was very quiet indeed, and I was obviously concerned that this was a result of my lack of experience. I needn't have worried, as the rest of the group were having similarly lean pickings aboard the nearby *Terranova,* despite her more experienced skipper.

Things picked up very slightly as the day wore on, with a trickle of fish being hooked over the Ascog Patches. The day's haul was far from impressive, though. We had sometimes caught as many fish casually during our cruises, using hand-lines with rusty hooks and Kit-Kat wrappers. Despite the efforts of well-equipped, experienced anglers, single-figure totals of Whiting and Saithe were the sum total of the day's catch.

As we headed back to Rothesay, the few fish we had caught were cleaned and the unwanted bits thrown overboard. Among the gulls was another white-winged bird hot on the heels of the Glaucous Gull the previous week in Tarbert. This one was smaller with an all-black bill, making it an Iceland Gull, and it kept us company for the remainder of our trip into harbour. The fishing punters were perhaps not as appreciative of the finer qualities of this bird as our more discerning wildlife holidaymakers. One asked if he was allowed to shoot it.

The fishermen didn't stay on board for the night, and had all booked into bed and breakfast accommodation in Rothesay. As we entered the small inner harbour, I noticed a couple of police officers on the pier, and as we tied up, it became apparent that it was me whom they wanted to see. I felt rather confused, unsettled, and not a little embarrassed, and I wanted to make sure that all of the fishermen were safely ashore before we got down to the detail of their business.

One of the officers put his hands behind his back and flexed his knees. "A vessel of dark blue or black colour, similar in shape to yours, was seen to be associated with an orange inflatable dinghy, similar to yours, causing a disturbance to yachts in the Loch Riddon area last week," he began. It was not clear exactly what the seriousness of the charge was, but it was an open and shut case as far as the officers were concerned. The *Glendale* was the only boat in the Clyde which matched that description.

I was thrown off-balance by the allegation, but composed myself and asked when the alleged incident had (allegedly) occurred. A bit of quick-thinking later, I was grateful for the Skipper's insistence on diligently recording all of our movements in a log book. I was able to provide evidence that at the time of the crime, we were halfway down the Kintyre peninsula, and the coastguard would back me up on that should an alibi be needed.

I could sense the disappointment of the officers in seeing their good detective work drawing a blank. I never did hear anything more of the incident. It seemed strange that someone had gone to the trouble of filing a complaint to the police, and also odd that the police saw fit to deploy two officers to follow up the claim. I can only think that it was combination of someone up to some mischief, and a particularly slow day in Rothesay police station.

Cleared of any wrongdoing, we were free to welcome the party back aboard the following morning. Despite not doing anything overtly different compared to the previous day, we were much more successful, and landed around 80 fish in half a day. Even I managed to hook a few mackerel for my lunch. The fishermen returned south with some tall tales, some beer in their bellies, and a few fish to feed on over the following days.

18.   Grouse or Duck

Every birder has his bogey bird. Carl had a blind spot for skuas, but I could have stood on a Black Grouse and never known it was there. I really should have seen one by then. I was brought up near to their strongholds in the northern Pennines, and the locals in Tighnabruaich often casually mentioned seeing them walking around the golf course as if they were Pheasants. Carl mentioned a lek (display ground) just behind the village. My only excuse was that I rarely got out of bed early enough to see them, as they are notoriously early birds, and are usually tucked up somewhere under a bush by 7am.

I knew that there were Black Grouse about. But despite a number of walks in the upland valley behind Tighnabruaich, all I had found were a lot of Red Grouse, which chuckled and mocked from perches around the valley. To make matters worse, I had found a lot of berry-laden guano, probably fresh from the backsides of Black Grouse, on rocks at the sides of the path. Then came a lovely October afternoon, during the week after my cruise with Peter as crew. Peter joined me for a walk, along with faithful dog, a huge, chestnut-coloured Rhodesian Ridgeback named Maura.

The views on this walk were particularly spectacular, as the air was crystal-clear and the Kyles were flat-calm. As we climbed, we could see straight over the low hills of Bute to the mainland beyond. The little Bull Loch on the north end, where we had taken our punters to see the nesting divers, could now be seen, reflecting the clear blue sky.

Maura ran on ahead as we carried on to the head of the valley. A fine male Hen Harrier drifted over the moors ahead of us, its grey wings held in a high 'V' as it stalled and dropped onto unseen prey. We then climbed on to the cairn at the top of the hill at the head of the valley. Peter pointed out the site of an eagle's eyrie, which was still occasionally used by a local pair, although they had chosen a different site in the season that had just ended. The view from the peak was truly glorious.

It was good to get a different perspective on our cruising area which stretched out before us to the south and west, but I was most impressed with the view to the north. We could now see right over Kintyre to the hills of Islay and the heaving Paps of Jura. On the north-west horizon, the tall mountains of Mull could clearly be seen, and a little closer, the conical peak of Scarba nestled between Jura and Mull. This was another world, close to our cruising area, yet unreachable during our weeks at sea.

We descended from the summit. As we walked down the valley, I looked over my shoulder for no apparent reason, perhaps to see if any eagles were visible. I was glad that I did. The distinctive shape of a male Black Grouse flew by, with its strange, lyre-shaped tail and broad white stripes on its black wings. Far below, on board the *Glendale*, a sign adorned the big oak beam, warning punters to 'Duck or Grouse'. At last I had now broken my grouse duck. And to add icing to the cake, as we made our final descent into Tighnabruaich, a magnificent young Golden Eagle soared across the hillside above us.

The following afternoon, Peter and Jill had asked me up to their house with their usual, relaxed hospitality.

"A nice day," I noted to Peter on the front doorstep. He stepped forward and scanned the skies and the horizon to the west.

"There'll be rain by seven," he concluded, based on signs which were completely invisible to me. Such was the conviction in his voice, though, that I had no reason to doubt that, in four hours' time, the rain would indeed arrive.

Peter was busy, so Jill asked if I would mind walking Maura, which was obviously not a problem at all. There was a snag, however. This fine specimen of a Ridgeback bitch was in heat. I kept her on the lead until we got as far as the edge of town, which was marked by the boatyard. There was no-one around, so the coast was clear to let her run free.

No sooner had I done this, than a face appeared at the window of the boatyard office. It was the hairy, scruffy face of a little mutt, which belonged to a carpenter who worked at the boatyard. My heart sank — how would I ever explain this when I got back? Perhaps it was best just to hope that the mongrel didn't have it in him to make any puppies. I called Maura to my side, but she ignored me. The mutt was watching her. I waited for him to make his move. Thankfully, it never happened. Either he had an attack of nerves, or he was actually locked into the office, but I was able to put some distance between Maura and the mongrel. We returned later, with Maura firmly on the lead and with her dignity intact. And two Black Grouse flew over. Would you believe it?

At 18:57 precisely, the first drops fell to herald a drizzly, rainy remainder to the evening.

19. Putting the *Glendale* to Bed

The Skipper returned after almost a fortnight away to help make preparations for the final cruise of the year, in the last week of October. Our guests that week were a family of four. Both Dave and Angela were hairdressers, who insisted on calling the saloon the 'salon', while the elder of the two sons was a keen Arsenal fan, particularly keen on reminding me that Arsenal had beaten Newcastle that very afternoon.

We ran a rather unusual cruise that week. A combination of a poor weather forecast and the hairdressing dad's fondness of seafood meant that we headed north instead of south. We made our way up Loch Fyne via Tarbert to Inveraray, and then on to the seafood centre at Cairndow, right at the top of the loch. This was the furthest north it was possible to travel in Clyde waters, and was a pleasant cruise on a sunny afternoon.

Dave was mad-keen on oysters, and we bought three dozen fresh ones for consumption back on the boat. Neither Angela nor the kids were keen, so it would be down to Dave, the Skipper and me to eat them while they were fresh. It was my first experience of eating live oysters, and I was not overly impressed. It was somehow reminiscent of similar sensations from the last time I had had a nasty cold on my chest. I tried a few with lemon juice and a couple with Tabasco, but I could not really get over the texture. I had six. The remaining 30 were shared between the Skipper and Dave.

There was still time for one last Beagle First of the season to be added on this trip. As we made our way back down Loch Fyne towards Lochranza, I was surprised to see what appeared to be a fledgling Guillemot so late in the year. I was even more surprised when it pattered across the water and took flight. A Little Auk on the West Coast in October was a good find.

On our last visit of the year to Lochranza, for the only time in the season, the eagles did not appear for us. The punters were not the keenest of naturalists, although the boys had said that they would like to see the eagles. It was most unlike them to let us down like this, but they had performed admirably all through the year, so perhaps they were due to take a well-earned rest.

Just four days after the final cruise of the season, I found myself single-handedly taking the *Glendale* on her last voyage of 1987, back around the Kyles to where the season had begun, at the boatyard at Port Bannatyne. The Skipper, meanwhile, took his faithful rusty Volvo via the short ferry onto Bute from Colintraive, with *Gordon* towing behind. He made it to the boatyard before me, and was able to radio me to confirm that everything was ready for me to bring the *Glendale* into shore.

What I didn't realise at the time was that I came incredibly close to ending the season by running the Glendale aground en route to Port Bannatyne. It would be difficult to describe chugging along at six knots as joy-riding in any way. Maybe it was because my spirits were raised by the beautifully calm conditions that I decided to go on a last tour of duty.

I made a small diversion, which I had never made in *Glendale* but had done many times in *Gordon*, through the idyllic natural harbour at Caladh. It wasn't until I passed this way again in *Gordon*, many months later at low tide, that I realised just why we didn't take the big boat through. Right in the middle of the northern exit of the harbour, a huge, domed rock sat in the channel. I had passed at high tide in *Glendale*, and I still shudder when I think how close I must have come to unwittingly getting impaled on that rock.

The sea was glassy-calm as I safely rounded Ardmaleish and floated into Port Bannatyne Bay. I could see the Volvo at the boatyard, and the Skipper radioed to give me the go-ahead to bring her into the slipway.

I had to let the *Glendale* drift into its cradle as gently as possible – a sudden breeze or too much propulsion would have meant that the boat might not balance on the narrow planking, or at the least be sat at a slightly embarrassing angle for passers-by to comment upon during the winter. In the end, I judged it very well, and drifted dead slowly between the cradle's posts, coming to rest right on the slipway. As the tide dropped, the team from the boatyard quickly set about placing wedges under the keel and trussed us up safe and ready for a winter out of the water.

I was secretly bursting with pride to have managed to keep the boat so straight on her cradle. As the hull emerged from the falling tide, I realised that the last time I had seen Glendale looking like this had been back in February. My relationship with the boat had changed completely in the ensuing months. I had first looked upon her on the slipway as an apprehensive novice, but she had safely brought me through a season's voyage of discovery, and I had even, for a short while as Skipper, become her master.

The cruises may have been over, but I still had one more task to complete on behalf of my employer. Every year, a newsletter was sent to all former punters, along with brochures and pricelists for the upcoming season. The Skipper asked me to contribute a 'Ship's Naturalist's Report' on the season passed, and I was more than happy to oblige. It gave me an opportunity to reflect on what had been an amazing year, and the wildlife highlights poured from my biro one after another. Wryneck and Pomarine Skuas topped the bird list, but the biggest highlight had been the dolphin encounter off Arran. Just as important as the stars of the show was the supporting cast of regular fare, and I gave the readers a round-up of the comings and goings of our local eagles, sharks and Puffins.

The Skipper authored the remainder of the newsletter, which covered the less natural events, including our first man overboard drill with a real man. There was also a paragraph for the benefit of former punters who had not visited in the summer of '87, in which he introduced me to those whom I had not met. As a Beagle employee, there was no appraisal process, but I was more than happy to read that I had "taken to life on board like a duck to water."

Also accompanying the brochures that winter was a copy of a newspaper cutting from the Liverpool Echo. Stan, the journalist who had visited the *Glendale* back in May, had produced an article along with a black and white photograph of the *Glendale*, under a headline of 'Slow Boat with a Touch of Class'. The article described me as a 'six-foot-five ornithologist with the eyes of a hawk', and was full of praise for everything about his cruise experience. Despite Stan's problems at mealtimes, he informed his readers that the sea-sick tablets remained in their packets, and described the food as 'spectacular', and 'rivalling many a five-star hotel in quality and quantity'.

All of this was a little at odds with my memories of Stan's mealtime struggles, but we were more than grateful and a little moved by this glowing testimonial. The anticipated flood of bookings from Scousers never did materialise, but we were delighted to see the article, and it gave us a boost to our morale.

The winter break seemed all-too-brief, as I attempted to catch up on my social life as well as making visits to Birmingham. New Year was seen in, as it always was back then, in Whitley Bay, before taking a freezing, two-mile walk back to the open houses of my friends. I managed to get out and about to do some birding in Northumberland, and spent a fortnight travelling around Wales with Yvonne. Our route had taken in such famous Welsh attractions such as Kenfig Pool, Tregaron rubbish dump and South Stack, which, in turn, just happened to be sites to see Pied-billed Grebe, Red Kites (still very rare in 1988) and a single Chough clinging to a cliff face.

It was an easy life, spending the money I had made during the summer for the four months of the off-season, in the knowledge that I would be starting again for another season soon. A year ago, I hadn't known what I was about to let myself in for. Now, with a season's experience behind me, I could hardly wait for the chance to get started on the next set of adventures.

20. New Crew for a New Season

There was never a proper discussion about returning for a second year. I never asked, the Skipper never offered, but it seemed that we both understood that I would be staying on. But the death of the Skipper's father meant that things had changed.

Beagle Cruises now had some personnel issues to address. The Skipper had decided that the best solution to fill the administrative void left by the passing of his father would be for him to spend more time at home dealing with day-to-day operation of the Beagle business. For my second season, we would hire an extra crew member, and operate in shifts, with four weeks on and two weeks off. And I was to be handed the first promotion of my career - I would be Skipper for a third of the new season.

The Skipper told me that there would be no need to arrange any interviews, as a new crew member had already been appointed. Somewhat unsettlingly, I learned that Dylan had actually been selected ahead of me when I had applied at the start of the year, but he had decided to take another job elsewhere. He was available again now, though, and keen to join us as the third crew member.

We met in Sedgefield during the winter. Dylan was a Welshman of quite striking appearance. He was 34 (which seemed ancient to me, eleven years his junior), and his prematurely bald head was surrounded by a thick ruff of black hair. His resemblance to a large egg in a nest of twigs was accentuated by a bristly black beard and moustache.

Like me, Dylan had no boating and limited cooking experience, but was an experienced naturalist. He was an expert on my former bogey-bird, the Black Grouse, having studied its population and ecology in his native Wales and contributed to several papers on the species. He seemed to be ideally suited to the job, and while we didn't exactly hit it off and get along riotously, I looked forward to getting to know him in the months ahead.

Plans were laid to start the pre-season preparation a little later than in the previous year, for two reasons. Firstly, the newly acquired additional manpower would mean that we could complete the pre-season activities more quickly. Secondly, the generator which had been installed during the previous pre-season was now in operation, which meant that we could live on board in relative comfort. We would not, therefore, need accommodation, and our working day could start a little earlier and end a little later.

In March, we travelled back to Port Bannatyne to start work. I was glad of the extra pair of hands that Dylan offered, and barnacle-stripping and painting tasks were accomplished much more quickly and painlessly than in the previous year. Somehow, though, some of the magic seemed to have worn off for me, and what had been the beginning of the big adventure the previous year had become more mundane - more like real work, perhaps.

Living on board whilst on the slipway made for a very different experience to the relative luxury we'd experienced the previous year in the hotel. We each chose one of the guests' cabins for the duration, and while it was cold on board, we could run the central heating from time to time to take the edge off the chill. Cooking was to nowhere near the same standard as we would serve to our punters, and we survived largely on Fray Bentos pies and a huge joint of gammon, which had been provided by the Skipper's mother.

The three of us were getting along reasonably well, but a series of incidents led to the beginnings of some cracks in the veneer. Dylan accidentally kicked over a large pot of brown emulsion, and I could see that his apparent 'couldn't care less' reaction was rankling with the Skipper. The damage was limited to the replacement of a few carpet tiles, but a growing tension was beginning to build within the ship's company.

I realised that Dylan's induction must have felt quite different to mine. While he had avoided a 'conventional' career, he was far more au fait with the ways of the big wide world. Unlike me, he could wire a plug and turn a screwdriver the right way, and the prospect of starting out in working life and being paid a wage held no novelty for him.

Despite this worldly wisdom, he still had to endure the reality of being bottom of the Beagle pecking order, an impression which was reinforced by the knowledge that I would be Skipper when the Skipper was not around. I could sense some of Dylan's unease, and a level of competitiveness which caused me to view him with an increasing guardedness. Nothing was said, but we could all sense that something was building in the atmosphere.

We all needed some time off, and during our second spring on the slipway, I managed to find a couple of opportunities to explore the Isle of Bute on foot. Directly across the island from the slip was St Ninian's Bay, which overlooked Inchmarnock, and this made for a very pleasant stroll from Port Bannatyne. I stopped to watch a flock of Fieldfares, the cold winter light highlighting the contrast between frosty blue-grey and warm chestnut feathers. They hopped around heavily, their chacking calls giving the impression that they had caught chesty coughs in the cold weather.

As I watched, there was a sudden, loud whoosh of wings, as a male Sparrowhawk saw its chance to use me as a screen from behind which to make its attack. The action was almost too quick to follow, but a single alarm 'chack!' was sufficient to scatter the Fieldfares. The Hawk sped on across the landscape, no doubt to plan another ambush on another flock of unsuspecting small birds. On the other side of the bay, a 'ringtail' Hen Harrier slowly drifted over the marshy land. At times like these, away from the chores on board the *Glendale*, it was still hard to believe I was being paid to be here.

I decided to carry on walking towards the reservoirs in the middle of the island, and at each crossroads, I seemed to choose the longer route. The reservoirs were the only large areas of freshwater in our cruising area, and they hosted decent numbers of common water-birds such as Tufted Duck and Coot, which we seldom encountered during our season. It wasn't until skeins of Greylag Geese began to fly in to roost that I realised time was getting on and darkness was gathering.

It was almost completely dark by the time I got back to Rothesay, and I set off along the sea front to walk the last mile and a half to Port Bannatyne. I decided to pause along the way and give Yvonne a call, which, with hindsight, was not the most thoughtful decision of the day. I finally made it back to the boatyard to find the boat deserted, and the Volvo was nowhere to be seen. A pang of guilt struck the back of my mind, as I realised that I had been missing for about four hours, and that the Skipper and Dylan must be out searching for me.

It turned out that they must have driven straight past the phone box on the way out, and when they returned some twenty minutes later I was given a stern lecture by the Skipper. I felt a little embarrassed and patronised, but he was right – my safety was his responsibility, and I had not given any indication that I would be away for much more than an hour.

Neither the Skipper nor Dylan shared my passion for football, but they had no objections to my request one weekend to go alone to the bar, just along the road from the boatyard, to watch the latest 'Old Firm' game live on television. I was used to the fervour of games between Newcastle and Sunderland, but there seemed to be an extra level of animosity between Celtic and Rangers due to what could best be described as religious tribalism.

I was aware that I was in a Rangers stronghold, having read the prevailing graffiti in the area, and sure enough, the bar was packed with ardent 'blue-noses'. It seemed that there was no such thing as a neutral in this affair, so I kept quietly to myself and watched the crowd in the pub with almost as much curiosity as the match itself. The Old Firm game was played out at least four times in each season, which I thought might dampen the enthusiasm, but it was obvious by the levels of anxiety among the locals that this was, as usual, a life or death battle. Celtic had nudged ahead in the title race, and victory today would be Rangers' last realistic chance of overhauling them.

The barmaid served me, keeping one eye on the goings-on on the small screen as she did so.

"MacAvennie. I even hate his name," she muttered as she poured my pint of heavy. The mood in the bar didn't get any lighter, as Rangers could only rally briefly in a 2-1 home defeat. I stayed hidden behind my pint, doing my best not to give away my neutrality.

*

Preparations were completed, and launch day came and went without the drama of the previous year. The *Glendale* once more cut through the Kyles, her diesel engine drumming out its familiar chugging rhythm across the waters.

As well as the generator and a new crew member, we had added a few gadgets and gizmos to the *Glendale* for my second season. Perhaps the simplest of these was rather incongruous at first sight. A doorbell had been installed in the wheelhouse, connected to a bell below decks, with the aim of letting the crew quickly alert any punters and other crew below decks that something of interest was in view.

The biggest and best gadget caught Peter's attention when he paid a visit to the wheelhouse, shortly after our arrival in Tighnabruaich. This was a new positioning system, based on radio signals rather than satellite, which provided stats on bearings to destinations, cruising speed, and improved our estimates for arrival times. It has to be said, though, that it would have been difficult to get lost in the Clyde.

Peter was very much against unnecessary mod cons of any kind on a boat. Here was someone who had navigated the Pacific using little more than a compass and dead reckoning, and who would rather have a fridge in a yacht than an outboard engine. All of these accessories were cheating as far as he was concerned.

"W – Wh – Why did you spend all that money on the electronic?" he asked the Skipper.

The real answer was that the Skipper could not resist such a fantastic new gadget toy, but sensing Peter's disdain, he made up an answer.

"It's because I will be away a lot this year and it will help Steve to know where he is."

"Really?" boomed Peter, dubiously. "I think that Steve knows perfectly well where he is."

It was good to be back in Tighnabruaich, and I was determined to take advantage of this rare opportunity to live in such glorious surroundings. In my first year, I had fallen into a pattern of going to bed late and getting up late, and I had not fully appreciated the beauty of the hills and valleys behind the village until my walks with Peter the previous autumn. I decided to put Dylan's Black Grouse expertise to the test, and arranged a dawn walk on a crisp April morning.

Sure enough, as we emerged from the village, I heard, for the first time, the strange bubbling and hissing noises from the puffed-up throat of a male Black Grouse. This call had even given rise to a new verb in some bird books, where it was described as 'roo-cooing'. Dylan and I began to scan the hillside, and it was Dylan's expert eye that picked out the silhouette of a lone grouse up on the horizon. He strutted around for a short while, lyre-shaped tail brazenly raised over a ruffled fan of white feathers, before quietly slipping away over the horizon.

Unfortunately, we only found the one grouse. Perhaps there were others, out of sight over the brow of the hill, but I had been told by Carl that there was quite a healthy 'lek' (display ground) which had been active just three years earlier. The Black Grouse was in decline, and this, I hoped, was not first-hand evidence of that fact.

We continued our walk up the brae, and paused to take in the ever-stunning views down the Kyles. The songs of Skylarks gushed from the clear blue heavens above, and Pipits parachuted down onto nearby boulders. The imminent arrival of spring was confirmed by the presence of a dapper male Wheatear which perched prominently on the peaks of exposed rocks.

Across the Kyle and up the hillside came the low, croaking call of a Red-throated Diver. It was almost certainly one of the birds from the Bull Loch on Bute, and I scanned for its shape over the water almost a mile away. It almost eluded us as it passed in front of the equally dark, heather-covered hillsides of Bute, but I was thrilled to pick out its reflection in the glassy surface of the Kyle, arrowing down towards the open sea.

21. Second Shakedown

Despite the fact that the *Glendale* was in her fifth season, we continued to be on the lookout for new places to go ashore. We tended to venture no further south east than the coast of Arran, which left a long stretch of Ayrshire coast within our cruising area but completely unexplored.

Our limited visits to the area had also left a poor impression of the industrial areas on the northern Ayrshire coast, most notably Ardrossan, the port from which the Arran ferry ran. On my only visit to Ardrossan, during my polytechnic field trip almost four years previously, an early arrival had meant that we were able to get a bite to eat. A few of us went to a local chip shop for battered haggis and chips, in an effort to settle our stomachs for the sea voyage ahead. It was a decent bit of haggis, but Ardrossan was not a pretty place, and not the sort of location that we'd expect our punters to have in mind for a holiday amid West Coast scenery.

There were some practical reasons which made it difficult to extend our cruising range to this coast. The most obvious of these was the extra distance needed to take in Ayrshire to the east and Kintyre to the west within a week's cruising itinerary. And the west-facing shore was more exposed than most in the Clyde to the effects of the prevailing wind, lacking the shelter which we regularly enjoyed elsewhere.

Before the season's shakedown cruise, we decided to put aside our prejudices to give Ayrshire a closer look, and headed south from Millport to Troon harbour. The breeze was quite light from the west, but we could still feel the effects of the greater 'fetch' (the distance over which the wind had travelled unhindered across the sea to build waves). As we approached Troon, we wallowed outside the harbour entrance for a minute while the Skipper hailed the harbour master on the radio. The reply was terse and slightly sarcastic, as we were instructed to tie up alongside a coaster, which in turn had tied up to the harbour wall.

First impressions were not good. We stepped across the deck of the rusting coaster to find that instead of a ladder for us to ascend to the quay, there was a set of three tyres arranged vertically. It was more like something from an enclosure at Monkey World than a cosy port to which we should bring fare-paying guests.

The Skipper, Dylan and I managed to scramble ashore, and decided to take a walk to see if the place improved away from the port. We had walked barely fifty yards when we noticed one of the locals trying to get our attention in an animated manner.

"Is that your boat tied up down there?" he shouted, and pointed in the direction from which we had come. "Coz if it is, then your boat's on fire." Sure enough, smoke was billowing from the *Glendale*'s every orifice, making her look like a scene from a Viking funeral ceremony.

It was undoubtedly an alarming sight, but my initial panic was quickly calmed by the Skipper's reaction. To him, this seemed to be little more than an irritation. We swung back down the tyres, scrambled across the coaster's decks, and back on board our smoking boat. She was not actually on fire, as it happened, but a very nasty problem had developed with the on-board central heating system. I switched the heating off, and we decided there and then to give up on our brief Ayrshire experiment. The Skipper repaired the offending gasket as we set a course back towards the familiar surroundings of Brodick.

This unpleasant episode left the whole interior of the boat even more smoke-saturated and smelly than ever. Below decks was designated as a 'no-smoking area', but even at the best of times, smoky salmon aromas and diesel fumes invaded every corner, persisting in hair and on clothes for days during time off.

Just before the season's shakedown, I had a brief visit from Yvonne, who immediately commented that I smelled more of diesel than usual. Despite my best efforts, I had failed in my PR attempts, and she never did return as a paying customer. Instead, we had to make do with a short break, starting with a visit to the boat in Tighnabruaich, and then something of a novelty - a trip across to Tarbert by car. As the crow flies, the two towns are only six miles apart. In the boat, the journey involved a twelve-mile voyage down the Kyles and then up Loch Fyne, which took around two hours. By car, the distance increased to over 80 miles around the top of Loch Fyne, which, when added to the drive up from Birmingham, meant that Yvonne was quite exhausted when we reached Tarbert.

Refreshed after a Bed & Breakfast breakfast, Yvonne was ready for a much shorter drive the following day. Being in a car gave us the opportunity to escape the confines of the Clyde-facing shores which formed the limits of the *Glendale*'s known universe. Within a few minutes of leaving the B&B, we were driving along the uncharted shores of the West Loch en route to the west coast of Kintyre. As soon as we emerged onto the open coast, there was a distinctly Hebridean atmosphere to the cool, bright, April morning, perhaps due to the broad, watery horizon to the west, and the clear views across to the sunlit hillsides of Islay and Jura. We drove on to Tayinloan, where we left the car and caught a ferry across to the southernmost Hebride, Gigha. The birds were different, too, with much higher numbers of Great Northern Divers, and flocks of Greenland White-fronted Geese, a bird which we never encountered on the eastern shore of Kintyre, just three miles away.

I pointed out the White-fronts to Yvonne. "Did you say Y-fronts?" she asked. The fact that 'White-fronts' sounds a lot like 'Y-fronts' had never even crossed my mind, which was rather sad, but then perhaps it was to be expected, considering that I had been very fond of Great Tits before I was old enough to be childish.

Yvonne's visit was all-too-brief, and she had to be on the road early for her journey back to Birmingham, so we decided to stay in Dunoon for the evening before her departure. There was plenty of accommodation to choose from, whose custom came from the steady stream of American guests, visiting their friends or relatives from the US Naval bases in the Holy Loch. We had no problems in finding a room, and enjoyed the sophisticated delights of a Chinese restaurant, serenaded by a Chinese version of Billy Joel's 'Uptown Girl' being piped quietly through a nearby speaker.

I said my farewells to Yvonne, as she caught an early CalMac ferry from Dunoon, before I caught the Postman Pat-style Post Bus back to Tighnabruaich. This was the only public transport which linked Tighnabruaich to the outside world, and ran a couple of times a day, giving a combined total of about twenty people per day the chance to travel to the village. I had had my last break, and now it was time to get busy again with one last push to get the boat ready for the new season.

The shakedown cruise began on 12th April, almost a month later than in the previous year, and the weather was noticeably more clement. Binge was with us again, and this time he had given a lift to Chris, my old school friend from Tyneside without whose diligent job searching I would never have even known about the Beagle career, let alone lived it. Chris emerged from Binge's car, shell-shocked after an almost literally break-neck drive over from Dunoon.

Also on board for the week were Carl and his girlfriend, Jan, but their presence as guests belied the fact that Carl was no longer a Beagle employee. The Arran Land Rover venture, while great fun and fairly busy, was losing money, and he decided to return to his native Nottingham to resume a life on the fringes of the music scene, producing mixing consoles for various bands.

We made sure that Carl would get a chance to return to his old base at Lochranza, which was our destination on our first full day. Dylan and I led a walk up the valley, and watched the eagles' nesting ledge carefully. There was no sign of activity there, so we broadened our scan. Eventually, two huge dots appeared, and glided gradually towards us. They then engaged in a spectacular aerial display, going into a steep dive before towering skywards, and repeating the stunt time and time again in front of the snow-capped peaks of Arran. The birds then retreated around the back of the tor, to the ledge on which they had chosen to build their nest for the year.

The weather was kind to us, which meant we could make the trip to Sanda. The island immediately cast its spell again as soon as we arrived, and it was wonderful to look into Morag's big, brown eyes and long eyelashes again. The Chinese Geese were still in residence, but did not share our delight at our re-union, as they honked their disapproval from the small lochan.

The second shakedown passed enjoyably and smoothly, almost sedately, without any major events, which was perhaps a good thing for a shakedown cruise. With hindsight, though, the drama of the previous year had prepared me well for my first season. Dylan acquitted himself well enough in the galley, producing a decent shepherd's pie, but I wondered whether he had really learned a lot from the week.

22.　Eating the Wildlife

The new season was soon underway, and we put our new shift-working rota system into practice. Within a couple of weeks of my last pre-season break, I actually started the season with a fortnight off, followed by two weeks with the previous season's 'dream team' working with the Skipper. It would not be until week 5 that I would assume command of the *Glendale* with Dylan as my mate.

I enjoyed the time off, and the chance to spend time with friends at home and in Birmingham, and attending friends' weddings in Cumbria and Lancashire on consecutive April weekends. All of the time, though, there was something a little dissatisfying about knowing that I was missing some of the action on the *Glendale*. Every cruise was an adventure in its own right, and not being part of a third of the season's trips meant that I was missing out on a sizeable part of Beagle history for the year.

Particularly disappointing were the occasions when I missed returning guests from my previous season. Bill and PJ had been itching to get back from Iowa for another Beagle fix, and could wait no longer than the second cruise of the season for their return. While I had a chance to catch up with them briefly when I arrived in Tighnabruaich on the Friday night, I could only listen with some envy to the new season's new anecdotes in which I had played no part.

I was soon back into my stride on my return, though, and despite the new crew and the altered working arrangements, the basic Beagle formula remained unchanged. My first walk of the season was on a typically enchanting evening at Ormidale. I was as thrilled as ever to walk through the woods, and was able to point out a furtive Red Squirrel which managed to hide most of its body, but not its bushy tail, behind the trunk of a pine tree. A Redstart shivered its tail and gave its rather hurried, mechanical warble from a low branch, while higher up, the shimmering song of a Wood

Warbler set the young oak leaves trembling. Last year it had been the novelty which had provided the thrill, but now there was a different buzz to be had through knowing the scene and its players so well, and in confidently imparting my experience to the punters.

We had a lively family of five from Essex on board; the father was a small man, but he had produced an enormous but very placid fourteen-year-old son called Mark. Mark had the habit of picking up large rocks from the beach, then finding even larger rocks against which to smash them, before quietly examining the resulting shards.

"Are you interested in geology?" I asked Mark.

"No, I just like smashing rocks," was Mark's straightforward response.

During my first season, our encounters with creatures from the deep had been limited to those which we could tempt into our fleet of prawn creels. Ever on the lookout for ways to access more underwater species, the Skipper secured a pair of scallop nets, donated to us by a local fisherman from a trawler called the *Girl Anne*. They were formidable-looking objects, complete with spring-loaded rakes at the entrances to their rusty jaws. Scallops were a favourite quarry for the local fleet now that the prawns had learned not to get themselves caught by walking around the prawn creels (that was according to local fishermen – nothing to do with overfishing, of course).

Professional scallop trawling was performed with four pairs of these nets being deployed at once. They would reap scallops by the sackful, but did untold damage to the seabed. We would sometimes see the sacks piled on deck, but the crew were always very secretive about the best sites for fishing their lucrative delicacy.

We tried trawling for scallops a couple of times around Arran, and we were able to put Mark's brawn to good use when deploying the nets off Catacol. We had very limited success, and judging by the number of rocks and smashed sea-urchins we brought in, it was obvious that we were doing no good whatsoever to the local wildlife on the sea bed.

After we winched our two scallop nets back aboard, we headed up to Tarbert, where, as chance would have it, the *Girl Anne was* unloading her impressive catch from the day. We bumped into her skipper, Wee Phil and his crew in the Islay Frigate that evening.

"We did a spot of scallop trawling ourselves today," the Skipper proudly announced.

"Really? How did you get on?" asked the *Girl Anne*'s skipper.

"We got six."

"Six sacks?" asked Wee Phil.

"Well, no."

"Six kilos then?" asked Wee Phil.

"No. Six scallops." The crew were still on the floor when we left the pub. Our six scallops fried up nicely with onions, bacon and a bit of garlic, but didn't really provide a full meal for the seven people on board.

Far less spectacular and nautical than the scallop dredges, but in its way just as revolutionary, was the acquisition of another new toy. As well as the main generator, which put out 24 volts to integrate with the electricity provided by the engine and alternator, we now carried a smaller, 240-volt generator on board, and had installed a couple of sockets in the saloon to allow the use of day-to-day electrical appliances. The sound of hair-driers was heard for the first time on board, as was the whirring of a food blender.

In the corner of the saloon was a small library, comprising three shelves of reference material. Mostly, the subjects covered were related to wildlife or various nautical themes, but among them was a dusty old Victorian tome, a cookbook which contained some 'traditional' Scottish recipes. One of these suggested a way to serve Capercaillie, the turkey-sized grouse of the Highlands. The 'method' went something like this:

-   Shove a whole onion into the 'body cavity' of a Capercaillie

-   Bury the bird for a week.

-   Dig it out of the ground.

-   Remove the onion to use in stock.

-   Throw away the Capercaillie.

The ingredients for this recipe were not readily available in our cruising area, and while we did consider swapping Cormorant for Capercaillie, we quickly concluded that we would give this one a miss. However, we did undertake to follow a slightly more practical, if painful recipe from the pages of the same book, and we would put the blender to use to achieve this.

Rubber gloves were distributed to the punters before a walk ashore at Carradale. Our quarry was to be nettles, and on the menu for lunch was nettle soup. Instructions were quite specific – only take the youngest growth in the top two or three inches of the nettle, nip it off firmly, and cook while still fresh. Mark and his family delicately tiptoed through the undergrowth and stuffed large quantities of young nettle leaves into plastic bags, before returning to the boat.

The nettles were duly whizzed up in the blender, and mixed with rather more traditional soupy ingredients such as stock, peas, lentils and onions. The end result was quite tasty, if nondescript, and certainly not stinging.

Our experiment was a guarded success, although perhaps we couldn't, hand-on-heart, say that the effort, and indeed danger of injury, could justify the end product.

Vickie and Winnie were back for their annual visit the following week, arriving early on the Saturday afternoon, and making themselves at home on board while we waited for the rest of the punters to arrive. The tide was low, and the afternoon sun penetrated through the crystal-clear waters, down between the old timbers of the pier below the water line to the sea bed. I stood on deck with Vickie and Winnie as we picked out all manner of sea life. Dead Man's Fingers grew in profusion low on the wood, while masses of starfish and brittle stars grazed the sea floor between them. On the other side of the boat, jellyfish swarmed in the deeper water, and patches of the glass-calm surface shimmered and boiled with a shoal of whitebait.

The ship's microscope normally stayed in its box until we were well into our holiday, but today it was put to good use straight away to examine some of these marine critters. Collecting samples on a day like this was an incredibly straightforward procedure, as the boat seemed to be surrounded by a thick jellyfish soup. This was made up almost exclusively of the non-stinging Common or Moon Jellyfish, which could be collected for closer examination by using some hi-tech equipment, namely a bucket on a string which was thrown over the side.

Related to the jellyfish were the comb-jellies, the commonest of which rejoiced in the name of *Bolinopsis infundibulum*. These were fantastic under the microscope, as they propelled themselves along with their ribbed bodies flashing with rainbow-coloured fluorescent stripes.

Too big for the microscope, and often to fit in the bucket, were Lion's Mane Jellyfish, complete with their long, stinging tentacles. The locals had a much more evocative name for these animals, referring to them as 'Scouders'. As the Scouders drifted through the sea below us, their long tentacles would snag on anything that got in their way. This included our anchor and creel ropes, and when these were taut, as was often the case, a sudden twang would send sting-juice flying in all directions, sometimes into the winch-operator's face. While it was unpleasant, the sting was not a lot more painful than that of a nettle, but it was still not something that you would choose to have on your eyelid while handling ropes and anchors.

Our remaining punters arrived at a more conventional time towards the evening. Among their number was Wally, who had served in the Navy during the war, who had seemingly undergone a transfusion of sea water into his bloodstream. I knew that Beagle Cruises had a wide appeal, but Wally created a punter category to himself, as he seemed to have chosen our holiday purely for the nostalgia of spending some time on a boat.

At frequent intervals, Wally would introduce a nautical quip into the conversation. Occasionally this would be relevant. No-one could mention the time without Wally translating it into a number of bells. When he was on deck, we were treated to him ringing out the time on the ship's bell.

"What time is it?" (at 3pm).

"Six bells! Ding-ding, ding-ding, ding-ding! Aharr, shiver me timbers."

Wally was even responsible for introducing a new 'tradition' that week. He was desperately keen to contribute to the running of the boat at every opportunity, becoming a kind of honorary crew member within a couple of days. Despite his advanced years, he scampered ashore to catch ropes, and manned the winch when we pulled in the prawn creels. The Skipper eventually found a way to keep him constructively occupied. He dug out an old tin of Brasso from the store cupboard and handed it to Wally along with a couple of cloths. The ship's bell had become tarnished over the years, and Wally's task was to make it shine again.

This request seemed to stir Wally's naval instincts, and he was suddenly on a mission to remove every last speck of tarnish from the bell. He spent the rest of the cruise furiously polishing, and succeeded in restoring the bell to its former glory. Not satisfied with that, he spotted another piece of tarnished brass on deck, this time an ornamental funnel, and soon we could all see our reflections in that, too. A new tradition had been born, and in future cruises, we would look for a volunteer to keep the brass shining.

Aside from brass-polishing and nautical nostalgia, marine biology was the big theme for the week, having been set by that microscope session on the first afternoon. Marine flora featured as much as the fauna, and I particularly enjoyed introducing the punters to the world of seaweed. Seaweed arranged itself in an orderly fashion up and down the shore. To adapt to the amount of sunlight they received through varying depths of water, green seaweeds were at the top, brown in the middle and red in some of the pools around the low water mark.

And they had great names. *Enteromorpha intestinalis* was the brightest green, slippery stuff at the very top of the shoreline, always near a source of fresh water. Then came *Pelvetia canaliculata* (channel wrack) on the rocks and sea walls at the back of the beach. *Ascophylum nodosum* (egg wrack) and *Fucus vesiculosis* (bladder wrack) both had little inbuilt bubbles to keep their fronds afloat in shallow water. *Fucus serratus* (serrated, or toothed wrack) was abundant a little lower. There was even a rarity to be found in the Clyde, a subspecies of *Ascophylum nodosum*, called Variety *mackaii* and lacking in bubbles, which we could find behind the castle in Lochranza.

Not content with just showing punters the seaweed, we just had to try eating some. Vickie and Winnie helped search through the *Glendale*'s cookbooks for a recipe. Eventually, a seaweed soup was chosen, which gave the Skipper another excuse to wheel out the blender. Not just any old seaweed would do. We needed to harvest some dabberlocks.

Dabberlocks was a long-fronded seaweed, a bit like kelp, but less hardy and restricted to sheltered waters. It could be distinguished from the more abundant kelp by a distinctive rib which ran up the middle of each frond, but to make things a little complicated, it was to be found almost exclusively below the low-water mark. The most accessible place with suitable conditions for dabberlocks was the bay at Sanda. But there was no way we would be able to harvest enough to make a meal by simply paddling or dabbling for dabberlocks.

Ever the showman, the Skipper donned a dry-suit, snorkel and flippers, and launched himself off the jetty on Sanda, an act which may well have been the reason behind a spate of reported sightings of Bottlenosed Whales in the North Channel, and a minor tsunami being detected as far away as Dublin. The seals gathered around to watch, presumably to have a bit of a laugh. After much splashing and snorting, the Skipper returned from the deep clutching a couple of handfuls of fresh dabberlocks.

While searching for the seaweed, the Skipper had chanced across some other small beasts which starred in another memorable microscope session at anchor off Sanda. We started by admiring some multi-coloured sea-slugs, or nudibranchs. Two of these were exquisitely coloured, with blue, yellow or orange tips to various odd appendages, packed full of venom from ingested sea anemones, and designed to ward off the attention of potential predators. Even a commoner sea slug species was spectacular under the microscope, with a covering of orange spikes along its back.

I had studied marine biology at school, so I was quite familiar with a lot of the creatures which we came across. There were some, however, which, like the sea-slugs, were new to me, and none better than the spectacular, but tiny, Blue-ray Limpets. The Skipper had done well to pick these out amongst the kelp, and he detached small sections of the fronds in order to minimise disruption to the limpets. On closer examination under a microscope, these tiny shellfish could be seen to have three stripes of the brightest electric-blue across their otherwise drab brown-green shells.

We returned our microscopic menagerie to the shallow waters by the pier, and I then set about preparing our novel new soup. By the time the seaweed had been whizzed in the blender, boiled for a couple of hours and mixed with other ingredients remarkably similar to those used for the nettle soup, our seaweed soup was once more rather nondescript, if browner than the previous week's dish. Still, it was a real novelty which was made all-the-more enjoyable for the fact that we had 'caught' the ingredients. We were, as Vickie and Winnie pointed out, the only wildlife holiday on which you actually ate the wildlife.

We had one further culinary treat in store for our regulars that week. A surprising number of recipes in our cookbooks involved porridge, and these extended far beyond the breakfast table. We often threatened punters with the 'porridge drawer', in which leftovers from breakfast were put into thin trays, then stored in a drawer and allowed to cool and congeal through the day. The theory was that the solidified porridge could then be sliced, and served with either sweet or savoury ingredients. Winnie and Vickie had heard of this delicacy during their earlier cruises, and this week they challenged us to produce it.

I added an extra couple of cupfuls of porridge to the morning's breakfast pan, so that we would have plenty left over for the drawer. Next, we greased two small baking trays, and slopped our rather generous breakfast left-overs into them. The Skipper emptied a drawer, and we popped the trays in.

Several hours passed after lunch, and we were all beginning to feel peckish. With no little excitement, the drawers were opened and the trays were brought back into the daylight. The porridge looked suitably insipid after spending much of the day deprived of light and air. It was duly sliced and served with strawberry jam. We all tried very hard to enjoy it, but in the end, there was no denying that it actually tasted like cold, slimy, lumpy porridge, and we would never inflict this 'tradition' on our punters again.

23.   Conquering Ailsa

Despite the prevalence of windy spells during that summer, there were weeks when the weather treated us well. On a calm, clear day, Dylan and I took the *Glendale* from Brodick to Ailsa Craig. As we approached the sheer cliffs, the sights and sounds of Gannets filled the skies above. These birds had entertained us with their death-defying high dives earlier in the week, but now we were treated to another, rarer spectacle.

Newly-fledged Gannets were taking their maiden flights. These juveniles had no practise at flying before launching themselves into the air from nests several hundred feet up. Their plumage was entirely dark grey, speckled with white, but what really made them stand out was their ungainliness in contrast to the effortless wheeling of the white, adult birds. They rocked and swayed on wobbly wings, descending quickly towards the sea where they crash-landed into the surf. They would then have to swim for days, living off their fat reserves, before hunger would drive them to take to the air again to learn to dive for their food.

Time and weather were in our favour, so we decided to try something a little different – today, I would lead a small group of punters to the summit of Ailsa Craig. The anchorage off Ailsa was not great, as the sea floor was strewn with boulders and chunks of basalt column which had tumbled from the cliffs over the millennia. There was a risk that the anchor could get snagged among the rocks, but conditions were good, so we decided to take that chance.

Dylan ran the landing party ashore, dropping us off below the unmanned lighthouse by running *Gordon* up the shingle spit. We were alone on Ailsa Craig, and today, we would conquer the summit. Despite Ailsa's appearance as a sheer pinnacle of rock, the climb up the east face was surprisingly easy. There was a well-worn system of tracks leading up to and around the quarry from which the granite used to make the world's curling stones had been hewn.

Above the quarry, the grassy slopes became progressively gentler towards the summit, which was marked with a whitewashed triangulation point. The views from the top made it well worth the climb. The closest coast was that of Ayrshire to the east, where we could see Girvan and Turnberry Point. Northern Ireland was sharp and clear to the west, while our cruising haunts of Kintyre and Arran stretched off to the north. We were standing atop 'Paddy's Milestone', and it was easy to see from the summit that we were indeed about half-way between Glasgow and Belfast. Below us the green slopes dropped away towards the cliffs, which were completely invisible from our vantage point. A multitude of Gannets wheeled below, Persil-white against the dark sea.

I was a little concerned, as I could feel that a breeze had kicked in while we had been on the rock. We hurried back down the slope and past the quarry, and I radioed Dylan to come and pick us up. The *Glendale* was out of sight around the corner from the lighthouse, and we waited on the spit for a few minutes for *Gordon* to appear.

Just as I was beginning to wonder if Dylan was having problems, *Gordon* emerged from behind the headland, slowly making her way towards us through the surf. I felt sure that she handled much more effectively and comfortably when driven at full throttle, but Dylan had never really got into the spirit of driving *Gordon* for fun.

We climbed aboard, and then splashed slowly along back towards the *Glendale*. I itched to take the helm, but Dylan was driving, and had a face like thunder, so I didn't say anything.

As the *Glendale* bobbed into view, I could have sworn that she had blown a little closer inshore during our absence. Dashed on the rocks of Ailsa Craig – I could have thought of worse places to be marooned, but I had no wish to suffer that fate, nor have to explain to the Skipper what had happened to his boat. We hurriedly weighed anchor, which had thankfully not become wedged among the rocks below, and steamed off towards the evening sun and Campbeltown.

I was alone in the wheelhouse, about three miles east of Sanda, and seven or eight short of Campbeltown. As usual, my eyes were watching the sea for any unusual movement which might betray a seabird, shark or sea mammal. I noticed a disturbance in the water some way off, towards Arran. I was too late to catch it with my binoculars, but scanned again to see if it reappeared. There it was again. This time I got my binoculars onto it, in time to see a long, black back, with a little fin following towards its rear. Definitely a Minke Whale. I rang the new alarm bell, which immediately summoned Dylan and the punters onto the deck. But I was unable to relocate it.

"Whale indeed ..." muttered the ever-cheerful Dylan. And it was hard for me to explain to the punters that I had actually lost a whale.

One of the unexpected upshots of our shift system was that while I crewed fewer cruises during my second year, I actually got to do almost all of the 'driving' as I still called it. When I was skipper, Dylan showed no interest in learning or studying for his boatman's licence. And when the Skipper was skipper and I was mate, he was happy to take a break from the wheel and leave me in charge.

I took great pride in my docking manoeuvres, and would modify the ship's log book to record these events. "18:35, docked, Ormidale" was the Skipper's entry, with the word "majestically" inserted later by me. My crowning glory came during a week when I was skipper, as we approached the pier at Millport. Our favoured berth at the end of the pier had been reserved by the *Keppel*, which was due to arrive shortly on its regular pleasure trip from Glasgow. The harbour wall was fully occupied by yachts, so I hailed the crew of the largest of these. They agreed to release their headline and swung out to give me space to nudge between them and the quay. The ensuing gap was barely wide enough to accommodate the *Glendale*, but I was able to swing us through 270 degrees to gently settle against the harbour wall in one controlled movement. I'm not one to boast, but it was a truly magnificent piece of boat-handling.

The crew of a cabin cruiser in the bay had evidently not performed its calculations quite so carefully. Only the tip of its mast showed above the water next to its mooring among the local fleet in the bay. Amazingly, after a breezy night and a high tide, dawn revealed that a second boat had sunk during the night right next to the first. I dutifully alerted the Coastguard, as the punters looked on in awe. Evidently sunken boats were another deliverer of punter value, a sort of marine equivalent of motorway rubber-necking.

*

During our two-week breaks, the three Beagle crew members led quite different lives. The Skipper would travel back to Sedgefield and tend to business and family matters. I would get the train back to Tyneside and spend time with family and friends. Dylan, on the other hand, had found himself an additional part-time job on a yacht running holidays in the Hebrides.

Despite a few minor tensions, things had gone reasonably well initially among our three-man team, but I was becoming increasingly worried about Dylan. His personality seemed to be quite changeable, most noticeably between times when the Skipper was and wasn't present. When the Skipper was around, Dylan was sweetness and light, and professionalism personified. When he was absent, I could see that he was not a happy chap.

Beagle cruises ran comfortable holidays for people who wanted to be well-fed and well looked after. Dylan had a more 'Lonely Planet' view of how wildlife holidays should be run. I could sympathise with this to some extent, but having seen it in action for over a year, I was fully bought into the Beagle way of doing things. He started to complain about what was being spent on stilton and whisky, or on wine glasses and cutlery. He had a point, but at the same time was missing the point.

Dylan's head seemed to be turned by his yachting breaks, which only served to confirm in his mind that the Beagle approach was not the right one. As he became more disenchanted with his role on board, his lack of enthusiasm began to affect the punters' holiday experiences. He didn't like porridge, but continued to produce a lumpy version of our signature breakfast dish. At times, it was painfully evident that the punters had tuned in to the fact that Dylan saw all of this as a time-wasting chore.

"Do you enjoy cooking, Dylan?" a punter once asked politely.

"Hate it," was the reply, and the conversation went no further.

Despite all of this, I still tried hard to rub along with Dylan. We had, after all, enough in common to have ticked the boxes to succeed in our interviews, and been hired to crew the *Glendale*. I had hoped that our common interest in birds might give us something to talk about, but even this was not as straightforward as it really should have been. Dylan explained that he didn't like to mix work with pleasure. Birds were part of his work, and, by his grumpy reckoning, not to be enjoyed.

Dylan's demons were never too far away, and finally seemed to be coming in to roost after just a handful of cruises. One evening, he had gone back to the boat early while I went for a drink with the punters in Campbeltown. When I got back, there were some unearthly noises coming from the crews' heads. Dylan emerged, pale-faced and red-eyed, muttering something about radioactive fish being served on board.

He switched the light off and pointed out that the smoked haddock by the fridge, which was left over from the evening's fish pie, was glowing slightly. He was convinced this was another symptom of the shambolic running of the enterprise, and that we were feeding the punters fish which had grown fat and radioactive at the nuclear wastepipes of Hunterston or maybe Sellafield. As it happened, the fish had just eaten too many of the old bioluminescent dinoflagellates, luminous bits and all. The only real issue was Dylan's growing paranoia.

While Dylan and I could just about tolerate one another, the clash in personalities between him and the Skipper had become all-too-apparent. Matters came to a head in May. The Skipper had been on the lookout for some time for a new fleet of prawn creels to replace some which had been stolen two winters before. He had seen a fleet advertised, and had agreed a price with the seller. Unfortunately, the pots were up in Oban, and someone would have to go up the coast to fetch them. I didn't have a car, and the Skipper didn't have the time. It seemed reasonable, therefore, that he should ask Dylan to go.

This didn't fit in with Dylan's plans, as he had made other arrangements during that fortnight off. The Skipper dug in his heels. As his primary employer, he insisted that Dylan should give the *Glendale* his first priority, even during his 'down time'. Then the Skipper gave what could have been construed as an ultimatum, and Dylan misconstrued this as being notice of termination of contract.

It was an unholy mess, and cracks were papered over, but the tensions remained during the rest of the season. I became a kind of agony aunt, listening both to the Skipper complaining about how miserable Dylan always seemed, and to Dylan moaning about the Skipper's profligacy.

One of my duties while I was in charge was to find a phone-box and call the Skipper to give him regular updates on how things were progressing during his weeks off. Even on the end of a line a hundred miles away, I could feel his anxiety building when the time for him to return was approaching. I couldn't resist such an easy opportunity for a wind-up, so I would make a point of letting him know that Dylan was in a particularly foul mood each time we were due to swap shifts.

24.   Looking down on the King of the Skies

There really was no such thing as a 'typical' Beagle punter, and it is fair to say that during our time, we had all sorts of people on board. Young couples and families with small children mixed with pensioners and octogenarians. That being said, there were undoubtedly more middle-class and middle- to late middle-aged people than in your average cross-section of society.

It was therefore all-the-more unusual when a pair of teenage girls returned for a second holiday. Susan and Emma had previously been on board with their families, and had decided to come back for an adventure on their own this time. Their parents had seen them onto the ferry at Gourock, and after their experience two years earlier, they could be confident that they would have a good, wholesome experience messing about on boats and walking in the hills.

Also on board that week were a couple who were, frankly, more typical Beagle punters. Alan and Joan were quite middle-classed and middle-aged, but brought their own energy and enthusiasm to the week's cruise. With a younger-than-average group, I decided to try something a bit different on our trip to Lochranza.

Eagle-watching was normally a fairly static affair, which involved sitting or standing on a hillside, and waiting for something to happen. Despite their reputation for shyness and nesting in remote areas, our eagles seemed to have tolerated seemingly disturbing levels of disturbance during the previous season, including rock climbers passing within a few metres of the nesting ledge. I had always been wary of going too close to the eyrie, but now that they had moved their home a mile up the neighbouring valley, my conscience was sufficiently clear to take a party up the hill and into the eagles' domain.

I led the party on the usual route from the loch and up the road, but we carried straight on past our regular vantage-point on the flat, grassy area at the foot of the tor, a spot which is now home to the Arran Distillery. We paused to pay our respects to a dead Red Deer stag in the stream, which I had observed in various stages of decomposition over the course of the summer. I often wondered if the distillery would use this as a selling point in years to come –

"... the purest water for our unique whisky has tumbled down from granite mountains, trickled through peaty soils, dissolved the iodine from the sea air and been filtered by the rib cage of a 20-year-old Red Deer stag to extract the very essence of the Monarch of the Glen ...."

I was disappointed to find that the late stag was not given any credit on the label when the whisky finally appeared in the shops some 15 years later, but it was nice to see that the eagles did get a mention. And the whisky turned out to be well worth waiting for too.

The craggy face of the tor was steep, but it formed the sharp drop at one end of a very long, shallowly-sloping escarpment. I decided that the best way to climb it would be to walk up the gently-sloping floor of Glen Easan Biorach, which flanked the tor. The further we walked up the glen, the shorter the slope became for us to ascend to get onto the plateau atop the escarpment.

We had to find a way of crossing the burn (which would later provide its 'unique' water to the distillery). It was too wide to jump, but was strewn with handy boulders, a few of which were flat enough to use as stepping stones. Eventually, after we had walked for a mile or so up the glen, we found a decent crossing place, and carefully negotiated our way to the other side. Joan managed to collect a walking-boot-full of water, so we paused briefly while she emptied the boot and wrung out her sock.

Unperturbed, we made the short climb up the heather-clad hillside. My attention was attracted by a high-pitched squeak from almost underfoot.

232

Parting the heather, I found a nest full of almost fully-grown Meadow Pipit chicks, drawing a chorus of 'Aahs' from the appreciative punters. We all had a peep, then left the pipits in peace to wait for their parents to return.

As we reached the plateau, we paused to take in the view. We had a close-up view of the distinctive skyline of northern Arran, dominated as it was by the 'Sleeping Warrior'. He was still snoozing, the peak of his helmet pointing skywards, and his large belly moving up and down almost imperceptibly as he snored. The weather was quite dull, and there was not a lot of wildlife to be seen. This was prime adder country, but not prime adder-watching weather.

As we approached the brow of the escarpment, a small group of Red Grouse exploded from the heather beneath our feet. The sea began to emerge into view from behind the hilltop, before finally, the *Glendale* could be seen at anchor, far away in the bay below. Then came an unforgettable moment.

An adult Golden Eagle had been resting on the crag near the old nest-site, just out of sight behind the brow of the tor. It chose this moment to launch itself into the air, completing a few circles in front of us and giving a rare chance to look down on its broad, golden-spangled wings. It watched us casually as it climbed to our eye-level, and then quickly ascended into the grey sky above to regain its rightful lofty position above us earthbound humans. Having made what use it could of the updraughts from the face of the cliff, it glided off towards the far side of the valley. It had been a thrilling encounter.

The euphoria of the moment then suddenly vanished. I had been so distracted watching the eagle disappear into the distance that I had lost track of where all of the punters had gone. I realised that I could not see Emma, and then, with growing panic, that no-one else knew where she was. The cliff dropped away almost vertically down a rock face below, and to me, it began to look distinctly possible that she may have stumbled and disappeared over the edge.

We started to stomp around, rather aimlessly, calling Emma's name. I radioed the Skipper and asked him to scan the cliff to see if he could see Emma's yellow coat from the bay. This was a bit of a desperate measure, especially as the light was not great and the Skipper was using an old pair of ship's binoculars two miles away, but his reply that he could not see her only served to increase the anxiety levels. Susan had somehow managed to stay calm up to this point, but I could see that she was becoming increasingly agitated.

Then Alan spotted her, quietly sitting on a rock below the brow of the hill, and completely oblivious to the panic she had caused. I called the Skipper to tell him that the emergency was over, and he urged me to read the riot act to Emma about staying in view. I had seldom felt the burden of responsibility weighing so heavily, but in the end, I was just relieved and happy that the search had ended this way.

Panic over, the descent of the escarpment face was a good deal quicker than the ascent. Going up had taken around two hours. Coming down was completed in three minutes, as the youngsters among us decided to yomp back down the steep slope. It was great fun, and the perfect way to release some of the tension and stress after our 'missing person' incident. We bounced and bounded over the tussocks and emerged unscathed from the odd tumble. We had a few minutes at the bottom of the slope to get our breath back, but my thighs would ache for days afterwards.

The age of our young punters meant that we weren't able to follow our usual Lochranza Hotel visiting routine that evening. The sun had finally come out, and the *Glendale* seemed to be an ideal platform from which to enjoy the scenery. Some of the wildlife seemed to think so, too.

The tide was high, leaving no rocks on which the local Common Seals could bask. Instead, we could see three of them 'hauled out' on dinghies, although none ever managed to climb into *Gordon*. *Gordon* did attract other visitors, though. A young Shag kept us entertained by sitting on one of the tender's oars for a while, and occasionally lifting its tail to paint another streak of white guano on her orange rubber side. This youngster was immortalised by Joan in a poem in the guest's logbook as 'Seamus the Shag, who sat and sh@t.'

Early the next morning, in Tarbert, I was aware of distress calls from some Herring Gulls nearby. This was far from unusual, as Herring Gulls would get distressed about just about anything. Sometimes this could mean good news for us, as it might be the signal that a passing Peregrine, or even an eagle was in view overhead. Most of the time, though, they just seemed to get distressed among themselves.

On this morning, the calls were more persistent than usual. Something was not quite right, so I went up on deck to see what was causing the commotion. I could immediately see two wretched adult Herring Gulls, flapping about in the water next to a nearby trawler. What wasn't so obvious was why they were behaving in this way. The trawler had left a long, nylon fishing line on deck, loosely covered by a tarpaulin. Several of the large, barbed hooks on the line were still baited, and the gulls had each swallowed a hook, meaning they were now tethered to the line and in serious trouble.

I called the Skipper and we devised a rescue plan. We jumped into *Gordon*, and slowly drifted towards the stricken seabirds. Then I grabbed one, and held it tight around the wings to prevent it from struggling. The hook was huge, with a jagged barb preventing it from being pulled back out of the bird's bill. The solution was to take some pliers, and cut the hook at a point where it protruded through the skin under the beak. The rest of the hook then followed, leaving a neat little hole in the bird's throat. We released the first bird, and quickly repeated the process for the second.

On regaining their freedom, both birds flopped pathetically across the harbour, their plumage waterlogged, and they heaved themselves out onto a pontoon to rest.   As we returned to the *Glendale*, a local fisherman watched on, puzzled as to why we had gone to such trouble to rescue some vermin.

In truth, neither bird seemed likely to survive.   From their state of exhaustion, I guessed that they must have been struggling for some time. One had a badly damaged tongue, and both now had wounds where the hooks had pierced their skin.   Still, there was life, and therefore hope. Tarbert Harbour had quite a collection of invalid wildlife, the stars being a one-eyed bull Grey Seal and a Great Black-backed Gull with a broken wing. Perhaps they could keep our unhooked Herring Gulls company while they convalesced.

25. Clyde Puffer

While the idea of a wildlife holiday on board a boat was not entirely unique, competition for the *Glendale* was minimal, especially on our home patch of the Clyde. The only other boating holiday offering in our cruising area was aimed primarily at steam enthusiasts. The *VIC32* was a wartime Clyde Puffer, built only a couple of years before the *Glendale*, but to a much older design, much like the *Vital Spark* of Para Handy fame. The VIC was, at 66 feet long, significantly bigger than the *Glendale*, and she could take up to twelve guests on board at a time. Puffers were designed with flat bottoms so that they could stay upright on a flat beach for unloading at low tide. In other words, they were not built for the open sea, so the VIC had to stay in inshore waters in the northern reaches of the Clyde.

As a result of these limitations, the only port in which we encountered the Puffer with any regularity was Tarbert. If there were a lot of trawlers in port, the *Glendale* and the Puffer would single one another out as a friendly neighbour against which to tie up. The respective skippers were by now old acquaintances, and got on well, but as a rule, the same could not be said for the punters.

We invited one another's punters on board for a look around. The Puffer punters, who were sold on nostalgia and classic steam engineering, could not understand why anyone would want to spend a holiday on a work-a-day diesel trawler. The *Glendale* group had not the slightest interest in watching pistons and wing-nuts, and wondered why anyone could travel to this wonderful area and forego the opportunity to see the wildlife spectacle on the islands to the south of the Clyde. Perhaps each group had an unspoken tribal loyalty to the brand they had chosen, leading to the slightly uneasy stand-off which often arose during these exchanges.

There was no doubt that the Puffer holiday franchise was a bigger one than that of Beagle Cruises, and I felt secretly rather envious of the merchandise on offer on the VIC. Puffer punters could buy mugs, coasters and sweatshirts, emblazoned with a picture of the boat, along with the catchy phrase 'VIC32 – toot – toot!' Try as I might, I could not think of a suitable onomatopoeic slogan for the *Glendale*. 'Glendale – chug – chug – chug!' simply did not have the same ring to it.

For slightly less enthusiastic steam enthusiasts, another treat was available in our cruising area. The famous paddle steamer *Waverley* ran a programme of summer cruises in the Clyde, and we would bump into her during several of our holidays. One of her regular ports of call was Tighnabruaich pier on a Saturday lunchtime, and her arrival each week was a bit of an inconvenience for us. It meant that we had to vacate the end of the pier and retreat to our nearby mooring for an hour or so, while the *Waverley's* day trippers took a walk into the village to the tearooms.

The *Waverley* cut an elegant figure as she steamed down the Kyles, and we often saw her during the summer, paddling determinedly towards the Mull of Kintyre at 16 knots. Her cruising speed was almost three times that of ours, meaning that most of the Clyde cruising area was within striking distance for a day-trip from Glasgow.

When the *Waverley* was off-duty or occupied on a national tour, an alternative ship was sometimes laid on. The *Southsea* was similar in size to the *Waverley*, and painted in Sealink colours. She would act as a 'steamer', but was distinctly lacking in paddles, and surely a poor substitute for the real deal. Several smaller boats also offered pleasure trips. The *Keppel* was a little Caledonian MacBrayne ship, while the *Second Snark* ran unabashed booze cruises from Glasgow.

Thankfully, I was only on the pier for one visit by the *Second Snark*. Dylan had taken the punters off on a walk behind Tighnabruaich, while I stayed on board on cooking duty. The *Snark* was a lot bigger than the *Glendale*, but was still able to tie up outside us when she arrived on the pier. I moved *Gordon* out of the way to prevent her from getting crushed between the boats. There then followed a clatter of feet on deck as the *Snark's* punters went ashore in search of a local pub to continue their day's itinerary.

I was praying that Dylan would return with our party before the *Snark's* punters arrived back at the pier, and it was a relief when they did. I could already see some booze cruisers staggering back along the coast road, so we wasted no time in untying ourselves from the *Snark* and the pier, nudging our way out and leaving her dangling by a single head line. I did the decent thing, and used *Gordon* to push the pleasure boat back into the pier so that one of her crew could go ashore and attach a stern line.

Job done, I returned to the *Glendale*, which was now waiting offshore. It was in the nick of time, as the first, extremely inebriated day-trippers had assembled at the end of the pier. They had taken offence at my departure, and were shouting some barely-comprehensible sweary-words after us as we left. I gave a cheery wave, and sped off in *Gordon*.

*

There was no doubt that Golden Eagles were the most sought-after birds during our cruises, but they were supported by a strong cast of other types of raptor. Kestrel, Buzzard and Sparrowhawk were the mainstays of the bird of prey fraternity, while Hen Harriers, although much scarcer, had a measured, unspectacular way of going about their hunting lives.

Peregrines, on the other hand, always turned heads. We encountered them throughout our cruising area, sometimes even several miles out to sea, where they dashed low over the surface in pursuit of our abundant seabird life. This was at a time not long after pesticide pollution had decimated their UK population, and Peregrines were still a rare sight, especially in England. Before joining the *Glendale*, I had only seen them three times in over ten years of birding, but I soon became familiar with their distinctive flight silhouette. Commonly described as 'anchor-shaped', there was something of a classic, timeless look about them, which brought to my mind a World War II fighter plane. Then the veteran flying machine suddenly changed shape, transforming into an ultra-modern, swing-wing jet, as it pinned back its wings and hurtled head-long into a stoop.

We tended not to be up early enough to see Peregrines hunting at their most active time, early in the morning. More often, we saw them soaring or gliding over cliff-tops, peerless in their agility and mastery of the air. Small birds would queue up to mob Buzzards and Kestrels, or chase the tail of a passing Sparrowhawk, but they all gave the Peregrines a wide berth. Only the local Ravens, with their huge beaks and aerobatic prowess, ever dared to engage Peregrines in a sparring match.

The sight of a Peregrine in full stoop, hurtling towards waders feeding on the Dhorlin at Campbeltown, was one of the highest accumulators of PV. A quite different Peregrine encounter, which rivalled the stoop in its preciousness, came during a walk around Sanda. Dylan and I could hear the jittery call of an adult nearby, which would normally be a prompt to point our eyes skywards to look for one of the birds defending its territory. In this case, though, the sound was not from above, and seemed to be coming from the ground off to the side of the path. We were half way up Sanda's eastern slopes, and I instructed the punters to lie low as we edged towards a ridge.

And there it was, perhaps twenty-five metres away. Only its head was visible above banks covered in grass and pink sea thrift. The black executioner's hood and bright yellow base to the bill could be clearly seen, as could an equally bright yellow ring around its piercing eye. I was amazed that we had managed to stay undetected by that eye, but as the first punter joined us, the tiercel took flight, and the moment was gone.

*

In August, we took a family party out for the week. The weather was good, and we were able to plan a full week without being restricted by adverse conditions. At Sanda, we had lunch at anchor, and I took the party ashore for a walk. There was a good variety of birds on show, including a ringtail

Hen Harrier and a young Peregrine on the wing with its parents. Early migrants passing through included Whinchats, Whitethroats and a recently-fledged, juvenile Redstart.

The family were underwhelmed by the birds, but loved the island. Nothing was ever particularly compulsory on our walks, but when we had mixed groups, we tended to diplomatically reach a consensus and all go along together. Within this family group, most opted not to exert themselves and climb the small hill, and instead chose to stay down at shore level, exploring the beach and watching seals.

Seal identification was quite easy with practise, and was made all the more so by the fact that there were only two species to choose from. Adult male Greys were especially easy to pick out, being so much bigger, with long, 'Roman' noses. The Commons were smaller, and attracted descriptions such as 'cute' or 'more dog-like'. Identification of bobbing seal heads at sea was followed by the chance to compare both species side-by-side out of the water at Sanda. Commons hauled out on a spit on the main island, while Greys were on exposed, seaweed-covered reefs over on nearby Glunimore. The Greys were much noisier, their howling and moaning calls drifting across the water.

Once the visible distinguishing features had been established, we moved on to the behavioural differences. I would entertain the punters, first by 'talking' back to the seals with their easily-imitated wails, although I have no idea what I might have been saying to them. This was followed by lying down on a rock in a seal-like fashion, feet down for a Grey, and curled up for a Common. I had an occasional scratch just to complete the effect.

Only the father of the punter family volunteered to accompany me on the short climb up Sanda's hill, so we left the rest to explore the shore and watch the seals. We had plenty of time for a rest on the summit to soak in the superb views on a flat-calm day, with the auks easy to pick out on the glassy water, and we could see distant flocks of Manx Shearwaters becalmed on the surface. As I scanned, I noticed a disturbance in the corner of my field of view, some way off in the direction of Ailsa Craig. The surface broke again, followed by a large fin, and then another. A small pod of dolphins was making its way towards us.

They passed about a mile offshore, making for the open Atlantic via the North Channel. Through the telescope, we could see five or six large dolphins, plain grey in colour, and with dome-shaped heads with no visible beaks. These were Risso's Dolphins, or Grampus to give them their old name. This was blissful; a clear calm day on Sanda, and lying back watching dolphins. The father was thrilled and excitedly told his family about our good fortune when we met them again by the jetty, but his enthusiasm was apparently wasted on the younger family members.

We made our way back around the bay and the Skipper made the short trip from the *Glendale* to pick us up in *Gordon*. I climbed aboard the mother ship, and gave the punters a helping hand up the wooden boarding ladder. This was the moment when my concentration slipped, perhaps as a consequence of just how benign and calm the conditions seemed to be.

Over the preceding eighteen months, I had learned a lot about ropes. On day one, the Skipper had shown me the most basic technique of tying off a rope. It involved wrapping it around a cleat in a figure-of-eight, which was probably secure enough in itself, but just to make sure, a flick of the wrist ensured that the rope was neatly 'cleated off'. I could not for the life of me work out how this was done. It was a bit like teaching a four-year-old how to tie shoelaces. I knew that if I was to instil any confidence at all in the punters, I would have to show that I could handle ropes proficiently, and I did, eventually, get the hang of them.

Even after a year and a half during which rope-handling had become almost second-nature, concentration was still needed. On our return to the *Glendale* after our trip ashore that day, I had made a schoolboy error in deciding to make a 'temporary' knot to tie *Gordon* to a guard-rail pole while the punters re-boarded the *Glendale*. Normally, I would have re-set the guard rail and then moved *Gordon* back to the stern, where there was a permanent metal cleat on one of the old gantries. Perhaps I was too keen to get aboard and tell the Skipper about the dolphins, but my lapse in concentration was to have some unexpected and unfortunate consequences.

The bay at Sanda was usually a sheltered enough spot in which to spend a comfortable night at anchor, and the first couple of times we stayed overnight there proved peaceful enough. For some reason though, perhaps a function of the odd tides that ran around the Mull of Kintyre, a swell could suddenly arise from nowhere during the night. With little breeze to swing us into the wind on our anchor rope, the boat turned side-on to the swell and rolled, sometimes quite violently, to give us an uncomfortable night. We spent the early hours of one morning cleaning up a broken flask of formaldehyde on the wheelhouse floor, which we kept on board just in case we ever felt the need to pickle a specimen (which we never did). The rocking of the boat caused it to fall from its shelf, and the choking fumes filled the wheelhouse, as we donned tea-towels over our mouths to try to reduce the streaming of our eyes.

Once more on this occasion, the sea had been calm when we turned in, but Sanda's mysterious swell arose again later that night. I knew that the anchor would hold firm, and that there was nothing for the boat to bump into in this bay, so my main concern was for the comfort of the punters who were being rocked rather vigorously in their coffins. I managed to get some sleep, but we were unexpectedly awoken early in the morning by shouts from outside.

At first, I thought I must be dreaming – how could there be voices coming across the water from an uninhabited island? Then I heard the rush of the propeller of another boat. I emerged from the wheelhouse and saw that a small trawler had come alongside, but I immediately sensed that something was missing. As I took my bearings, I was horrified to realise that *Gordon* was nowhere to be seen.

My absent-minded failure to make permanent the temporary knot, coupled with the night's heavy rolling, had led to her slipping away in the darkness.

Thankfully, all was not lost, and it turned out that our luck was (partially) in. *Gordon* had been washed up on the rocks on Sanda. A few short metres to the north, and she would have been off into the North Channel, en route for Northern Ireland or even the open Atlantic beyond.

After a quick chat with the crew of the fishing boat, we arranged a lift ashore. One or two of the punters had been woken by the commotion, so the Skipper explained the situation and went on to say that we would leave them on board while we went to retrieve *Gordon*.

The trawler came alongside, and the Skipper and I managed to step onto it, before we were ferried across to the little concrete jetty. The swell was still running, and the only way to disembark was to leap down from the bow of the boat onto the jetty. The Skipper went first, and timed his jump well, escaping with a few splashes to his clothing. I waited for my chance for what seemed like an age to find a gap in the waves breaking on the jetty, which were now exaggerated by the wash from our boat which had overtaken us. Eventually I saw my chance, and leapt. It felt like I was airborne for several seconds, but I stumbled when I came down on the concrete, allowing just enough time for the next wave to catch me. My wellies were full to the brim, and my jeans were drenched.

Job done, the small trawler promptly steamed away and continued with its day's business. It was a typical example of the camaraderie which was to be found among the seafaring community – a crew whom we had never previously met, nor would ever see again, had gone out of their way to help when they saw another boat in trouble.

After I'd emptied my wellies, we walked along the shore to where *Gordon* was stranded. She must have floated away several hours earlier, as the falling tide had dropped enough to leave her high and dry. We would have to wait for some time for the waters to rise again before floating her off. Meanwhile, I was getting colder and colder. Morag the cow watched us curiously as we entered the derelict farm house, seeking shelter from the chilling wind. I was shocked by just how cold I had become in such a short time, especially as temperatures were not particularly low. Fortunately, we had had the presence of mind to retrieve a first-aid kit from *Gordon*, which included a foil blanket.

The blanket was removed from a tiny packet, and unravelled to a size which was comfortably big enough to cover me. Almost instantly, I was warm again. The Skipper hailed the punters on the radio, and gave them an update on our progress. We let them know that we would be ashore for some time and set an expectation of a long wait.

Perhaps it was the boredom, or maybe some energy had returned after the warming effects of the foil blanket, but after a short time kicking our heels in the farmhouse, we returned to *Gordon* and summoned superhuman strength to dislodge her from the rocks. This was slightly risky as we could easily have damaged her rubber hull, but the prospect of another few hours ashore was just too dull to contemplate. We were soon back on board and resumed the week's cruise. If the Skipper was angry, he hid it well – perhaps he could sense from my embarrassment that I had learned my lesson about temporary knots.

26. Mayday

Discipline to an almost military level was something to which I had found difficult to adjust, especially as I still had very little first-hand experience of what could go wrong on a boat. In the case of my poorly-tied knot, the consequences were not too severe, and had resulted in nothing worse than a soaking, a short delay to a cruise, and a loss of face in front of the punters. I knew that life on fishing boats could be dangerous – I had seen a couple of locals with crippled thumbs, and heard how auld Wullie McPhee had fallen and been crushed and killed between trawlers at Crinan. But for the first time, on the next cruise, I was to feel the danger very much closer to home.

We left Tarbert on a routine run towards Lochranza. Our cruising speed of six knots would see us make the 12-mile journey in about two hours, in time for a late lunch and a walk to look for eagles. We were about half an hour out of port when I heard a garbled distress call on the radio. The Coastguard asked the sender to repeat his message, but I had already heard the words 'Mayday' and 'Tarbert', 'man in the water' and 'not breathing'. I swung the *Glendale* around and opened up the throttle. The Skipper, sensing that something was amiss, shot up through the hatch.

A fisherman was in the water, having fallen overboard not far from the mouth of East Loch Tarbert. I calculated that we must have travelled about three miles in the half-hour since leaving Tarbert. Even if I could get to the scene flat out at eight knots, I knew we would be too late to help. This was a job for *Gordon*.

I could now see the stricken boat, a 20-footer which had been creel fishing about a mile from the harbour mouth. Checking the radar, I confirmed that the boat was indeed three miles away. The Skipper jumped into *Gordon*, and sped off towards the little boat. I called the Coastguard, as did two other boats nearby. At eighteen knots, *Gordon* would make rendezvous in ten minutes, and the two other yachts making their way to assist would arrive at about the same time. The Coastguard asked me to relay messages to Gordon, as the hand-held radio was not sufficiently powerful for its signal to be received at their headquarters in Gourock.

I could only watch helplessly as the drama unfolded. As predicted, ten minutes later, the three rescue boats converged on the scene. The punters seemed a little bemused by this inconvenient interruption to their holiday, and watched on in silence. One of the yachts had a doctor on board, who attempted to resuscitate the victim, but it was decided to transfer the lad into *Gordon* and get him ashore as quickly as possible.

By the time I took *Glendale* into Tarbert some fifteen minutes later, the ambulance had been and gone, and an empty *Gordon* was tied to a little slipway at the top of the harbour. While I had undoubtedly had a much easier experience than the Skipper, I was very rattled, and made a hash of my solo docking manoeuvre, bumping the *Glendale* heavily against the empty quay wall. The Skipper was waiting for us, looking even more ashen-faced than I was feeling.

The lad was 25, about two years older than me. He had been wearing the same style of yellow oilskins as those which I regularly wore. He had been dragged under after getting tangled in the ropes while throwing prawn creels back into the water. One of the locals, who knew the Skipper, had watched as the lad was loaded into the ambulance, by which time attempts to save him had already been abandoned.

"Was that your mate?" he asked. It wasn't. But it felt as if it so easily could have been.

We took a short while to compose ourselves, and then we were on our way again. The Coastguard thanked us as we made our way back out to sea. We were both shaken by the incident for some time afterwards, and our prawn creels lay untouched on the sea bed for the next four weeks.

27.   Two Birthdays

September had come around all-too quickly, and my 24th birthday arrived on a changeover day. The Skipper was on the road back to Sedgefield, and had left me to give a present from the boat to another birthday boy, Peter, who would be 66 on the following Tuesday. I went up to their house to collect this week's smoked salmon, and handed over a present which I knew was guaranteed to go down well. It was a bottle of Highland Park, Peter's favourite malt.

"That's terribly kind," he said. "How on earth did you remember that it was my birthday?" My answer was truthful, but a little tactless.

"I remembered yours because today is mine."

Peter looked crestfallen, and wracked with guilt, but I assured him that there was really nothing to worry about.

I returned to the boat to resume preparation for the impending arrival of the next punters, and tuned in the radio on my Walkman to catch up on football commentary from St James's Park. There was coverage of Paul Gascoigne's first return to Newcastle following his summer transfer to Tottenham. The main talking point from the game was the reception which Gazza was given, and especially the nature of the missiles that were thrown onto the pitch.

"I believe they are Mars bars" observed the commentator.

"Yes, and they can really hurt," explained expert summariser Jack Charlton. "Especially when they've been kept in the fridge."

The punters soon arrived and Dylan and I welcomed them aboard, before making the regular thirty-minute Saturday afternoon chug up the Kyles and

Loch Riddon to Ormidale. As we passed the fish farm, the little pier came into view. This spot was normally deserted, but two familiar figures appeared, ready to help us to tie up. Peter had told Jill of his birthday embarrassment, and she handed me a cake which she had baked for me in double-quick time. I was more than touched by yet another gesture of kindness from them.

The weather during the second season never seemed to settle. The following cruise was spent entirely in the northern lochs, hiding from the relentless pounding of westerly and north-westerly gales. I felt particularly sorry for John, a birdwatcher who lived not far from Glasgow, who had come especially to take the chance to explore the marine bird-life from a different perspective. Instead, we were restricted to Lochs Fyne, Striven and Long, places which he could access readily by car on any weekend.

A particularly sheltered spot was Loch Goil, where the old wooden pier under the imposing Carrick Castle had been replaced by a small, concrete jetty, primarily for use by the navy. There were few boats at sea due to the awful weather, and I was relieved to see that the pier was available for us to tie up for the evening. The face of the pier, unusually, was shorter than the length of the *Glendale*. With the gale howling against our stern, I decided to put out a stern line and two 'spring' lines, one from the stern forward and the other from the bow backward. As well as being more secure, these ropes give us leverage to 'spring' away from the pier if the wind was still strong when the time came to leave. I would not need a head line, because of the strength of the wind on the stern, and anyway, the other lines would probably compensate for its absence. I had made another silly mistake.

We went for a short walk before dusk, while Dylan prepared our evening meal. There was very little to look at other than the spectacle of the wind whipping the tops off the waves in the loch. An exhausted Fulmar sat at the water's edge, displaced from the open sea, and I empathised with its plight. I did not really want to be on this beach either, but hopefully we were making the most of a bad deal.

The dishes were stowed after dinner, and I took a walk around the deck, checking that all of the ropes were properly set. The wind was still very strong, but we had chosen a good, sheltered spot for the night, and I retired to my bunk satisfied that all was safe and sound.

At 3:30am, I awoke with a start. I could hear some loud creaks from on deck, and I was alarmed to sense that the boat was listing slightly. I quickly threw on some clothes and raced up the ladder and onto deck. As I emerged, I was completely disorientated. The wind had dropped, and the boat must have swung through 90° as the falling tide flowed out of the loch. The tide was now rising again, and instead of being on the end of the pier, we were now alongside the end of it. The tyres had wedged under the concrete edge of the pier, and the boat had started to list.

I tried to push us free, but it was no use. I was going to need help from the engine. I started her up, praying that the punters would not be awoken by the noise, especially a know-it-all yachtie who was on board that week. The plan worked, and with some gentle persuasion and horsepower, the tyres were freed, and we bobbed back to an even keel.

As I tended to the ropes, the hatch door slid open, and out popped the know-it-all yachtie's head. "Now I don't believe you wanted to do that!" he said, or words to that effect. I muttered something about everything being under control, which was technically true, but inside, I knew that there was no escaping from the fact that I had made a basic error in not securing a headline when we had first arrived.

Dawn arrived the next morning, and the gale had reawoken too. Now it had swung around more to the east, and was pinning us to the pier head. I faced a new problem, as my normal routine for leaving a pier might not work due to a combination of a short pier head and the onshore wind. The margin for error was reduced further by the huge rock on which Carrick

Castle perched, just a few metres off our port bow. I saw this, perhaps subconsciously, as an opportunity to redeem myself and show my yachtie punter that I did, in fact, actually know what I was doing.

I was going to try a manoeuvre I'd never done before, and use one of the spring lines to swing the boat away from the pier. The idea was that this rope would not actually be tied to the pier, but could be looped around a bollard and retrieved by a swift yank from deck by Dylan. Things started well, and the bow was pointing in a promising direction, away from the pier, and from the castle's rock. I gave Dylan the signal to pull in the rope. Nothing happened. The rope had snagged on the pier, and was now joining forces with the wind to swing us alarmingly back towards the huge rock.

I had to think fast. One thing I didn't know (and would probably rather not think about) was the shape of the rock beneath the water level. As far as I knew, we could have run aground at any moment. If I gave Dylan the order to drop the rope into the sea, there was a real danger that it could fall under the boat and snag the propeller. The ensuing lack of power would mean that we would certainly run aground. I was quickly running out of options.

I was about to shout to Dylan to jettison the rope, when it suddenly broke free. It trailed safely in the water as I accelerated away from the rock. Dylan managed to quickly pull it back on board, and disaster was averted. One of the most uncomfortable, and frightening, episodes of my skippership was brought to a close.

The forecast remained grim, so we were forced to keep to the sheltered waters of the sea lochs to the north of the Clyde. The southerly gales had blown huge quantities of plastic bags to the head of Loch Long, giving it an untidy feel as we anchored off Arrochar, and providing our holidaymakers with an unwelcome reminder of our proximity to civilisation. This visit gave us a rare opportunity to visit somewhere much more a part of the tourist trail than the rest of our cruising area. Arrochar was a strange portal onto this other world, from where a short walk would bring us to the shores of Loch Lomond.

I've been back to Loch Lomond since, and been impressed by its scenery and atmosphere, but after two years on the sea, there was something distinctly second-best about a mere freshwater loch. Here, there were no tides and no heady mix of salt and seaweed aromas. There were no Eiders bobbing around, no chance of a Porpoise's back or a seal's head emerging from the waves, and indeed no real waves to talk about. My transformation into a salty sea dog had evidently taken effect.

Our local punter had been to Loch Lomond plenty of times, and could go there whenever he pleased. While I sympathised with his position, I knew that the safety and comfort of all of the guests was my responsibility alone. I was not about to risk either safety or comfort on the off-chance that we may encounter a Sabine's Gull in a Force 9 off the Mull of Kintyre.

We finally ventured out of the Kyles and across a choppy Loch Fyne to Tarbert, in the hope that the weather would improve, but on the contrary, the winds just got stronger and turned to an even more unfavourable southerly quarter. I always liked Tarbert, but even my view was being challenged after being trapped there by the weather for three days and nights.

The rigging of yachts in the marina clanged out rhythmically across the harbour day and night, a sound which could not be escaped above or below decks. For once, the noise from our generator was actually welcome as it gave some relief from the monotonous clanging. I looked up out of the hatch, and could see the Auxiliary Coastguard flag blowing rigidly horizontal, almost visibly being frayed by the gale. This tiny window onto the outside world somehow reminded me of a scene from an Antarctic expedition, and I imagined that the punters could not be enjoying this unplanned extended stay.

Every morning, Donald the Water Man appeared and called down to me. I don't know what he thought we did on board, but even he must have realised that five punters and two crew were not likely to consume 500 gallons of water quite that quickly. I had already handed over his ration of McEwan's Export on the first day, and my generosity didn't extend to rewarding him for his subsequent enquiries.

Eventually, the wind abated a little, but it was too late (and the seas probably still too swollen) for us to head south. Instead, we turned to port when we finally left Tarbert harbour. We didn't often stop at Inveraray, but its position on the west shore well up towards the top of Loch Fyne made it a handy bolt-hole when the weather turned nasty. It was a pleasant cruise up Loch Fyne, through the narrows at Minard and past the huge quarry at Furnace.

I was always surprised by how many marine birds could be found so far 'inland', but this was just as much a part of the sea as any other stretch. Gannets and auks could be found right at the northern end of the loch, and I was pleased to see a Bonxie over Minard. Baby Puffins swimming nearby were good to see, even if they couldn't meet the bright-billed expectations of their parents, with their scruffy, sooty faces and dull bills. They had emerged from their burrows at night, and then proceeded to put as much distance between themselves and their homes as possible, although this sometimes led to them being funnelled into the narrow waters of Loch Fyne.

On our stormy cruise, the punters had gone off their various ways to go shopping or to visit Inveraray Castle. Dylan and I took the opportunity to dive into the George Hotel for a swift pint. The pub was quiet, except for one curious patron, who insisted on sitting with us at our table and staring at us, quizzically. He ignored our initial offerings of crisps, and turned his nose up at an ashtray-full of beer. Instead, he put his chin on the table, with eyes fixed on me and ears pricked. The barman called across.

"I shouldn't tell you this, really," he said, "but try throwing a beermat." I frisbeed a beermat across the bar, and quick as a flash, the sheepdog darted across the room and leapt to capture it. He then brought it back and carefully set it down again on the table ready for the next round of the game. By the time we left, there were a large number of half-chewed beermats on our table, soggy with dog slobber. We said our goodbyes to the dog, and the wait was underway for him to find a new friend to play with.

On returning to Tighnabruaich at the end of the week, an unfamiliar boat could be seen among the yachts moored near the pier. Its hull was conventional, but at the stern was an odd piece of equipment, and when the sail was deployed, she was really quite a striking sight. This was Peter's new boat, *Bamboo*, which employed a junk-rig, and a brown sail that would have looked quite at home in Hong Kong harbour. The odd-looking contraption at the stern was a self-steering mechanism, which had been patented by Peter's close, and recently-departed friend, 'Blondie' Hasler. Acquiring this boat was Peter's tribute to a man who had been a national hero, as one of only two who had survived a daring raid to become known as the Cockleshell Heroes during World War II.

Peter and Jill were to spend a lot of time bobbing about in the Kyles in *Bamboo*, but Peter had bigger plans in mind for her. The first task was to do a little conversion work, which meant throwing away the engine. Yachts were for sailing. Engines were dirty, noisy things for lazy people who couldn't sail. The space and weight that were saved could be much better used by a bigger fresh water tank and a beer-filled fridge.

It had been over thirty years since Peter and Jill had got as far as Tahiti on their around-the-world honeymoon. Now Peter was getting itchy feet. He knew he had one more solo voyage left in him, and one day, he set off from Tighnabruaich in *Bamboo*, and did not return until he had completed a lap of Ireland. The weather had not been kind to him, and he was quite exhausted after struggling through storms off the west coast. His arrival coincided with a dawn exercise by the Royal Marines in the Kyles, and Jill thought that delirium had set in when he staggered home, with stories of arriving ashore among landing craft.

Peter's sailing days were all but over, but he retained a refreshingly energetic outlook on life whenever he spoke. It was clear that his life had been almost one long adventure. In a moment of reflection over a rather large whisky at his house one evening, he commented on this very fact.

"You know," he boomed, "sometimes I look back on my life, and I've bloody enjoyed it!"

28. Capsized *Gordon*

I did my best to get on with Dylan, but the shifts when I was working with the Skipper always seemed to be more enjoyable. Perhaps it was because I had a little less responsibility, or the fact that the atmosphere on board tended to be more relaxed. And the cruises always seemed to be more memorable and eventful – I sometimes wondered to what degree the slightly strained atmosphere with Dylan around rubbed off on the punters.

The Skipper had returned for another stint in September, having undergone surgery on his sinuses during his week off. I led a walk along the shore at Skipness on a pleasant afternoon, and radioed the *Glendale* to say that we were nearing our pick-up place on the shore. The reply sounded a little unclear, but I could just about make out enough words to establish that he was on his way.

As *Gordon* rounded the little headland, I could see that something was not quite right. The Skipper was leaning right out over the side of *Gordon*, and as he approached the shore, I could see why. The after-effects of his sinus operation had suddenly kicked in, and blood was literally gushing from his nose. We got the punters into *Gordon*, and headed back to the *Glendale*. The Skipper did not look too good at all, as the colour drained from his face. After consultation with the punters, it was agreed that some fairly drastic action would be needed.

The nearest town of any size was Lochranza, about three miles to our south. Getting there in *Glendale* would have taken half an hour, so for the second time in just a few cruises, we decided to take the unusual step of leaving the *Glendale* at anchor in the hands of the punters. I raced across to Lochranza with the Skipper in *Gordon*. We would call a doctor when we got there, and hopefully he would not lose too much more blood.

I ran *Gordon* up the beach and helped the Skipper up to the lounge of the Lochranza Hotel. The bar staff found a quiet corner and sat the Skipper down there, giving him a cup of sugary tea while I had a restorative pint of 80/-. As it happened, the bleeding had slowed quite significantly. After the cup and pint were finished, the Skipper felt well enough to carry on, even if he was short of something like a pint of blood. The punters had been in charge of the *Glendale* for about an hour and a half by the time we returned, and had successfully managed to keep her afloat without any further mishaps.

The following week, we were cruising out of Loch Fyne into an area near Skipness, where the sea still ran red with the Skipper's blood. Over the radio, we heard a conversation between the Coastguard and a yacht which was drifting towards some rocks on Inchmarnock. It seemed that the yacht's crew had no experience in sailing, and a fault had developed with its engine. Unable to raise a sail, their only means of propulsion was now a brisk wind, which was pushing them towards the rocky west shore of Inchmarnock. We were about four miles from the scene. A tattered Auxiliary Coastguard flag fluttered forlornly from our mast. It was our duty to offer our assistance.

The seas were quite swollen, rough enough for us to have taken a course to tack into the waves at an angle en route to Lochranza. The stricken craft was due east of us, so we changed course, and found ourselves rolling along with the swell with a strong westerly wind blowing along behind us. Shortly after we changed course, there was a loud crash and splash from our stern. *Gordon's* rope had been left too long for the conditions, and she had capsized, flooding her engine, and sending some of the items on board to the sea floor.

We stopped and considered our options. Without *Gordon*, we were much less capable of offering any help to the yacht, and aside from completely abandoning our trusty tender, we had no option but to radio the coastguard and call off our mission. There was some confusion as I explained to the Coastguard that our tender had capsized, but their panic subsided when they realised that she was actually still attached, with no-one on board, when she flipped over.

Dragging *Gordon* through the water upside down for any distance was not going to do her any good at all, and there was a real risk that her precious outboard engine could come off and sink to the sea bed. Never one to shirk a challenge, the Skipper decided that we couldn't afford this risk. He took it upon himself to perform a death-defying manoeuvre. He secured himself to the *Glendale* and to a burly punter using a lifeline, before hurling himself onto *Gordon's* soaking, slippery, upturned hull, and attaching a rope by which we could winch her back over. It was a highly risky operation, bordering on the reckless.

My job was to concentrate on driving the boat as slowly as possible, keeping the bows pointing straight into the wind, and minimising the boat's movement. While the Skipper was defying the elements, risking his life and battling with the flashing brine, I watched as a Storm Petrel fluttered across our bows. I quietly berated myself for getting my priorities somewhat misplaced, but it was the best view I'd had of a Storm Petrel for quite a few weeks.

The petrel disappeared from view, and my focus switched back to the life or death struggle which was going on at the stern. The Skipper managed to get safely back on board, having successfully attached a rope to the far side of *Gordon's* hull. The winch was engaged, and *Gordon* was righted. Meanwhile, the boat which had called for help was already being rescued, so our actions which had proved so costly wouldn't have served any purpose anyway. We had to divert to Tighnabruaich for repairs to *Gordon*, and made do with oar-power rather than a 55 horsepower outboard for the rest of the week.

29. Decision Time

My time on board the *Glendale* had been truly life-changing, but there was one thing which was completely clear to me before and during my career there. This was not a livelihood, and never could be, and I would only spend one, or a maximum of two years on board. The first year went so well that I didn't have any second thoughts in deciding to return for a second term. But as the second year progressed, my thoughts began to turn, slowly, to life after Beagle Cruises.

Because of the shift system we had adopted, I could spend more of my time at home. A lot of this was misspent as usual, but I did have the need for a 'proper' career at the back of my mind. I was still enjoying my adventure, but everyone and everything seemed to tell me it had to come to an end after my second season. Partly, this was a case of being true to my own word. When I had embarked on this career, I had set myself a maximum term of two years. I also had to consider my parents, as despite my apparent independence, I still could not really support myself financially, and had no fixed abode other than my old bedroom at home. I had also discussed this with Yvonne, and I had learned that maintaining a relationship while constantly out of contact at sea would always be difficult.

As well as the human reminders, the sea herself had shown me that she could be a fickle beast. So benign and playful on calm days, she had increasingly shown me her darker side, claiming the life of the young fisherman off Tarbert, and battering the boat when the mood took her to unleash a storm.

Job prospects were still limited in my native north-east, but my brother had got wind of an opportunity with a previous employer of his down south. My future life after the *Glendale* was to be shaped during my last fortnight's shore-leave. Once more, I found myself on the platform at

Newcastle Central Station, but instead of heading north to Edinburgh Waverley, I was looking for a train to take me to London.

It was not as if I had never been to London before, but the mass of humanity on the platform at Kings Cross came as a shock when compared to my favoured habitat of remote, Scottish Islands. I descended into the bowels of the city, and took the Piccadilly Line towards Ealing. My brother was waiting for me in a bar near Ealing Broadway station, and I took some much-needed refreshment before continuing to my base for the trip, his flat in Hanwell.

I took the chance to spend a few days in the capital, and even managed to take in another insipid performance by Newcastle United at Charlton on the Saturday. The Seoul Olympics were underway, complete with Ben Johnson's startling victory in the 100m, and an even more startling revelation afterwards, as news emerged of his failed drugs test.

Despite expectations, I found myself getting a favourable impression of the unexpectedly homely feel of Ealing and Hanwell. I felt even more at home in the local pub, when I saw the picture which hung in pride of place above the fire. It was a large painting of the *Waverley*, resplendent with her familiar white, black and red funnels, pulling away from Tighnabruaich Pier with the Kyles and the low hills of Bute in the background. If I had stared any longer, I'm sure I would have fallen into the picture and been transported home, Narnia-style.

I had to return to earth quite promptly the following morning. It was time for my interview, and time to see if I was really cut out for the real world. The train crossed Hanwell Viaduct, passing through an oasis of leafy treetops amid the seemingly endless urban sprawl. Still, even these trees were almost alien when compared to my current place of work, dominated as they were by horse chestnuts as opposed to the birches, oaks and conifers we encountered on our cruises. I disembarked at the next station,

Southall, and walked the last mile through a residential area to an unremarkable, low-rise office on the Heathrow edge of town.

The role for which I would be interviewed was titled 'Systems Support Officer'. I knew precious little about what it would entail, other than that it was something to do with helping people with computers and making their printers work. Apart from programming the *Glendale's* navigation system, I couldn't claim to have any IT experience at all. While the new job description could hardly have been further removed from a Ship's Naturalist, there were some parallels with my Beagle interview, two years earlier. In both cases, I knew little or nothing about what to expect, but I knew that a lot would be down to how I got on with the people I would meet.

The format of the interview was rather more conventional than my only previous one. I met with The Boss and a representative from Personnel (as that function was still known then), but most of my time was spent with the two people with whom I would be working should my application be successful. I enjoyed the day and liked my potential colleagues, although at the end of the day, I still didn't really understand quite what the job would involve.

I went out with my brother to meet a group of future colleagues socially that evening at the Adam & Eve in Hayes, and again, I enjoyed the company. The day had gone well, and all indications seemed to be that the job was there for the taking.

The significance of this trip reached further than its professional implications, as Yvonne called off a planned liaison in London as the final act of our relationship. The long-distance arrangement had led to a series of misunderstandings, and in truth, this was the conclusion of a steady decline since Easter. The final straw was that Yvonne, who had actually investigated getting an office transfer to the North East, didn't like the prospect of me even considering working in London.

Back in North Shields, the offer of employment fell on the doormat just a couple of days later. If I accepted, my income was set to rise by over 500%. Accommodation would not be an issue, as a vacancy was coming up at a flat near my brother's place in Ealing Broadway. But my feet were getting cold. This would be a huge change, and one which would take me in a completely unexpected direction. I picked up the phone, and put it down. Then I picked up again, and this time I dialled and accepted the offer. The deed was done.

Almost as difficult as making the fateful phone call to London was breaking the news to the Skipper on my return to the *Glendale*. When I had arrived to start my working life on the *Glendale*, neither of us was at all sure how things would work out. Our backgrounds had been so different, with me being a comprehensive kid and he a product of a public school. At the age of 22, he had taken a decision to buy and convert a trawler and embark on an entrepreneurial life, while my response when confronted by similar life choices at the same age was to go into the garage for a game of darts against myself. But give or take a few arguments over the two years, we had got along together very well, and I felt that the mutual respect we had for one another had developed into a true friendship.

I had been quite open about my plans to attend the interview and look for a new career, but now, the prospect of confirming my impending departure felt like a breach of loyalty. I needn't have worried, as the Skipper respected my decision, although he did ask whether I would be interested in taking on the Beagle venture when he was making plans to move on himself the following year. My impending departure had put recruitment back on the agenda, so job ads were re-drafted, and the applications came flooding in.

30. Awesome

The end of my second and final season was fast approaching, but there was still time for one last hurrah. An all-star cast was assembled. Carl, whose four-year Beagle career had come to an end the previous year, returned with his wife-to-be Jan. And the Hollicks were back, Al with a few more silver whiskers in his black beard, and Jill, just as excited about being on board as on the first day they set foot on the *Glendale*.

We settled in the saloon on the first night, and drew up grand plans for the week ahead. Carl and Al were keen birders, and Jan and Jill had taken up the hobby too. This week, there would be an attempt to break the record for the number of species seen in a week, a record which stood at 85. With a few waders at Davaar and a massive arrival of assorted migrants on Sanda, we convinced ourselves that a total in excess of 100 species was possible.

It quickly became obvious that the ton would be way beyond our reach. The forecast was poor – wind, rain, then more rain and wind, followed by severe gales and torrential rain. We decided to use the tried and tested tactic of pushing south as quickly as possible, to give us the best chance of visiting Sanda, where something good was bound to turn up.

Campbeltown was grey and windswept, and the forecast was for a force 7 south-westerly. There was not going to be a visit to Sanda on the next day. Instead, we took a walk around Campbeltown Loch, all the way to Davaar. An adult Glaucous Gull was an early bonus, hanging on the strong breeze along the sea wall near the town, frosty-white against the grey sky. There was a decent variety of waders on the Dhorlin, until they were all terrorised by one of the local Peregrines. Davaar yielded a Short-eared Owl, and as we passed the naval fuelling jetty en route back to the boat, we watched a Dipper flying low over Campbeltown Loch on whirring wings. What had promised to be a washout at the start of the day had turned out to be quite productive. We still believed, just, in our quest for three figures.

The wind had dropped a little and the sun appeared on the following morning, so we went ahead with our planned trip to Sanda. The calm waters of Campbeltown Loch gave way to a steady swell as we left, and things became choppier as we rounded the splendidly-named headland on southern Kintyre, called 'The Bastard'.

To maximise time ashore, we decided to prepare a large fry-up lunch, which was to be served as soon as we anchored at Sanda. I was 'on' cooking duties, and duly went down to the galley to prepare the food bought that morning in Campbeltown. On the menu was a traditional Scottish brunch, including black pudding and squares of sliced sausage.

The Skipper was at the helm, and did what he could to tack into the wind to reduce the effects of the choppy sea, but the boat was bouncing around; one minute pitching, rolling the next. Huge quantities of fat oozed out of the frying black pudding and sausage meat, and I was soon chasing slices around the pan as they floated around in the thickening slick of lard. The galley lurched around me as I crouched under its low roof, getting a face-full of fry-up fumes for my troubles. This was not good.

I had never actually been sea-sick in my life, but now I felt worse than ever before, and began to doubt the strength of my stomach. I was therefore hugely grateful to Carl, who saw the greenness of my face, and took over galley duties while I gingerly climbed up through the hatch to take a breath of fresh air and set my sights firmly on the horizon.

My stomach was back on an even keel as we anchored in Sanda's wonderfully calm bay. Our unhealthy lunch was hastily devoured, as the Beagle Connoisseurs on board were impatient to get ashore on their favourite island.

Sanda was its usual thoroughly enchanting self. We set off on what had become a familiar walk, around the harbour, past the wee loch, through some low bushes and over the top of the little hill. It was now a gloriously bright, sunny, blustery day. Below in the bay, the *Glendale* was swinging gently on her anchor, while *Gordon* was an orange spot next to the concrete jetty. Morag grazed, happy in the company of sheep behind the farmhouse. It was a view which was almost recklessly perfect, and one which would condemn all of those who gazed upon it to pangs of yearning over years to come.

We paused on the hilltop, drinking in the views, when suddenly, a Merlin exploded almost vertically into the air above us. Presumably it had been chasing a pipit or lark up the hillside, and had climbed abruptly when it noticed us nearby.

I always liked Merlins – perhaps my favourite bird. Their presence is always electrifying, a Billy Whiz of a bird, never resting, always on the lookout for a small bird to chase. As we descended along the lighthouse road, the Merlin appeared again, this time hurtling across the sheep fields and up the opposite slope, stopping only to pick a fight with a visiting Sparrowhawk. Although there were certainly a few Merlins resident in our cruising area, this bird was another Beagle First, which only added to the enjoyment of the encounter. Most likely it was a young bird, which had migrated down from its upland nesting grounds to try its luck in catching some of the fellow migrants at the coast.

With heavy hearts, we made our way back to the boat and raised the anchor. The wind was behind us as we headed around the southern tip of Arran to Brodick for the night. The wind grew stronger and the waves started to look threatening, but with them at our stern, the effect was merely to buffet us, and occasionally push *Gordon* up alongside the boat. We were unable to use the pier at Brodick, as the ferry, the *Isle of Arran*, had already tied up there for the night instead of at her usual berth on the mainland at Ardrossan. Here she was out of harm's way in the shelter of

Arran's hills, and snugly tied to the pier by a large number of massive ropes. It was too late, and the seas too rough, for us to go anywhere else for the night. We were going to have to spend the night at anchor in Brodick Bay.

Depth alarms were set to go off if the water became shallower than ten metres or deeper than twenty, but we decided not to put our faith entirely in this system. This would be the first and only night which I had to spend on active anchor-watch. The Skipper and I took turns to sleep, and then would spend a couple of hours in the wheelhouse, making sure that the boat stayed in one place. Boredom was relieved, and sleep averted, by occasional excursions out onto the blowy deck, where we tugged on the anchor rope to check for signs of dragging.

The wind howled between the looming black mountains of Arran. Glen Rosa seemed to act as a funnel out of which the gusts were focused across the bay and in our direction. We swung from side to side on our rope, but the anchor was stuck firm in the sandy sea bed.

Dawn broke, and the long night ended uneventfully but with the gale still blowing. The wind meant that an ascent of Goat Fell, Arran's highest peak at 2,868 feet, was not a realistic option. I was rather disappointed, as I wanted a last attempt at finding the elusive Ptarmigan, but we had to content ourselves with a walk around Brodick Castle gardens. A few woodland birds were added to our list, and overhead, flocks of Redwings, newly arrived from Scandinavia, swirled with the autumn leaves.

On returning to the *Glendale*, we faced another dilemma. The wind had not abated, but our decision to set sail was based not on sound judgement, but on our half-baked idea that seeing 100 bird species was still an outside possibility. Besides, the sea would be following us, and I had recently made a similar crossing as skipper under conditions that were comparable. On that occasion, we completed our passage without any ill-effect, and had in fact been treated to a good show of seabirds, including several Bonxies and Storm Petrels and a Sooty Shearwater.

When I had been skipper, I had decided to use the shelter of Arran's north-east coast as far as possible, and ensured that the wind would be right behind us before striking out east across the open water. This time, though, the Skipper set a course directly for Garroch Head at the southern end of Bute. He knew best, though, so I didn't really think to question our tactics. Arran's mountains provided shelter from the wind which extended well offshore, and while the horizon looked lumpy and turbulent, somehow we still didn't really see what was coming.

We reached the rougher water, which was now being blown unhindered by any obstruction between us and the mouth of Loch Fyne. This was still not a great distance – five or six miles, perhaps, but the ferocity of the gale was enough to whip up some big, short waves. The anemometer was steady at around 40 knots, and with some gusts, it was off the scale at over 50. And this was with a following wind, so our six knots could be added to any of these measures. A conservative guess would be that we were in a force 9, gusting 11, rather than the forecast 7 to 9.

As long as the wind was at our stern, we were reasonably comfortable. The Skipper asked me to shorten *Gordon's* rope, so there would be less danger of her capsizing, as had happened just a few weeks earlier. As I exited the wheelhouse, a squally shower passed through. It was as if I'd been sent, fully clothed, into a freezing power-shower, and I was drenched by the time I returned indoors, just a few seconds later.

I looked towards Garroch Head, to see how long it would be before we reached the shelter of Bute. But I could see that all was not going to plan. The Skipper had misjudged the wind direction, and our heading was taking us towards the Ayrshire coast to the south of Little Cumbrae. Were we to change course towards Garroch Head, we would have turned beam-on to the waves, which would have been at best ill-advised, and at worst suicidal.

Our concrete ballast meant that on the one hand, the boat would quickly right itself after being tipped to one side, but on the other hand, a prolonged spell of rolling could build up sufficient momentum to tip the boat over. The weight of this same concrete would then take effect to ensure that our final journey to the sea-bed would be a quick one, but that really didn't bear thinking about.

The further we went, the more perilous our situation became. The waves were getting bigger and bigger, as the wind refused to relent, and the fetch of the waves from the Kintyre shore increased. We were going to have to do something fairly drastic to retrieve the situation.

Our heading was now hopelessly too far south, and our bows were pointing the wrong side of Hunterston nuclear power station on the horizon. Our only available option would be to tack back into the wind. We would have to turn into the waves, and continue until our bearing towards Garroch Head would allow safe passage with a following sea. Looking at the charts and the radar, and assessing the direction in which the wind and waves were moving, we calculated that we would need to be around a mile and a half to the north west before we could turn again and resume our course. At normal cruising speed, it would take about fifteen minutes to reach that spot, although we expected that on this occasion, we would be slowed by wind and waves.

The tacking manoeuvre would start and end with 'storm turns', whereby the Skipper watched the waves and tried to identify a lull. He would then turn the wheel hard and up the throttle, to minimise the time spent side-on to the waves. The tension mounted as the Skipper watched the waves for a lull, waiting to choose his moment. Then the revs surged, and my heart leapt into my mouth as we turned through almost 180°, listing as we went. We were battered, beam-on, by a couple of sizable waves, but our momentum carried us through, and the manoeuvre was completed successfully.

The seascape now changed completely. Instead of being overtaken by the waves as we rolled along in their surf, we were now heading almost straight into them. The bow was engulfed by wave after wave, and a fraction of a second after each one was broken, the wheelhouse window was hit by a wall of blinding brine. On numerous occasions, the boat felt as if it was stopping dead in the water, or even being knocked backwards by the force of the waves. It was a relentless battering and the anemometer was now locked on 50 knots.

It was very quiet in the wheelhouse, until Jill piped up with a suggestion to the Skipper.

"Do you think we should call the Coastguard?" she asked.

"We are the Coastguard," was the Skipper's terse response.

I stood with Carl, and we watched as the evening sun repeatedly dipped behind the crests of the onrushing waves. It was as if the sea had heard that I would be leaving, and had summoned a storm to give me one final display of her strength.

"Awesome," I said, and not in the American sense of the word.

The engine lacked its usual, reassuring heartbeat, as the Skipper constantly adjusted the throttle, slowing down each time a particularly big wave or trough had to be negotiated. Every time the revs dropped, I braced myself for the next thud of mountainous sea on larch.

The Skipper gave me the unprecedented order to distribute the life jackets. Everyone had crowded into the wheelhouse, but no one said anything as I disappeared below decks. Down below, the effects of the waves were no less dramatic. I retrieved an armful of lifejackets from a cupboard and ducked to avoid the big oak beam. At precisely that moment, we toppled off the crest of a big wave, and I was momentarily weightless. My feet left the ground and my head hit the beam. The floor then rose back abruptly and I found myself lying, unhurt, but face-down among a pile of lifejackets.

I struggled back up through the hatch with the lifejackets, and squeezed into a packed wheelhouse. The atmosphere was heavy with anxiety and fear.

We could see a large cargo ship leaving the Clyde ahead of us, which was not apparently being affected by the short, quick waves which were giving us such a rough time. Through the spray, the ship's name, 'North Star' could be read. The Skipper now had to make another decision which would have been unprecedented on Beagle Cruises – was our predicament sufficiently perilous to issue a distress call? Our situation was not immediately life-threatening, so rather than the better-known 'Mayday', the Skipper could have chosen to begin his call with the less critical, but still highly urgent 'Pan-pan'. In the end, he decided that we were still in control, and that things were actually progressing according to our hastily-assembled plans. No distress call would be issued, but we would call up the *North Star* to see if she could offer any help.

"*North Star, North Star, North Star.* This is *Glendale, Glendale, Glendale.* Do you read me, over?"

The call went out on channel 16, meaning that any nearby ship or coastguard should pick it up. The roar of waves and lurching of timbers continued unabated, but there was silence from the radio. Eventually, a foreign skipper's voice gave a tentative response, and agreed to continue the exchange on a working channel.

Now on Channel 06, the Skipper put forward his request for assistance. If the skipper of *North Star* agreed, she would change course and escort us to sheltered waters in her lee. There was another silence while *North Star* considered her position. The *Glendale* must have been visible from her bridge, about a mile off the starboard bow, obscured from full view by a veil of waves and spray.

Despite the evidence before him, the skipper of the *North Star* came back to us, and explained in broken English that he was unable to offer any assistance. There was something about not wanting to put himself behind schedule, but the message was clear enough. We were on our own.

"Are we all going to die?" asked Jill. It was not an overly constructive question, but in fairness, it was a reasonable one, which went unanswered. Then an argument broke out between Jill and the Skipper.

"You just swore at me," said Jill.

"I only asked you to move your bloody handbag," explained the Skipper. Jill had put her handbag on a shelf next to the ship's wheel, and the strap had become tangled in one of the spokes, hindering the Skipper's attempts to keep the boat under control among the huge waves.

Meanwhile, Al Hollick had been quieter than usual, and his face was beginning to take on a greenish hue under his Tarbert fisherman's hat. He suddenly darted for a window, sliding it down just in time before thrusting his head out through it. After a few seconds, his head came back into the wheelhouse, dripping with sea spray and lacking a Tarbert fisherman's hat. His bolt for the window had been with such speed that his hat had flown off, and it was now lying upside down on the deck by the wheelhouse, filled with the erstwhile contents of his stomach.

"I haven't felt this ill since I was in a coma with hepatitis," quipped Al.

At this point, I decided to vacate the wheelhouse. I sat alone on the generator box at the stern, holding onto a couple of metal stanchions, and watching as the sun-lit spray hurtled overhead and carried on parallel to the sea's surface into the distance. If it hadn't been so frightening, it would have been a fantastic spectacle. It is one which I am never expecting to forget.

It took us fifty minutes to travel the mile and a half to the point at which we were ready for the second storm turn. Again, the Skipper successfully found a slight lull in the onslaught, and made the turn safely. The wind and waves were again at our stern, and once we had settled onto our new bearing, we could see that Little Cumbrae was now straight ahead. To have made for Garroch Head as per our original plan would still have proven uncomfortable, so we chose the longer, safer route to get to the calm waters behind Little Cumbrae.

It was a huge relief as we rounded the southern tip of the island, bringing our ordeal to an end. Shags lined the rocky ridge just as they had done the during the previous year's Hollick cruise, but no-one had the energy to make any jokes about androids this time.

The huge waves had been toying with us for nearly three hours, leaving everyone physically and emotionally wrung out. The Skipper disappeared below for a few minutes, and then emerged from the hatch, carrying a bottle of the Campbeltown malt, Springbank, and a tray of glasses. This was partially to celebrate our safe passage but also to calm frayed nerves.

We took a look at Millport as an option for spending the night instead of Rothesay, but despite its sheltered outlook, we could see that the sea in the harbour was still swollen, so we pushed on to Rothesay. Even on the short crossing between the Cumbraes and Bute, the spray was easily breaking over the bows, but compared to what had gone before, this was trivial.

Dusk was gathering rapidly as we docked at Rothesay, and we were all grateful to be reacquainted with terra firma. For the only ever time on a Beagle cruise, we ate in a restaurant rather than preparing a meal on the boat that evening. Al quickly recovered from his sea-sickness, and the colour returned to his cheeks. Our Chinese meal, served by Angie, our oriental hostess from the far east (of Bute), was enjoyed by all.

As we reflected on an extraordinary day, the Skipper quietly shook his head.

"Who would have thought we would be in here this evening?" he wondered.

"Not me," replied Al. "I thought I'd still be bobbing around somewhere out there, blowing into my little whistle."

*

The gale was still in full blow the next morning, and was now accompanied by torrential rain. We still had a bird record to chase, so after breakfast, we set off on a walk to a reservoir just inland of Rothesay. We allocated the crew's oilskins to the punters, so I went out wearing just jeans and a completely porous grey and black cagoule with a Newcastle United badge embroidered on it. I was already soaked to the skin by the time we made it to Rothesay Castle on the far side of the town centre, and became progressively wetter and wetter as the day went on.

The path became a slippery quagmire, and members of the party frequently lost their footing. Jill, who was wearing oilskin dungarees, slipped in a particularly big muddy puddle.

"It went right up to me gusset," she informed us, the Lichfield tones enriching the exclamation.

Birding conditions were nigh-on impossible, and our optics were rendered almost useless by the driving wind and rain. We did manage to squint between the raindrops on fogged-up lenses and add a couple of species to the list. Pochard, Shoveler and Coot were the 'highlights', which led us to question whether the effort, cold and wet, and indeed the danger of the previous day, had all been worthwhile.

We had cracked the record, but still fell well short of the 100 target. It was Friday, and time to make our way back to Tighnabruaich. The wind had swung around further to the north, and was now blowing straight down the East Kyle. The anemometer stayed up at around fifty knots as we took turns to sit in the bow and let the spray fly past. The theory was that it would be possible to stay dry up in the bows with the waves breaking either side of us, but in practice, several soakings were had.

The cruise was over, and as usual, we had served up a memorable one for our favourite guests, even if things had not quite gone to plan. It was difficult to gauge exactly how much danger we had exposed ourselves to on the trip. While the boat had taken a fearsome battering, not a single mug or plate had been broken on board. The *Glendale* had, no doubt, seen much more severe conditions than these in her time as a working trawler. But it had been quite an ordeal for everyone who had been on board. Some time later, the Skipper showed me something which unnerved me. The throttle lever in the wheelhouse operated a larger lever in the engine room, to which it was connected by a small hinge. Forty years at sea had seen this hinge erode, and it was now wafer-thin. Had it chosen to give way during this episode, the outcome could have been much, much worse.

31. Sailing Away

Dylan had had enough. His simmering dispute with the Skipper had rumbled on since the Oban prawn creel affair, and he departed without any goodbyes. I was only too happy to forfeit my last week of holiday, and step in to crew for the final cruise of the season. The Skipper came to collect me from Dunoon on the Friday evening. As we drove along past the viewpoint at the top of the Kyles, the Tighnabruaich eagles greeted us. We pulled into the lay-by and watched as they drifted off to hunt on Bute's low hills, one of them making a brief diversion to terrorise a passing Cormorant with a half-hearted stoop.

We didn't make it to Sanda on my last cruise, as the weather was not looking too clever. I had some unfinished business to attend to on Arran, though. The high mountains there were home to a relict, but healthy, isolated population of Ptarmigan. These high arctic Grouse are quite common in the Cairngorms and in the far north of Scotland, and Arran represented a remote southerly outpost to their range in the UK. A few weeks earlier, Dylan had found three on Arran's tallest mountain, Goat Fell. But I had never seen one, despite previous trips up Goat Fell and nearby Beinn Nuis.

We landed in *Gordon* on the shore below Brodick Castle, meaning that our ascent of the mountain would cover all of the 2,868 feet from sea level to summit. The path up the hill was well-trodden, easily accessible to tourists, and for the most part, had quite a gentle incline. The final few hundred feet were steeper, and involved dodging among some huge granite boulders. The view from the summit was glorious. The granite slopes fell away abruptly below us into several spectacular deep glacial valleys. Gigha, Islay and Jura could be seen, with clear water between them and the west coast of Kintyre. To the south, Ailsa Craig seemed to float eerily in mid-air, as the indistinct horizon was making it difficult to distinguish between sea and sky.

I watched the rocks, hoping for a white wing to give away the presence of a Ptarmigan. Despite my best efforts, and willing some small lumps of granite to walk or fly away, it was not to be my day. I called the punters together, and began the descent as Ptarmiganless as I had been when we'd set out.

A small bird flitted across the path and up onto a nearby boulder. Its red tail quivered as it sat there, making it obvious that it was a Redstart, but it dropped down the hillside and out of sight before I could raise my binoculars. There are only two real choices when it comes to redstarts in the UK. Common Redstarts are quite common in the Clyde area, and Black Redstarts are not, so I assumed that it must have been the former. What did not occur to me until much later was that this was very late for a summer-visiting Common Redstart. What should have been even more obvious was that no self-respecting Common would be seen a couple of thousand feet up a mountain and miles from the nearest tree. I later learned that this is actually the preferred habitat of Black Redstart over much of its range. It is also a regular autumn migrant in Britain (albeit mainly in small numbers on the east coast), so I now have no hesitation in claiming one last posthumous Beagle First – Black Redstart.

A bank of Atlantic cloud had swept in overnight, and the last day of my last cruise dawned grey in Lochranza. The eagles performed for us one last time, soaring in a family of three over the tor, and soon it was time to return to the boat, pull up the anchor and head up towards Tighnabruaich.

I walked up the slope of the deck to the bows, and set to securing the still-dripping anchor to its cradle. As I did so, I noticed a Black Guillemot a little way ahead of us, paddling steadily away, but in increasing danger of being over-run by the accelerating boat. I paused to watch, and reflected on the fact that despite two years of nearly daily sightings of these 'Tysties', I had never tired of seeing them. It swam a little further and then, rather than flying off, it elected to dive, its bright red feet briefly breaking the surface as it propelled itself downward. I watched as its black body and wings blended with the inky water below me. Like the Cheshire Cat, soon all that could be seen were the white, oval patches on the wings, as it 'flew' deeper and deeper, before being lost to view beneath the bow.

The cruises were over, but my work was not yet done. We still had two vacancies to fill ready for the following season. It was quite intriguing for me to go through the interview process from the other side of the fence. Most of the applicants proved to be unsuitable, either through a lack of enough knowledge about nature, or, in a couple of cases, through downright weirdness. We narrowed the field down to five, and in the end, only three interviews were scheduled.

All three turned out to be good candidates. Stuart was first, an ex-warden from the Farne Islands. We got on well, and Stuart seemed to know his onions well enough. A Goshawk over the Burnt Islands helped liven up his interview, as did an eventful walk up the valley behind Tighnabruaich. We had not seen too many birds, but then I noticed some movement on the hillside, and watched a number of shapes moving around and coming together as a drama unfolded.

One of the shapes was that of a bald, white-haired man, clad in a blue boiler-suit and black wellies. This was obviously Peter. Another was a swift, brown quadruped; this was Maura, his Ridgeback. The white shapes scattering about the hillside were the local sheep flock. But one white shape had been picked out by Maura, and was isolated from the flock. Maura was harrying the sheep and looked to be closing in for a kill. Stuart and I hurried towards the scene.

We could now hear Peter shouting frantically at Maura, trying in vain to call her off. Maura had other ideas, and was having far too much fun letting her hunting instincts run wild. All looked to be lost for the sheep. At this point, I drew a deep breath and yelled at the top of my voice. "MAURA!!" echoed around the valley. The dog immediately stopped, confused by the strange voice which had suddenly called her name. Peter took the opportunity to catch up with her, and dragged her by the collar down the hill to meet us. I introduced Stuart to Peter.

"Hello," he said. Then he grabbed Maura tighter by the collar. "I'm terribly sorry about that," he explained, before swearing loudly at his dog and giving her a hefty clip behind the ear. Stuart would not forget his introduction to Peter any time soon, just as I didn't forget my first encounter some 20 months previously.

The next candidate to arrive was the early favourite for the post. Colin had an impeccable CV, and was supremely well-qualified for the role, having spent the summer working as a bird guide for the RSPB in the Highlands. Finally, we welcomed Don on board. He was a keen birder from Surrey, not as polished a performer as Colin, but a likeable chap, nonetheless. The highlight of his interview was in the pub, when he flipped a coin on the pool table to decide who would start the game. The coin spun, bounced off the baize, and flew straight down the centre pocket.

We agreed quite quickly that Stuart was going to be taken on, so it was a straight choice between Colin and Don for the vacant second spot. Colin definitely had the stronger CV, but for some reason, we both felt that Don was better suited to the job, and perhaps had more potential. So the choice, although a difficult one, had been made.

My last evening in Tighnabruaich was a clear one, and after a quiet few beers in the village, the Skipper and I strolled back along the front to the boat one last time. The moon hung low over Bute's hills, its light casting a shimmering silver path right across the Kyles, which seemed to link the island to our shore.

Tighnabruaich, like Sanda and Lochranza, was a place which had etched itself on my soul, and I knew I would miss it badly. But I knew that the *Glendale* would be here next year, and vowed to pay a visit again when I got the chance.

On the afternoon of my final day as a Beagle employee, the Skipper and I took the *Glendale* up Loch Striven to collect the prawn creels and take them out of the water for the winter. It was a beautiful calm day, the fiery red bracken and heather reflecting in the still waters of the loch. Gannets plunged close to the boat, having homed in on a shoal of fish, and one emerged alongside us grasping a shining mackerel in its bill.

We located the prawn creels, and set to work on pulling them on board. It was a good 'catch', and a shame that we had no punters with us to enjoy it. The highlights were not one, but two octopuses in the pots. As I freed one from the netting, it attached itself firmly to my oilskins in a strategically delicate position. I was entranced, until the Skipper pointed out that it possessed a powerful beak. I hurriedly peeled the beast sucker by sucker from my front, and dropped it overboard. At first, it parachuted through the black water, presumably making itself seem as large as possible to fend off the threat from me, but with a single flick, it pulled its eight tentacles together and jetted off out of sight back into the depths.

The slow pace of life aboard the *Glendale* always allowed plenty of time to think and reflect. I was alone in the wheelhouse, the only noise being the rhythmic chug of the engine and the rush of water past our hull. I looked out over the glassy-calm waters of the Kyles. I knew I was going to miss the sights and sounds of my time as the Beagle Bird Man, but I could congratulate myself on completing a job well done. What had started out as a huge leap into the unknown had turned into a fantastic experience, and, dare I say it, a bit of a triumph.

When my adventure had begun, I had been severely lacking in so many of the key facets of the job. In my two seasons, I had learned a little more about my specialist subject, birds, especially seabirds and eagles. I had learned more still about other aspects of nature, particularly botany and marine life, but this was another case of building on a foundation that already existed. I was amazed to think how much I had learned, and how much of this had been an utterly new experience to me. Now I was a competent boatman, and had several hundred hours at the helm behind me. But what use would these new skills be in the 'real' world that awaited?

What I had gained, which would be invaluable in later life, were some less obvious skills and experiences. Now I could cook. I might never have impressed my wife-to-be a year later had I not conjured up my signature *Glendale* dish of stuffed trout with baked tomatoes and horseradish sauce on our first date. I now knew how to put together and execute a plan, and I knew to put my punters, or customers, first. Others recognised the changes in me, too. When the Skipper discussed my imminent departure with Jill, she was moved to say that I had arrived in Tighnabruaich as a boy, but would leave as a man.

The day had started with a clear, calm November morning in the Kyles. All was quiet and the pace of life was as slow as usual, until an unusual fleet of vehicles emerged from the village, and made their way towards the pier. They stopped outside the pier house, and their occupants quickly disembarked and busied themselves, rushing around purposefully. Fishing nets, which had been carefully unravelled ready for repair work by a local fisherman, were unceremoniously 'tidied up' and removed. One of the men, wearing sharp clothes and black shades, summoned me onto the deck. He asked if he could use our hose to damp down the pier. This would have delayed our departure, so I politely declined to assist, pointing him in the direction of a tap on a nearby wall at the top of the pier.

These people were aliens from another planet, but it was a planet to which I knew I would be moving all-too-soon. They were marketing men from Renault, and Tighnabruaich Pier had been chosen as an idyllic spot in which to film an advert for the new Renault 19. I saw the finished article a few months later, on the television of my flat in Ealing. It started with a driver being tossed a set of keys. "Lucky man, you've got the north" said his boss. After taking in some of the country's more scenic upland roads, he finally rolled up on Tighnabruaich Pier. It was the pier that I knew so well, even though it was devoid of fishing nets, and its planks neatly hosed down. And there was no trawler home to a 6'5" Geordie ornithologist tied up at the end. By the time the filming had finished, I was on my way down south. I had been the lucky man.

Printed in Great Britain
by Amazon

83015948R00159